"This introduction to the Pauline Letters ␣␣␣␣␣␣␣␣␣␣␣␣␣␣␣␣␣␣ the most accessible of its kind. Complicated history of exegesis is presented simply and comprehensibly. Summary boxes in the text and questions for review and reflection facilitate understanding. A particular strength is the focus on the theology and ethics of each letter. A final chapter completes the picture with brief presentations of the legacy of Paul in the early centuries of the church."

— Carolyn Osiek, RSCJ
Charles Fischer Catholic Professor of New Testament, Emerita
*Brite* Divinity School

"At last, a responsible and interesting new volume on Paul's letters for students! I whole-heartedly recommend it."

— Clare K. Rothschild
Associate Professor, Scripture Studies
Lewis University, IL

"Daniel Scholz provides us with a very functional text that will work well for undergraduate or first-year seminary courses in Paul's letters. The occasion behind each letter is carefully set out, and the 'Theology' and 'Ethics' sections for each letter will prove helpful. The graphics within each chapter make it very user-friendly. The questions at the end of each chapter will allow this to be readily put to use in academic courses. The final chapter, on such writings as *Acts of Paul and Thecla, Third Corinthians,* and *Acts of Paul,* also provides a helpful introduction to Paul's legacy in early Christianity. I heartily recommend this book as a good candidate for courses on Paul's letters."

— Mark Reasoner
Associate professor of theology
Marian University

# AUTHOR ACKNOWLEDGMENTS

I offer my sincere thanks and gratitude to Kathleen Walsh and Maura Hagarty at Anselm Academic, and especially to Jim Kelhoffer, for their enormous editorial contributions that brought this book to completion. Most importantly, I thank my wife, Bonnie, and our three children, Raymond, Andrew, and Danielle, for their patience and support throughout this writing project.

## Publisher Acknowledgments

The publisher owes a special debt of gratitude to James A. Kelhoffer, PhD, who advised throughout this project. Dr. Kelhoffer's expertise and passion both as teacher and scholar contributed immeasurably to this work. Dr. Kelhoffer holds a PhD in New Testament and Early Christian Literature from the University of Chicago and is professor of Old and New Testament Exegesis at Uppsala University in Sweden.

The publisher also wishes to thank the following individual who reviewed this work in progress:

Jeffrey S. Siker
*Loyola Marymount University, Los Angeles, California*

# THE
# PAULINE
# LETTERS

## INTRODUCING THE NEW TESTAMENT

DANIEL J. SCHOLZ

JAMES A. KELHOFFER, ACADEMIC EDITOR

ANSELM
ACADEMIC

Created by the publishing team of Anselm Academic.

Cover art: Lorrain, Claude (Gellee) (1600–1682). *The Embarkation of St. Paul of Rome at Ostia.* Museo del Prado, Madrid, Spain. Scala / Art Resource, NY

Printed in the United States of America

7044

ISBN 978-1-59982-099-6

# CONTENTS

# Studying Paul and His Letters

Next to Jesus, no figure has had more influence in Christian tradition and history than Paul. In fact, studying Paul's letters is essential for understanding Christianity. Fortunately, the Christian Scriptures provide plenty of source material to understand and interpret Paul. Just as the four Gospels of Matthew, Mark, Luke, and John inform readers about Jesus, the thirteen Pauline letters in the New Testament provide information about Paul and his followers. In addition to these letters, the New Testament Acts of the Apostles also focus on Paul in its narrative of the early church's mission and development. Outside the Christian Scriptures, other letters and narratives contribute to understanding Paul and his impact in Christian tradition and history.

One of the most important and surprising features of the thirteen New Testament letters attributed to Paul is that some of these letters most likely do not come directly from Paul. Of the thirteen Pauline letters, scholars are convinced that seven are "undisputed letters" of Paul. The seven undisputed Pauline letters are Romans, 1 Corinthians, 2 Corinthians, Galatians, Philippians, 1 Thessalonians, and Philemon. Written between 50 and 60 CE, these letters provide direct access to Paul and offer insights into the world of the first Christians. These seven letters are the primary sources used today to understand and interpret Paul.

The six others Pauline letters fall into the category of the "deutero-Pauline letters": Colossians, Ephesians, 2 Thessalonians, 1 Timothy, 2 Timothy, and Titus. *Deutero-* is a Greek prefix meaning, "second" or "secondary." These six letters are widely regarded by scholars as written by followers of Paul sometime between 70 and

120 CE. For this reason, these letters are often referred to as the "disputed letters" of Paul.

## The Letters of Paul in the New Testament

In the New Testament, the thirteen letters attributed to Paul follow the four Gospels of Matthew, Mark, Luke, and John and the Acts of the Apostles.

The Pauline letters appear in the Bible not in chronological order but according to length of these letters. Thus, Romans, the longest of the letters with 7,111 words and 1,687 total verses, comes first. Philemon, with 335 words and only 25 verses, appears last in the Bible.

| Book | Abbreviation |
| --- | --- |
| Romans | Rom |
| 1 Corinthians | 1 Cor |
| 2 Corinthians | 2 Cor |
| Galatians | Gal |
| Ephesians | Eph |
| Philippians | Phil |
| Colossians | Col |
| 1 Thessalonians | 1 Thess |
| 2 Thessalonians | 2 Thess |
| 1 Timothy | 1 Tim |
| 2 Timothy | 2 Tim |
| Titus | Ti |
| Philemon | Phlm |

The Acts of the Apostles is another important source for understanding Paul. Written a generation or two after Paul by the same author who wrote the Gospel of Luke, Acts narrates events from the ascension of Jesus in Jerusalem to the imprisonment of Paul in Rome. The author, Luke, commits the entire second half of Acts to the missionary activities of Paul. Some of what is known about Paul from his authentic letters is supported by details from Acts. For example, the presence of Sosthenes and Crispus in Corinth in Acts 18 parallels references in 1 Corinthians to Sosthenes (1:1) and Crispus (1:14). Other times, however, details from Paul and Acts contradict. For instance, in Galatians 1:18, Paul explains that he waited three years after his call to go to Jerusalem. However, in Acts 9, Paul's visit to Jerusalem appears to occur much more quickly. Needless to say, these types of disagreements have led scholars to question the historical reliability of Acts. Given this, most scholars consider Acts as a secondary source for understanding Paul, as its presentation of Paul is shaped by Luke's theology and cannot consistently be cross-referenced with information from Paul's letters.

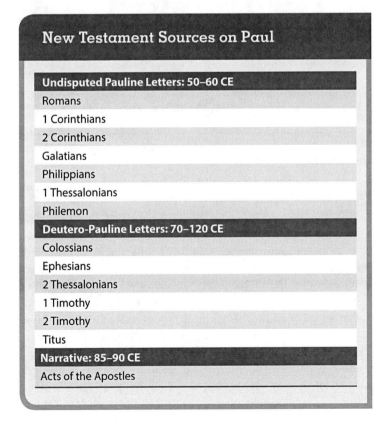

### New Testament Sources on Paul

**Undisputed Pauline Letters: 50–60 CE**

Romans

1 Corinthians

2 Corinthians

Galatians

Philippians

1 Thessalonians

Philemon

**Deutero-Pauline Letters: 70–120 CE**

Colossians

Ephesians

2 Thessalonians

1 Timothy

2 Timothy

Titus

**Narrative: 85–90 CE**

Acts of the Apostles

The remaining sources that help us to understand and interpret Paul fall into the category of extracanonical sources; that is, early source material not included in the canon of the Christian Scriptures. This source material is classified according to its literary form: letters, narratives, or apocalypses (end of the age stories). Written mostly in the second and third centuries CE, these sources highlight the legacy of Paul centuries after his death.

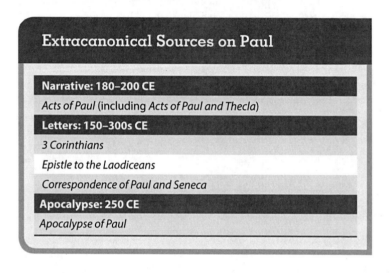

**Extracanonical Sources on Paul**

**Narrative: 180–200 CE**

*Acts of Paul* (including *Acts of Paul and Thecla*)

**Letters: 150–300s CE**

*3 Corinthians*

*Epistle to the Laodiceans*

*Correspondence of Paul and Seneca*

**Apocalypse: 250 CE**

*Apocalypse of Paul*

The New Testament sources reveal three important insights into Paul. First, Paul is complicated. Whether in his early years as a Jewish Pharisee who was a leader of the persecution of the original Christians or in his later years, when he challenged Jewish Christians to accept uncircumcised Gentile Christians as partners in faith, Paul was no stranger to facing controversy. Further, Paul's theological thinking, as seen in the letters, presents a remarkable integration of Jewish theology and Greek thought that is not easily understood today. Second, Paul had an enormous task to accomplish in proclaiming Jesus Christ to the Gentiles. In Paul's own words, he interpreted his encounter with the resurrected Christ as a call from God to "proclaim [Jesus] to the Gentiles" (Gal 1:16). In response to this call, Paul spent the next thirty years spreading the "good news" of Jesus Christ to Gentiles living in the eastern half of the Roman Empire.

Third, Paul's theology eventually influenced the course of Christian history and theology. Within Paul's lifetime, there were competing ideas and beliefs about Jesus. Paul's voice was one among many.

Despite the availability of the various New Testament and extracanonical sources, Paul remains elusive. However, with the rise of various scientific methods for studying the sources in the past two hundred years, theologians and scholars have learned much about how to better understand and interpret Paul and his letters. *The Pauline Letters* presents the fruits of this labor and addresses some of the context and background information needed for an informed understanding of Paul and his letters.

Chapter 1, "Paul of Tarsus," begins with a brief history of the modern interpretation of Paul. This chapter includes the criteria and sources used in this book for interpreting Paul as well as the first-century Jewish and Hellenistic contexts on him. The second half of the chapter summarizes what scholars know about the life of Paul and presents an overview of his letters and of ancient letter writing.

Chapter 1 lays the foundation for the two main parts of this book—part 1: the seven undisputed Pauline letters, and part 2: the disputed letters and post-Pauline writings. Part 1 consists of chapters 2–8 and takes up the seven undisputed letters of Paul. Although scholars debate about the dates and order of composition of the letters, part 1 of this book proceeds with the following hypothetical dates and order:

| | |
|---|---|
| 1 Thessalonians | 50 CE |
| 1 Corinthians | Spring 55 CE |
| 2 Corinthians | Fall 55 CE |
| Galatians | Late 55 CE |
| Romans | Spring 56 CE |
| Philippians | 60 CE |
| Philemon | Late 60 CE |

These chapters focus on the historical, social, and literary contexts of each letter as well as what these letters reveal about Paul's theology and ethics.

Part 2 begins by examining the six remaining letters attributed to Paul—but disputed by scholars—in the New Testament. Although scholars debate the dates and order of composition of these letters also, part 2 of this book proceeds with the following hypothetical dates:

| Colossians | 70–100 CE |
|---|---|
| Ephesians | 80–110 CE |
| 2 Thessalonians | 90–100 CE |
| 1 Timothy | 100 CE |
| 2 Timothy | 100 CE |
| Titus | 100 CE |

Chapter 9 focuses on the deutero-Pauline (or disputed) letters of Colossians, Ephesians, and 2 Thessalonians; and chapter 10 considers the disputed letters of 1 Timothy, 2 Timothy, and Titus, also known as the Pastoral Letters. These chapters discuss the developing historical, social, and literary contexts in which the letters were written as well as the theology and ethics of each letter. Chapter 11 provides a historical and theological overview of certain later letters, narratives, and an apocalypse that claim to convey traditions about Paul. Knowledge of these extracanonical sources is important for understanding the legacy of Paul in the second and third centuries.

Studying Paul and his letters will provide readers with much information and plenty of insights into Paul. The abundance of sources on Paul, canonical and extracanonical, will shed light on the obstacles and opportunities that the earliest Christians faced in spreading their versions of the good news of Jesus Christ throughout the Roman Empire.

# PART 1

## The Undisputed Pauline Letters

# CHAPTER 1

# Paul of Tarsus

## INTRODUCTION

This chapter examines the historical figure of Paul of Tarsus. The beginning of the chapter includes a brief survey of modern attempts to interpret Paul as well as the interpretative criteria to be used in this book. It also includes some details of the canonical and extra-canonical sources available for understanding Paul as well as the first-century Jewish and Hellenistic influences that shaped his life and work. The latter part presents a summary overview of Paul's life and some background information on his letters.

### The Reception of Paul
### in Christian History and Theology

The reception of Paul and his letters in the formation of the New Testament and throughout Christian history can hardly be overstated. Nearly half of the New Testament writings are attributed to him: thirteen of the twenty-seven books of the New Testament are traditionally associated with Paul, and his legacy stretches well beyond them. Leading figures from every period of church history have wrestled with the person of Paul and his theological thinking. From the writings of church fathers (such as Augustine of Hippo) to the theology of the sixteenth-century Reformers (such as Martin Luther) to the rise of the modern historical criticism (for example, F. C. Baur and Ernst Troeltsch) and the "new perspective" on Paul (such as E. P. Sanders), scholars have responded to the theology and person of Paul as reflected in his surviving letters.

## A Biblical Figure like No Other

Unlike any other figure in the New Testament, Paul can be known in a unique and distinctive way—through the seven letters that scholars are confident he wrote. Within the context of modern historical criticism of the Bible, such a claim can be said of no one else in the New Testament, including Jesus. To be sure, the four New Testament Gospels of Matthew, Mark, Luke, and John provide information about Jesus, but these are his words and deeds as preserved, recorded, and edited by later Gospel writers a generation removed from the actual events. Jesus himself left no written account of his words, thoughts, and deeds. This is true of Peter as well, another leading figure in the New Testament. The two letters attributed to Peter in the New Testament (1 Peter and 2 Peter) are, in fact, written by others in his name one or two generations after his death.

Paul's seven undisputed letters offer insights into his theology and the world of the early Christians. Through the lens of Paul's perspective, contemporary readers can see the hopes and the challenges of some of the original Christians who formed communities around their belief in Jesus as the Messiah and Son of God. In addition, the letters also show some of the earliest theological thinking to emerge in light of the Christians' belief in the death and Resurrection of Jesus.

## The Limits of Historical Inquiry

Despite the advantage and opportunity these letters offer for understanding both Paul of Tarsus and the Christians he associated with, they carry some limitations. Although Paul's actual missionary outreach to the Gentiles spanned nearly thirty years, from about 35 to 64 CE, the seven undisputed Pauline letters cover only a portion of those years, approximately 50 to 60 CE. If Paul wrote at all in the first half of his thirty-year missionary work, no letters have been discovered to date. Neither is there any record of undisputed letters dating to Paul's final years. Furthermore, the "occasional" nature of Paul's letters limits their usefulness. By *occasional*, scholars mean that Paul wrote to address specific situations—the particular problems and concerns of certain congregations. Paul's surviving letters never give a systematic summary of his theology. Indeed, he may be best understood as a pastoral theologian, applying the gospel to the changing situations he faced.

# UNDERSTANDING AND INTERPRETING PAUL

To understand and interpret Paul today requires a brief overview of the past two centuries of Pauline research. This section examines the established paradigms and perspectives that have shaped contemporary approaches to Paul. It also discusses the main sources for Paul, both canonical and extracanonical, that have informed these paradigms and perspectives. The section concludes with a closer look at some of the first-century Jewish and Hellenistic influences that shaped Paul.

## Brief History of Modern Interpretation

The work of Pauline scholars of the nineteenth and twentieth centuries finds it roots in the sixteenth-century Reformation period as well as the eighteenth-century Age of Enlightenment and Age of Reason that influenced the Western cultures of Europe and America. In his approach to the study of the Bible from a linguistic and historical perspective, sixteenth-century Reformer Martin Luther ignited some of the earliest studies of Jesus, Paul, and the early Christian communities. The work of Luther and other reformers laid the foundation for later biblical studies. In the eighteenth century, fundamental ideas and concepts in areas such as science, art, history, music, philosophy, and religion were being thought about in new and different ways. The Bible itself was not immune to these changes in thinking. Scholars began examining the Old and the New Testaments anew in terms of their literary, historical, and cultural dimensions. In short, human reason was now being applied to the study of the Bible. This new Western perception of reality even affected the understanding of the New Testament's central figures, Jesus and Paul.

Much of the discussion on Paul in the past two hundred years has centered upon the question of Paul's relationship to the Judaism of his day. Connecting Paul to Judaism dates back to the nineteenth century and the foundational studies generated by the early work of historical-critical scholarship. The research and writing of leading German scholars such as F. C. Baur (1792–1860), *Paul, the Apostle of Jesus Christ* (1845); Ferdinand Weber (1812–1860), *The Theological System of the Ancient Palestinian Synagogue Based on the Targum, Midrash and Talmud* (1880); Emil Schürer (1844–1910), *The History of the Jewish People in the Age of Christ* (1897); and Wilhelm Bousset (1865–1903), *The Judaic Religion in the New Testament Era* (1903), paint a portrait of ancient Judaism that shaped early interpretations of Paul.

## Pauline Terminology[1]

Understanding the vocabulary that Paul uses in his letters can be one of the more vexing problems that people encounter in trying to interpret Paul. The following list notes some common terms Paul used along with a general definition of each term and one or more passages in which the term appears.

Faith (Greek: *pistis*)—an absolute trust, belief in God

- Galatians 3:7—"Realize then that it is those who have faith who are children of Abraham."

Gospel (Greek: *euaggelion*)—good news, glad tidings. For Paul, it was a term that encompassed God's saving work in Jesus Christ.

- Romans 1:16—"For I am not ashamed of the gospel. It is the power of God for the salvation of everyone who believes; for Jew first, and then Greek."

Grace (Greek: *charis*)—favor, often divine favor freely given.

- 2 Corinthians 6:1—"Working together, then, we appeal to you not to receive the grace of God in vain."

*Continued*

---

1. For a good resource on Pauline terminology (e.g., *salvation, righteousness*, etc.), see Gerald F. Hawthorne, Ralph P. Martin, and Daniel G. Reid, eds. *Dictionary of Paul and His Letters: A Compendium of Contemporary Biblical Scholarship* (Downers Grove, IL: InterVarsity Press, 1993).

**Pauline Terminology** *Continued*

Justice/Righteousness (Greek: *dikaiosynē*)—what God required. For Paul, it is God's restoration of humanity through Jesus Christ. Paul often uses this term in its derivation, *justification* and interchangeably as *righteousness*.

- Galatians 2:21—"I do not nullify the grace of God; for if justification comes through the law, then Christ died for nothing."
- Romans 3:21–22—"[T]he righteousness of God has been manifested apart from the law . . . through faith in Jesus Christ."

Law (Greek: *nomos*)—law; God's instructions to Israel for proper relationship with God and others. The Mosaic Law, which prescribed the Jewish way of life, was defined in both oral and written form.

- Romans 7:25—"Thanks be to God through Jesus Christ our Lord. Therefore, I myself, with my mind, serve the law of God but, with my flesh, the law of sin."

Salvation (Greek: *sōtēria*)—the result of God's action in Jesus Christ, awaiting final fulfillment in God's coming kingdom.

- 1 Thessalonians 5:9—"For God did not destine us for wrath, but to gain salvation through our Lord Jesus Christ."

Sanctification (Greek: *haiasmos*)—a process of becoming holy because of faith in Christ.

- Romans 6:22—"But now that you have . . . become slaves of God, the benefit that you have leads to sanctification, and its end is eternal life."

Sin (Greek: *hamartia*)—An offense against God, literally meaning, "to miss the mark."

- 1 Corinthians 15:3—"For I handed on to you as of first importance what I also received: that Christ died for our sins in accordance with the scriptures."

These publications portrayed the Judaism of Paul's day in very negative terms—a narrow and legalistic system based on a rigid set of Torah-based demands that led to self-reliance on one's own works for salvation. The so-called late Judaism was seen to have undergone devolution from the lofty morals of the later Israelite prophets to the (supposedly) legalistic Pharisees. Rather than cultivating the human-divine relationship, it was argued, these religious structures prohibited direct access between God and the Israelites. Such a pejorative view of ancient Judaism provided the lens through which Paul was understood and interpreted. The research of these Christian scholars led to the conclusion that Paul became an "outsider" to his Jewish religion, even an anti-Jewish outsider. Paul had, in fact, become a "Christian," who offered to the world an alternative to the Jewish way and a restoration of the ideals of ancient Israelite religion that had become corrupted in the centuries before Jesus' birth. As the great (Christian) apostle to the Gentiles, Paul brought the Christian God revealed by Jesus to the non-Jewish world of the first century. Nineteenth-century New Testament scholarship was convinced that Paul fought the Judaism of his day by advocating that through Christ God was once again made accessible. Paul's emphasis that salvation was achieved not by works of the Mosaic Law but by faith in Christ became the great dividing line that showed Christianity's superiority over Judaism. Rudolf Bultmann (1884–1976) solidified this traditional view of both Paul and Judaism by the mid-twentieth century.[2]

In the late 1940s, Bultmann wrote two books that significantly contributed to standardizing the nineteenth-century negative assessment of the ancient Judaism of Paul's day: *The Theology of the New Testament* (1948) and *Primitive Christianity in Its Historical Setting* (1949).[3] Bultmann saw *justification by faith* as the center of Paul's

---

2. The emphasis on Paul's center of thought grounded in "justification by faith" by nineteenth- and twentieth-century German (Protestant) Pauline scholars originated in the work of the sixteenth-century Reformer Martin Luther.

3. See Rudolf Karl Bultmann, *Theologie des Neuen Testaments* (Tübingen: Mohr, 1948); ET: *Theology of the New Testament*, trans. Kendrick Grobel. (New York: Scribner, 1951) and *Das Urchristentum im Rahmen der antiken Religionen* (Zürich: Artemis, 1949); ET: *Primitive Christianity in Its Historical Setting*, trans. R. H. Fuller. (Philadelphia: Fortress Press, 1980). In one of Bultmann's earliest and most influential publications, *The History of the Synoptic Tradition* (1921), Bultmann employed a form-critical study of the Synoptic Gospels of Matthew, Mark, and Luke. Bultmann's research established the framework from which the activities of the early church and the formation of the oral and written gospel tradition would shape the training and education of students of biblical studies for generations.

thought. In his view, this Pauline doctrine was the linchpin that held together Paul's theology and best represented Paul's fundamental break from Judaism. According to Bultmann, ancient Judaism mistakenly understood justification as achieved through one's own merit, through one's work of the law. Paul contrasts this erroneous view of self-justification with justification by faith alone. Justification that leads to salvation cannot be merit-based; it is achieved only through faith in Jesus Christ. Faith in Christ is a gift, a grace bestowed by God.

This characterization of the split between ancient Judaism and Paul on the question of justification found support well into the second half of the twentieth century. Until the 1980s, almost all Pauline scholars held this view.[4]

## The Legacy of Paul

The life and letters of Paul created a legacy early on in Christianity. Evidence of this legacy can already be seen within the canon of the New Testament. Embedded within the Second Letter of Peter, dated by many scholars to the early second century CE, is a reference to Paul and his letters: 2 Peter 3:15–16. The author speaks of the wisdom given to Paul for his letter writing, as well as that in Paul's letters there are "some things hard to understand" and certain people "distort to their own destruction."

The publication of E. P. Sanders's 1977 book, *Paul and Palestinian Judaism*, marked a significant breakthrough in Pauline scholarship. Sanders successfully challenged the now centuries-old negative view of ancient Judaism as a narrow, legalistic religion centered on

---

4. Two of Bultmann's leading students, Ernst Käsemann (1906–1998) and Günther Bornkamm (1905–1990), held this view. In 1969, both scholars published influential books on Paul: Käsemann, *Perspectives on Paul* (Philadelphia: Fortress Press), and Bornkamm, *Paul* (Philadelphia: Fortress Press). Each perpetuated Bultmann's and other scholars' negative view of ancient Judaism and carried on the argument of justification by faith as the center of Paul's thought and the lens through which to view the split between Paul and the Judaism of his day.

self-justification achieved through works of the law.[5] His research of Palestinian Jewish literature facilitated a monumental shift in the discussion of ancient Judaism. In this literature, dated 200 BCE to 200 CE, Sanders noticed a "pattern of religion" within Palestinian Judaism and argued that the Judaism of Paul's day was actually a religion of "covenantal nomism."

In speaking of covenantal nomism, Sanders argued that Pauline scholarship had gotten it wrong by characterizing ancient Palestinian Judaism as a legalistic "works-righteousness" religion. Salvation was not something achieved by one's work through adherence to the law; rather, salvation was a grace, a gift from God established through the covenant with Israel. Justification was an act of divine grace. The law (*nomos* in Greek), or Torah, served as a means to remain (and return) to the right relationship with God as specified in the covenant. Knowing that all people sin and fall short of the covenant, ancient Palestinian Jews viewed observing the law as their covenantal obligation and as the means by which they can remain in right relationship with God. *Justification* or *righteousness* (from the same Greek word, *dikaiosynē*) could not be earned by one's merit; it was a gift to all Jews who desired to be in the covenant.

Sanders's argument that ancient Palestinian Judaism is better understood through the lens of covenantal nomism made such an impact in the field of Pauline scholarship that this approach came to be called the new perspective on Paul.[6] It offered a new generation of scholars an opportunity to see Paul and his relationship to the

---

5. For other instances, especially in the twentieth-century Pauline scholarship, in which the standard view of Paul and his relationship to ancient Judaism has been challenged: see Magnus Zetterholm, *Approaches to Paul: A Student's Guide to Recent Scholarship* (Minneapolis: Fortress Press, 2009), 90–93. Zetterholm discusses the work of three scholars in particular who challenged the research and conclusions of others who studied Paul in relation to rabbinic Judaism and rabbinic literature: Salomon Schechter, *Aspects of Rabbinic Theology* (London: Adam and Charles Black, 1909); Claude Joseph Goldsmid Montefiore, *Judaism and Saint Paul: Two Essays* (London: Goshen, 1914); George Foot Moore, "Christian Writers on Judaism," *Harvard Theological Review* 14 (1921): 197–254. In fact, as Zetterholm points out, much of Sanders's research is built upon the earlier critiques of Montefiore and Moore, 100–105, and more recently, Krister Stendahl, 97–102.

6. James D. G. Dunn is credited with coining the phrase "new perspective" in his 1982 lecture at the University of Manchester and subsequent publication, "The New Perspective of Paul," *Bulletin of the John Rylands University Library of Manchester* 65 (1983): 95–122. See also Krister Stendahl, *Paul Among Jews and Gentiles* (Philadelphia:

Judaism of his day in a different light. Scholars of the new perspective such as N. T. Wright, *What Saint Paul Really Said* (1997), and *Paul: In Fresh Perspective* (2005), and James D. G. Dunn, *The Theology of Paul the Apostle* (1998) no longer held the traditional view that Christianity was the religion of grace in opposition to the works-righteousness religion of Judaism. Sanders, Wright, Dunn, and other new-perspective scholars do not view Paul as anti-Jewish or as a religious reformer *outside* the Judaism of his day. Rather, they see Paul *within* the Judaism of his day, recognizing how a judgment of ancient Judaism as simply a legalistic "works-righteousness" religion unfairly distorts the Judaism that Paul and other believers in Jesus encountered and engaged.

This most recent generation of Pauline scholarship has given birth to "the radical new perspectives of Paul," which holds such positions that for Paul there were two covenants, one for Jews and one for Gentiles.[7] This most recent development in the reorientation of Paul to the Judaism of his day has created tension between the new perspective and the radical new perspective. The latter contends that the new perspective simply repeats the old paradigm, albeit in a new and creative way. The former argues that the radical new perspective too narrowly limits Paul to the Judaism of his day. Regardless of these varying positions, the reorientation of Paul has launched research and publication in areas such as Paul and the Roman Empire and Paul and economics.[8] These latest approaches to

---

Fortress Press, 1976), 78–96, and his essay "The Apostle Paul and the Introspective Conscience of the West," *Harvard Theological Review*, 56 (1963): 199–215, in which he argues twentieth-century perspectives, such as guilty conscience, are routinely and wrongly projected onto first-century Paul. These insights also helped shape the "new perspective."

7. See Zetterholm, chapter 5, "Beyond the New Perspective," 127–164, for a sampling of studies on this radical new perspective on Paul. See also the panel discussion "Newer Perspectives on Paul" at the 2004 Central States Society of Biblical Literature in Saint Louis. See Mark D. Givens, ed., *Paul Unbound: Other Perspectives on the Apostle* (Peabody, MA: Hendrickson, 2010): 1. See also John G. Gager, *Reinventing Paul* (Oxford: Oxford University Press, 2000), who offers an overview of the traditional and newer perspectives on Paul.

8. On Paul and the Roman Empire, see Neil Elliott, *The Arrogance of Nations: Reading Romans in the Shadow of the Empire* (Minneapolis: Fortress Press, 2008); on Paul and economics, see David J. Downs, *The Offering of the Gentiles: Paul's Collection for Jerusalem in Its Chronological, Cultural and Cultic Contexts* (2008); and on Paul and women, see Jorrun Økland, *Women in Their Place: Paul and the Corinthian Discourse of Gender and Sanctuary Space* (London: T & T Clark, 2004).

Paul illustrate well the contemporary trends in Pauline scholarship and the potential for future areas of exploration that have been facilitated by this new perspective on Paul in recent decades. These trends also illustrate the impact of post-Holocaust interpretation on biblical studies, as Christian scholars have sought to find salvific room for Jews apart from Christ.

## Pauline Christianity

Among the first generation of believers in Jesus as the Messiah and Son of God, Paul's voice was one among many. These voices offered diverse and competing ideas about Jesus. Paul's own insight into Jesus, which he wrote was "not of human origin . . . it came through a revelation of Jesus Christ" (Gal 1:11–12), was one of the distinguishing characteristics of his gospel and "Pauline Christianity."

Paul employed a variety of strategies to deal with these different ideas about Jesus. Sometimes Paul reacted angrily to these other voices, as when he heard that another gospel was swaying the Gentile churches of Galatia: "O stupid Galatians! Who has bewitched you?" (Gal 3:1). At other times, Paul countered by presenting a more detailed account of his gospel, as when he wrote his letter to the Romans, introducing himself and his gospel to the Christians in the city of Rome whom he had yet to meet.

## Criteria for Interpreting Paul

Regardless of whether scholars begin with the assumption that Paul was a convert outside the Judaism of his day or a reformer who remained within Judaism, all approaches to Paul embrace a set of criteria, either clearly stated or simply assumed. The set of criteria, in turn, then shapes the interpretative process. This book is no exception, employing its own criteria for interpreting Paul and his letters.

The first criterion used here has to do with the sources on Paul. Not all receive equal treatment; that is to say, some are considered more important primary sources, while others are considered less reliable. The primary sources, the seven undisputed Pauline letters, provide the best information for understanding and interpreting Paul. Additional sources—the remaining six New Testament letters attributed to Paul, the Acts of the Apostles, and extracanonical material (such as early church writings, archeological materials, and so on)—contribute to the interpretation of Paul. These other sources must be understood within the context of their place and time in the development of the early church and Pauline Christianity.

The handling of the sources leads to this book's second criterion. Because the letters of Paul are occasional letters, the information and details contained in each should be explored in light of its specific historical setting, theology, and ethics (that is, rules of conduct). Each Pauline letter must be allowed to stand on its own because each was written for a particular occasion. Further, sorting through the theology and ethics embedded in these letters requires close scrutiny. Some of Paul's thinking forms the basis of his larger theological framework (for example, justification by faith in Christ: Gal 2:15–12; Rom 3:21–28; Phil 3:7–11); some is very situational (such as the case of incest in Corinth, 1 Cor 5:1–13); and some belongs to a received tradition he inherited (for instance, the celebration of the Eucharist in Corinth, 1 Cor 11:23–26).

The occasional nature of Paul's letters, criterion two, connects directly to the third criterion: the chronological treatment of Paul and his letters. The history, theology, and ethics within Paul's letters is commonly handled either thematically or chronologically. Although both approaches have merit, this book proceeds with a chronological treatment, which reinforces the idea that these occasional letters are best understood within the chronology of Paul's life, the evolution of his own theological thinking, and the historical developments within the first and second generation of Christians.[9]

## Sources on Paul

Scholars categorize the source material on Paul in a variety of ways. The clearest division is between canonical sources (those within the

---

9. This chronological approach is advocated by some of the best contemporary treatments of Paul. See Udo Schnelle, *Apostle Paul: His Life and Theology*, trans. M. Eugene Boring (Grand Rapids, MI: Baker Academic, 2003). For a good example of a thematic approach to Paul, see James D. G. Dunn, *The Theology of Paul the Apostle* (Grand Rapids, MI, and Cambridge, UK: Eerdmans, 1998).

New Testament) and extracanonical sources (those outside the New Testament). Source material on Paul (and Pauline Christianity) within the canon of the New Testament is plentiful, with the most important source material in the canon being the seven undisputed letters of Paul. First Thessalonians, the earliest of the seven, was written from the city of Corinth in 50 CE, sometime after Paul was expelled from the city of Thessalonica. Paul probably wrote 1 Corinthians in the spring of 55 CE and his Second Letter to the Corinthians in the fall of 55 CE, possibly from the city of Ephesus. Shortly after 2 Corinthians, Paul wrote his Letter to the Galatians. Probably a year or two later, Paul wrote his Letter to the Romans in the spring of 56 CE. During one of his imprisonments (possibly in Ephesus, Caesarea, or Rome), Paul composed his Letter to the Philippians and his Letter to Philemon.

## Pseudepigraphy

Pseudepigraphy, from the Greek pseudēs, "false," and epigraphē, "inscription," is the act of writing in another's name. A common practice in the ancient world, pseudepigraphy was an attempt to deceive the recipients of the written work. An example of pseudepigraphy would include the first century CE "Letters of Socrates" which are presented as if Socrates (470–399 BCE) had written them.

Old Testament pseudepigrapha were quite popular between the years 200 BCE and 200 CE. Many Jewish writings were attributed to biblical characters such as Adam and Eve (Life of Adam and Eve), Moses (Assumption of Moses) and Isaiah (Martyrdom and Ascension of Isaiah). Early Christians carried on the tradition of pseudepigraphy in works such as the Gospel of Peter (mid-second century CE) and Paul's Epistle to the Laodiceans (mid-third century CE).

Most scholars acknowledge the likelihood of pseudepigraphic works in the New Testament. For example, the apostle Peter, martyred in the mid-60s CE, did not write the First and Second Letter of Peter, composed in the late first century and early second century CE, respectively. In the case of Paul's letters, the majority of scholars believe that later Pauline Christians writing in Paul's name composed the Pastoral Letters (1 Timothy, 2 Timothy, and Titus) and Ephesians. Scholars are less certain if this is the case with Colossians and 2 Thessalonians.

The remaining source material on Paul in the New Testament consists of the six deutero-Pauline letters of Colossians, Ephesians, 2 Thessalonians, 1 Timothy, 2 Timothy, and Titus, and the Acts of the Apostles.[10] Paul did not write the six remaining Pauline letters. Scholars speculate that the real authors may have been either close associates of Paul during his lifetime or contemporary leaders within the Pauline communities that survived after his death. These unknown authors were attempting to carry on the theology and ethics of Paul, adapting it to their new circumstances. Scholars debate the exact date and place of composition of these letters. They were likely written between the years 70 and 120 CE. There also appears to be some literary relationship among these Pauline letters; for example, Ephesians is a later expansion of Colossians. As a whole, these letters take up the concerns of the second and third generations of Pauline Christianity and reflect the legacy of Paul's influence in the early church.

An additional New Testament source for understanding and interpreting Paul is the Acts of the Apostles. Composed in the late first century CE by the same author who wrote the Gospel of Luke, this two-part narrative, Luke-Acts, tells the story of Christianity from the birth and infancy of Jesus (Luke 1–2) to Paul's imprisonment in Rome (Acts 28). Luke offers his perspective on Paul only decades removed from the actual historical events. Much of what Luke relates about Paul in the Acts of the Apostles can be verified from the authentic Pauline letters.

Source material on Paul (and Pauline Christianity) outside the New Testament is scarce. Scholars classify much of this source material as "apocryphal Pauline literature." *Apocryphal* here refers to early Christian writings not included in the New Testament. This source material includes letters, acts, and apocalypses (end of the age stories) that were written in Paul's name or about Paul, mostly from the second through the fourth century CE. These pseudepigraphic works include extracanonical letters (*3 Corinthians*, the *Epistle to the Laodiceans*, and the *Correspondences between Paul and Seneca*), an extracanonical narrative (the *Acts of Paul*, which includes the *Acts of Paul and Thecla*), and an extracanonical apocalypse

---

10. Jude, 1 Peter, and 2 Peter could be included here on the list, as many scholars regard these New Testament letters as additional post-Pauline trajectories.

(*Apocalypse of Paul*).[11] More so than actually disclosing information about Paul, this source material shows how the early church used Paul and his theology to address the concerns, debates, and issues of their times.

## Pauline Contexts: Jewish and Hellenistic

Modern approaches to Paul rightly consider both the Jewish and Hellenistic contexts that shaped his life and his worldview. Paul was ethnically a Jew (a Hebrew) of the tribe of Benjamin (Phil 3:5), born and raised in the Greek city of Tarsus in Cilicia (Acts 21:39), a region several hundred miles north of Jerusalem, outside of Palestine. Luke also presents Paul as a Roman citizen (Acts 22:22–29). Further, Paul and his fellow first-century CE Jews lived in a period of history heavily influenced by *Hellenism*—defined as the adoption of Greek language, literature, social customs, and ethical values. Both Judaism and Hellenism formed and informed Paul throughout his life.

### Diaspora Jews

*Diaspora* comes from a Greek term meaning "scattering." It is a reference to the dispersion of the Jews upon their return from exile in Babylon (587–538 BCE), although the prophet Jeremiah complains about such a development even before the Babylonian exile. Although many Jews returned to their homeland in Palestine after the exile, many others established Jewish communities in other parts of the Mediterranean area. Paul, born and raised in Tarsus of Cilicia, would have been counted among the scattered Jews. At the time of Jesus and Paul, in fact, most Jews lived in the diaspora in such cities as Antioch, Corinth, Rome, Ephesus, and Alexandria. (See map on p. 31.)

---

11. For a very good single-volume work that contains all the New Testament apocryphal writings, including the apocryphal Pauline literature, see J. K. Elliott, *The Apocryphal New Testament: A Collection of Apocryphal Christian Literature in an English Translation based on M. R. James* (Oxford: Clarendon Press, 1993). See also Richard I. Pervo, *The Making of Paul: Constructions of the Apostle in Early Christianity* (Minneapolis: Fortress Press, 2010).

Research in the past few decades has shown that the Judaism of Paul's day was quite diverse. Some Jews, for example, were born and raised in Palestine (Palestinian Jews), like Jesus and many of

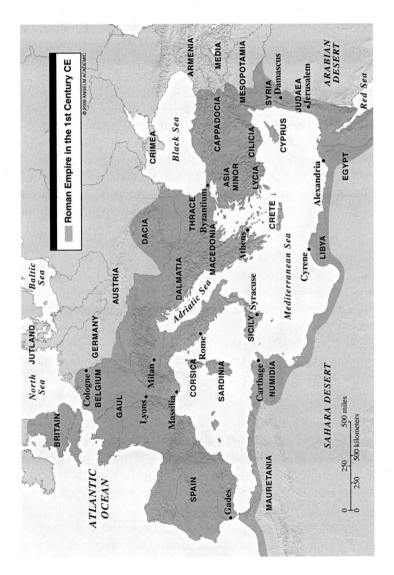

his Jewish followers, and spoke Aramaic. Other Jews were born and raised outside Palestine (diaspora Jews), like Paul and many other first-century CE Jews, and spoke Greek. Various other Jewish groups also had a presence in the first-century CE world. A small percentage of Palestinian and diaspora Jews belonged to the elite groups of the Sadducees (a conservative aristocracy), the Pharisees (interpreters of the oral and written Mosaic Law; the group to which Paul belonged—Phil 3:5; Acts 22:3), and the scribes (trained scholars). Most Palestinian Jews either lived in the Palestinian countryside and were simply referred to as the *'Am ha-'aretz* (in Hebrew, the "people of the land") or resided in the cities scattered throughout the Roman Empire. Some Palestinian Jews were revolutionaries trying to evict Romans from their Jewish homeland of Palestine (the Zealots and Sicarii), while others lived in isolated communities anticipating the Messianic Age (the Essenes). The differing religious and political views of these Jewish groups affected how they lived their Jewish faith. For example, different understandings of purity and the calendar was the subject of intense debate among the Jews.

Despite their diversity of beliefs and practices, the various Jewish groups agreed on four fundamental areas: belief in their covenantal relationship with a single God (YHWH); conviction in the divine election of Israel among all the other nations; reverence and adherence to the divinely revealed instructions of the Mosaic Law (the Torah); and devotion to the Temple in their capital city of Jerusalem. These defining characteristics separated Jews from the other nations, and they would be the very issues Paul would integrate into his message and missionary outreach to the Gentiles about the crucified and resurrected Messiah.

In addition to these Jewish influences, Paul was impacted by the Hellenistic culture that had engulfed the ancient Mediterranean world for centuries before he was born. Paul's Jewish religious belief in a single God (monotheism) was certainly not the norm of the Greco-Roman world. Nearly all people in the Roman Empire were polytheistic; that is, their religious observances were not restricted to a particular god or goddess (deity). Cities within the Roman Empire had sanctuaries, in which devotion to a deity took place by those trained for the proper ceremonial activities. Religious practices associated with the mystery cults of the Roman Empire were also common. Participants in these mystery cults kept secret the practices of the rites performed to their deity. Meals were often shared among the members of these mystery cults and their deity, with the assurance of the deity's protection and special knowledge for cult members. Among the most popular mystery cults within the Roman Empire were those of Dionysius, Mithras, and Isis.

## Artemis, the Goddess of Ephesus

In the city of Ephesus, there was the well-known temple devoted to Artemis, the goddess of fertility. Artemis was one of the most widely worshipped female gods in the province of Asia.

Acts 19 relates Paul's encounter in Ephesus with the silversmiths and artisans who made miniature silver shrines of Artemis. Paul publicly challenged the existence of Artemis or any god "made by human hands." Paul's words caused such chaos and confusion among the citizenry that a riot broke out in the city.

Paul also faced numerous Greek philosophies (worldviews) that shaped and defined the Hellenistic culture of his day. Among the more popular philosophies were Epicureanism, Stoicism, and Cynicism. Epicureanism stressed the material nature of all things (including the body and soul as perishable), the importance of inner peace and harmony, and the complete disconnect between the deities of the other world and this world. By comparison, Stoicism emphasized the divine spark in each person and the practice of virtue as the human ideal. In addition, it taught that the universe was held together by a controlling principle called the *logos* (*word*) and a vital spirit or soul called *pneuma* (*spirit*). Cynicism espoused that true human freedom would come from living a simple life, void of possession and material wealth.

Alongside these various worldviews, Paul the Pharisee most likely embraced the Jewish worldview of apocalypticism. As the Essenes also were, the Pharisees were Jewish apocalypticists who viewed the world as a duality between good and evil. Some first-century CE Jews anticipated an imminent end to this age (the eschaton), which would culminate in God's intervention in the world. God, in control of human history, would send someone to deliver his people from the forces of evil on Earth, set up God's kingdom, raise the dead, and judge the world. These Jews held an apocalyptic eschatology, but many Jews at this time had no such imminent eschatological expectation.

Paul and his contemporaries were immersed in a diverse arena of competing beliefs and philosophies. It was to this world that Paul would bring his gospel of Jesus Christ.

## Summary: Understanding and Interpreting Paul

### CORE CONCEPTS

- One of the main areas of research on Paul for the past two hundred years has been Paul's relation to the Judaism of his day.
- James D. G. Dunn coined the term the *new perspective* to describe recent Pauline scholarship that sees Paul more as a reformer within the Judaism of his day.
- E. P. Sanders's concept of covenantal nomism stemmed from a new perspective in studying Paul within the context of ancient Judaism.

### SUPPLEMENTAL INFORMATION

- Source material on Paul is plentiful.
- Most of the nineteenth- and twentieth-century New Testament scholarship portrayed the Judaism of Paul's day in negative terms.
- Paul and his letters are best understood within the chronology of his life, the evolution of his own theological thinking, and the historical developments within the first and second generations of Christians.
- The seven undisputed letters of Paul provide the primary source material on Paul.
- Both Jewish and Hellenistic influences shaped Paul's life and worldview.
- Paul can be understood as a Jewish apocalyptic Pharisee.

# THE LIFE AND LETTERS OF PAUL

The second part of this chapter begins with a chronological accounting of Paul's life, beginning with his birth and formative years, and then turning to his life as a Pharisee, his encounter with the risen Christ, and his missionary work as the apostle to the Gentiles. It then takes a closer look at the letters of Paul, which includes a discussion of letter writing in the ancient world and Paul's use of letter writing in his outreach to the Gentiles. This section concludes with a discussion of the composition and formation of what is known as the Pauline Corpus, the body of Paul's works.

## The Life of Paul

### Paul's Birth and Formative Years in Tarsus

Paul's letters and the Acts of the Apostles say nothing about when Paul was born and very little about his formative years. The only clue to the year of Paul's birth comes from an incidental comment Paul makes in his letter to Philemon, written around 60 CE. There, Paul refers to himself as an old man (Phlm 9), which would have made him perhaps fifty years old in the early 60s. This clue points to the possibility that Paul was born sometime between the years 5 and 15 of the first century CE. Nothing is written of Paul's parents or other relatives, aside from his parents being Jewish (Phil 3:5), but he did apparently have at least one sister (Acts 23:16). Paul never married (1 Cor 7:7–8), and so it is assumed that he had no children.

What scholars do know is that Paul claimed to be a descendent from the tribe of Benjamin (Rom 11:1; Phil 3:5) and, according to Acts, was born and raised in Tarsus, the capital city of Cilicia in the southeastern part of the province of Asia Minor (Acts 21:39, 22:3). Tarsus stood at the crossroads of major commerce and trade routes. A wealthy, metropolitan Hellenistic city with a large Jewish population, Tarsus was known for its Hellenistic school, which trained and educated the elite in philosophy, rhetoric, and poetry. As an urban Jew surrounded by Hellenistic culture, Paul was exposed to a multicultural environment during his formative years and was conversant in the oral and written dialect of *Koinē* (common Greek)—the

## Was Paul a Roman Citizen?

Luke writes in the Acts of the Apostles that Paul was a Roman citizen (Acts 16:37–38, 22:27, 23:27). Yet nowhere in any of Paul's undisputed letters does he mention his Roman citizenship. Roman citizenship could be obtained by means other than birth, such as adoption into a prominent Roman household or release from slavery. It is entirely plausible that Paul inherited Roman citizenship from his family ancestry of being freed Jewish slaves.

The tradition that Paul was martyred by being beheaded is consistent with Luke's statement of Paul's Roman citizenship, as Roman citizens found guilty of capital crimes against the state were spared torturous deaths. However, there is no reliable historical basis for this later apocryphal tradition. The tradition of Paul's martyrdom by decapitation could be based in part upon Acts, rather than any certain knowledge of the historical Paul.

language of his letters and the entire New Testament. According to Acts, Paul returned occasionally to his hometown after his conversion and during his missionary travels (Acts 9:30, 11:25).

Although Paul never speaks directly of any formal training and education he may have received, his letters point to the use of both Greco-Roman rhetorical style and Jewish interpretive practices. For example, in his letters, Paul employed the literary device of "diatribe," common to the Cynic and Stoic philosophers of his day, in which questions are put forth and then refuted (for instance, Rom 10:5–8). In addition, similar to the Jewish Pesher or Midrash (interpretation of Scripture) of his day, Paul applied the Jewish Scriptures to his new situation of faith in Christ as the Messiah and Son of God (such as 1 Cor 10:1–4).

### Paul the Pharisee

Paul refers to himself as a Pharisee (Phil 3:5). In fact, Paul says he was "a zealot for my ancestral traditions" and had "progressed in Judaism beyond many of my contemporaries among my race" (Gal 1:14). Pharisees were descendents of the Hasidim, a resistance movement that originated in response to the oppressive rule of Antiochus IV Epiphanes (175–163 BCE). Pharisees saw themselves as the interpreters, and the social enforcers, of the Mosaic Law and the oral law that evolved from its interpretation. Where Paul received his Pharisaic training is unknown, although Luke writes that Paul trained "at the feet of Gamaliel" (Acts 22:3), the well-known and respected teacher of Jerusalem. Paul himself gives no indication that he ever formally studied in Jerusalem under Gamaliel. As a Pharisee, Paul would have viewed the Torah (the written law) and his "ancestral traditions" (the oral law) as the center of his religious identity and life.

Paul's extremely zealous attitude toward the Mosaic Law most likely fueled his persecution of the early Christians, as he saw these Christ-believing Jews as a threat to the other Torah-observant Jews. Paul likely perceived this band of Jews' profession of faith in this man as blasphemy, which certainly provided enough justification to try to stop the spread of this dangerous message.

## Was Paul also Known by the Name *Saul*?

In the Acts of the Apostles, Luke sometimes refers to Paul as Saul. This mostly occurs in Luke's references to Paul before his encounter with Christ (Acts 7:58, 8:1–3, 9:1). Twice after he meets the resurrected Christ, Luke calls Paul by the name *Saul*. In Acts 13:9, Luke uses these names side by side, "But Saul, also known as Paul . . ." After Acts 13:9, he is always called Paul, except when Saul/Paul recounts his earlier vision of Jesus (Acts 22:7,13; 26:14).

The name *Paul* is the Greek equivalent to the Semitic name *Saul*. In other words, the name Paul reflects the Greco-Roman culture in which Paul was raised (the city of Tarsus, Cilicia), and the name *Saul* reflects Paul's Jewish heritage. Paul lived in both the Hellenistic and Jewish world.

Interestingly, Paul never refers to himself as Saul in his letters. This may simply be an indication of his largely Gentile audience who would know him only as Paul. It is more likely, however, that Paul never used the name *Saul* for himself, reflecting his life as a Hellenized Jew.

There are only glimpses of Paul the Pharisee during the period in which he persecuted the early Christians. Scholars can merely speculate that the Sanhedrin in Jerusalem authorized him to persecute the church. Paul himself says, "I persecuted the church of God beyond measure and tried to destroy it" (Gal 1:13), and "in zeal I persecuted the church" (Phil 3:6). In Acts, Luke introduces Paul at the stoning of Stephen, the first martyr in the Acts of the Apostles (Acts 7:58). Luke writes that at the stoning of Stephen, the witnesses "laid down their cloaks at the feet of a young man named Saul," an indication that Paul was the one who authorized the stoning. Luke paints a frightening picture of Paul in his persecution of the church. He notes that immediately following the stoning of Stephen, "a severe persecution of the church in Jerusalem" (Acts 8:1) broke out and that Paul was "trying to destroy the church; entering house after house and dragging out men and women, he handed them over for imprisonment" (Acts 8:3). In his persecution of the church, Luke indicates, Paul was "breathing murderous threats" (Acts 9:1). Much later in Acts (22:4, 26:9–11), Luke discloses even higher levels of violence that Paul directed against the church. As Paul himself reflected upon these actions years after his encounter with the resurrected Jesus, he expressed regret: "For I am the least of the apostles, not fit to be called an apostle, because I persecuted the church of God" (1 Cor 15:9). Luke's portrayal of Paul, before his conversion, as one who literally "breathes murder" is, therefore, probably accurate. In one of the later New Testament letters attributed to Paul, the author in 1 Timothy 1:13 offers an apologetic attempt to present Paul as ignorant about what he did in persecuting the church.

## Paul's Encounter with the Risen Jesus

Scholars debate about the length of Paul's persecution of the early church and the year in which Paul received his call and commission. Dating Jesus' crucifixion in the year 30 CE, and Paul's call and commission in the year 33 CE, is a common position.[12] Paul's conviction that God revealed the resurrected Jesus to him reshaped and reoriented his entire life and worldview. It is difficult to overestimate the impact this event made on Paul and his understanding of himself, Judaism, and the universe.

---

12. See Schnelle, 51.

## Did Paul Have a "Conversion" Experience?

Interpreters of Paul have traditionally thought that Paul had a "conversion" experience after meeting the resurrected Christ on the road to Damascus. By *conversion*, a change from one religion (in this case, Pharisaic Judaism) to another (Christianity) is meant. Yet neither Paul in his letters nor Luke in the Acts of the Apostles uses the language of *conversion* in this sense.

Most details of this event come from Luke. Three times Luke narrates the encounter between the resurrected Jesus and Paul in the telling of the story of the early church: Acts 9:1–19 (Paul on the road to Damascus to persecute Christians); Acts 22:3–16 (part of Paul's defense speech to the Jews in Jerusalem); and Acts 26:2–18 (part of Paul's defense speech to King Agrippa). In Acts 22:15, Luke says that Paul is to be the risen Christ's "witness" (*martus*) "before all to what you have seen and heard." The idea of "witness" is repeated in Acts 26:16.

In Galatians 1:11–16, Paul speaks of having a "revelation" (*apokalypsis*) of Jesus Christ, and being called by God "to preach" (*euangelizomai*) Jesus to the Gentiles. In this revelation and call, it is doubtful that Paul saw himself converting from one religion (Pharisaic Judaism) to another (Christianity).

The conversion Paul had was likely an internal one, of heart and mind, as he sought to reconstruct and redefine his understanding of God, Israel, and himself in light of the crucified and resurrected Christ. It should be noted that both *call* and *conversion* are modern terms and that neither is completely adequate for interpreting the accounts of Paul and Luke.

Paul speaks briefly to this event in his letters to the Galatians and the Corinthians, both written about twenty years after the event and in the specific context of Paul defending his apostolic status and authority. In 1 Corinthians, Paul writes, "Have I not seen Jesus our Lord?" (1 Cor 9:1), and "Last of all, as one born abnormally, he appeared to me" (1 Cor 15:8). In Galatians, as part of his autobiographical sketch, Paul writes that God "was pleased to reveal his Son to me, so that I might proclaim him to the Gentiles" (Gal 1:15–16).

That Paul does not discuss this life-changing event in the seven undisputed letters does not minimize its importance for the formation of Paul's theology. After all, in his occasional letters, Paul is writing to specific circumstances, most of which did not require any discussion of his original encounter with the risen Jesus.

## Paul, Called to Be the Apostle to the Gentiles

The revelation of the resurrected Christ fundamentally changed Paul's life. Paul spent the next thirty years fulfilling what he believed God had called him to do: preach the good news of Jesus Christ to Gentiles. This revelation and call made Paul's gospel distinct among all others who were spreading the "good news" of the death and Resurrection of Jesus. The following reconstruction of these thirty years is based upon what can be gleaned from Paul's letters, cross-referenced (when possible) with Luke's account of Paul's missionary journeys in the Acts of the Apostles. It begins in 33 CE, the approximate year Paul experienced the resurrected Christ.

Immediately following his revelation, Paul reports going into Arabia and returning to Damascus (Gal 1:17). Exactly how long Paul stayed in Arabia or how far he traveled into Arabia before returning to Damascus is unknown. However "after three years" (about 35 or 36 CE), Paul went to Jerusalem "to confer" with Cephas (Peter) and stayed with him for fifteen days (Gal 1:18). From there, Paul traveled in the regions of Syria and Cilicia, presumably on his initial missionary outreach to the Gentiles of that region (Gal 1:21–24), joined at some point by Barnabas and Titus. This entailed considerable travel by Paul. Jerusalem is about 200 miles south of Damascus. Paul's return north to the regions of Syria and Cilicia was closer to 400 miles.

Paul made his second trip to Jerusalem (the so-called Jerusalem conference) fourteen years later (about 49 CE), after receiving a revelation (Gal 2:2). This time he went with Barnabas (a Judaic Christ-believer) and Titus (an uncircumcised Gentile Christ-believer), to present to Peter, James, and John "the gospel" that he "preached to the Gentiles" in Syria, Cilicia, and elsewhere (Gal 2:1–10). The Jerusalem conference was likely intended to resolve the growing tensions between Judaic and Gentile Christians, specifically around the question of admitting Gentiles as equal members of the church.

## Paul's Autobiography

The closest thing to an autobiography of Paul is found in the undisputed letters of Galatians 1:11–24 and Philippians 3:4–11. These passages, although limited in scope, contain some details on Paul's life, in his own words:

- Born into the race of Israel, the tribe of Benjamin (Phil 3:5)
- Jewish parents (Phil 3:5)
- Circumcised on the eighth day (Phil 3:5)
- A Pharisee, zealous for his ancestral traditions (Gal 1:14; Phil 3:5)
- Progressed in Judaism beyond many of his peers (Gal 1:14)
- Blameless before the law (Phil 3:6)
- Zealously persecuted the church and tried to destroy it (Gal 1:13; Phil 3:6)
- Had a revelation of God's resurrected Son (Gal 1:16)
- Called to proclaim Jesus to the Gentiles (Gal 1:16)
- Visited with Peter in Jerusalem three years after his encounter with the risen Jesus (Gal 1:18)
- Was initially well known for going from persecutor of the churches to defender of the faith (Gal 1:22–23)

Peter and Paul apparently reached some kind of an agreement, shaking "their right hands in partnership," and concluding that Paul and Barnabas would continue their missionary work to the Gentiles, and Peter, James, and John would go "to the circumcised" (the Jews).

Precisely what was agreed at the Jerusalem meeting is uncertain. For example, a two-pronged mission to Jews (led by Peter) and Gentiles (led by Paul) does not address what kind of community the church would form among the many Jews living in the diaspora. Paul then met Peter in Antioch, where they argued over the issue of Jews sharing table-fellowship with Gentiles. Paul "opposed" Peter "to his face because he was clearly wrong" and acting hypocritically (along with Barnabas) over not dining with Gentiles (Gal 2:11–13). Paul and Barnabas went separate ways after they had a falling-out when Barnabas took the side of the circumcision faction. According to Luke, Paul chose Silas to replace Barnabas (Acts 15:36–41). Clearly, in Antioch different understandings of the Jerusalem agreement emerged. Does a mission to Gentiles mean accepting Gentiles as uncircumcised Gentiles who do not eat kosher foods? Do Judaic Christ-believers have to abandon the Mosaic Law when in fellowship with Gentile believers? Can there be one community comprised of Jews and Gentiles that can eat and worship together? Such questions would not be resolved within Paul's lifetime.

## The Gallio Inscription

Fragment of the "Gallio Inscription" with the Greek form of Gallio visible in the fourth line from the top

According to Acts 18:12–16, Paul was brought to trial before Lucius Gallio, the proconsul of Achaia, sometime during his eighteen-month stay in the city of Corinth. The "Gallio Inscription," an inscription documenting a letter from emperor Claudius addressed to Gallio's successor, offers reliable historical evidence that Gallio was in Corinth in the summer of 51 CE. This fact provides the only verifiable date in the chronology of Paul's life from which all other dates are calculated backward or forward.

## Paul the Tentmaker

As a missionary to the Gentiles, Paul worked for a living as an artisan. According to Acts, Paul was a tentmaker by trade (Acts 18:1–3). However, nowhere in Paul's letters does he attest to this trade.

Tentmaking in the ancient Mediterranean was hard, physical labor. Tents were sewn together with cloth and sometimes leather. It required strong hands, shoulders, and back to work effectively with these materials. Cities such as Tarsus, where Paul grew up, and Corinth, where Paul met Aquila and Prisca (also known as Priscilla) and stayed for a lengthy time, would have had a high demand for tents, because tourists, soldiers, sailors, and athletes all needed tents for travel and lodging.

Paul continued his Gentile missionary work with Silas (Silvanus) and Timothy, traveling through Asia Minor and crossing into Macedonia, where they established small house churches in Philippi, Thessalonica, and possibly Berea (Acts 16–17). It should be noted here that out of necessity, scholars follow the chronology of Acts, allowing for the possibility that some details may point more to Luke's theology than to Paul's life.

After being expelled from various Macedonian cities, they moved south to Achaia. Paul briefly visited the city of Athens but was unsuccessful there (Acts 17). The three then moved on to Corinth, the capital of Achaia, where they stayed for about eighteen months. There they met Prisca and Aquila, who were in Corinth after Emperor Claudius expelled them from Rome in 49 CE (Acts 18). It is plausible to infer that Paul wrote his First Letter to the Thessalonians from the city of Corinth in the year 50 CE.

After leaving Corinth, Paul next traveled through Asia Minor, then to Syria (including brief visits to Jerusalem and Antioch), and back again to Ephesus, the capital of Asia Minor (Acts 19). Paul stayed in Ephesus for at least twenty-seven months, preaching and strengthening the churches in the region (about 52 to 55 CE). Paul traveled personally, sending and receiving messengers and letters back and forth from Ephesus to Macedonia, Corinth, and other parts of Asia Minor. In the spring of 55 CE, Paul wrote his First Letter to the Corinthians, and in the fall of that year, wrote his Second Letter to the Corinthians and his Letter to the Galatians. Throughout his extended stay in Ephesus, Paul encountered significant opposition from both Jews and Gentiles and even spent some time in prison in Ephesus.

After his twenty-seven months in Ephesus, Paul made a third and final visit to Corinth. From there, he sent his Letter to the Romans in the spring of 56 CE. In the conclusion to his Letter to the Romans, Paul documented his upcoming plans to revisit Jerusalem and then stop back in Rome en route to Spain (Rom 15:23–29).

Establishing a timeline for the final years of Paul's life requires exploring a portion of Scripture written after Paul's death, Acts 21–28, which provides details that are impossible to verify from any of Paul's letters. During his third and final visit to Jerusalem, Paul was arrested and brought to trial before the Sanhedrin (Acts 22–23). Paul's trial caused such a commotion that he was transferred and imprisoned at Caesarea for two years under Antonius Felix and his successor, Porcius Festus (Acts 24) before being put on trial again, this time before King Agrippa (Acts 25–26). Agrippa found Paul guilty of "doing nothing at all that deserves death or imprisonment" (Acts 26:31). Paul was then transported under armed guard back to Rome, where he remained under house arrest for two years (Acts 27–28).

## The Persecution of Paul

In his Second Letter to the Corinthians, Paul catalogs the ways he suffered for responding to his call and commission to preach the good news of Jesus Christ to the Gentiles.

> Five times at the hands of the Jews I received forty lashes minus one. Three times I was beaten with rods, once I was stoned, three times I was shipwrecked, I passed a night and a day on the deep; on frequent journeys, in dangers from rivers, dangers from robbers, dangers from my own

*Continued*

The Persecution of Paul *Continued*

race, dangers from Gentiles, dangers in the city, dangers in the wilderness, dangers at sea, dangers among false brothers; in toil and hardship, through many sleepless nights, through hunger and thirst, through frequent fasting, through cold and exposure. And apart from these things, there is the daily pressure upon me of my anxiety for all the churches. (2 Cor 11:24–28)

Paul summarizes here twenty years of persecution, from his original revelation and call in 35 CE to the writing of 2 Corinthians in 55 CE.

Paul wrote two other letters—the Letter to the Philippians and the Letter to Philemon—while in prison. Late in his apostolic career, Paul was imprisoned in three cities at different times: Ephesus, Caesarea, and Rome. Scholars are uncertain of where Paul wrote these two imprisonment letters.

### The Death of Paul

The death of Paul remains the subject of speculation. Luke does not narrate Paul's death, choosing to end the Acts of the Apostles with Paul under house arrest, still very much alive and preaching his gospel. No canonical sources provide information about Paul's death, and only one extracanonical source from the early Christian tradition speaks of it. That source, the *First Letter of Clement*, dates to the end of the reign of Emperor Domitian, 95–96 CE, and presupposes Paul's death as a martyr in Rome. *First Clement* 5 offers an account (decades removed) of the death of Paul:

By reason of jealousy and strife Paul by his example pointed out the prize of patient endurance. After that he had been seven times in bonds, had been driven into exile, had been stoned, had preached in the East and in the West, he won the noble renown which was the reward of his faith, having taught righteousness unto the whole world and having reached the farthest bounds of the West; and when he had borne his testimony before the rulers, so he departed from the world and went unto the holy place, having been found a notable pattern of patient endurance.[13] (*1 Clement* 5:3–6)

The date of Paul's death remains uncertain, but early church tradition holds that Paul was beheaded in Rome during the reign of Emperor Nero (54–68 CE), most likely during the years between 62 and 64 CE, when persecution of Christians in Rome was widespread. In Romans 15, Paul mentions his hope to *visit* Rome (*not* in chains) and thereafter conduct missionary work in Spain. The accounts of Acts 28 (Paul under house arrest in Rome) and Romans 15 cannot be harmonized.

## The Letters of Paul

### Letters and Letter Writing in the Ancient World

The sending and receiving of letters was a common form of communication for people living in the Roman Empire. This certainly holds true in the case of the early Christians; indeed, twenty-one of the twenty-seven writings in the New Testament are classified as "letters."

### "Letters" or "Epistles"?

Past scholarship used to classify some of Paul's writings as letters and others as epistles, with letters thought to be read privately (like Paul's Letter to Philemon) and epistles read publicly (like Paul's Letter to the Romans). This historic distinction in nomenclature is no longer used today. This book will use the terms *letter* and *epistle* interchangeably.

A comparison of Paul's letters with those of the time clearly shows that Paul followed the literary conventions of his day. However, he did adapt his letters in some ways to the churches to which he wrote. For example, the salutation of Paul's Letter to the Romans

---

13. English translation from J. B. Lightfoot.

(1:1–7) includes not only the standard identified sender-recipient ("Paul . . . to all the beloved of God in Rome") and greeting but also a basic summary of his gospel and an explanation of his missionary outreach to the Gentiles (1:2–6). The length of the body of Paul's letters was also atypical for his day. The theology and ethics that Paul develops in the body often required extensive explanations, resulting in an unusually long letter.

Letter writers in Paul's day routinely followed a basic structure. Letters began with a salutation that included the name of the sender, the name of the intended recipient(s), and a brief greeting. After the salutation came a thanksgiving (oftentimes a prayer) and then the body of the letter that contained the main purpose for writing. Some type of command often signaled the closing of the body of the letter. The letter then ended with a conclusion that included a peace wish, a greeting to known acquaintances of the letter's recipient, and a benediction.

Letters were typically written on papyrus. Papyrus, a plant grown on the banks on the Nile River in Egypt, provided the raw materials for making paper. The center of the plant was split into thin strips, pressed, and dried in the sun. The strips were then joined together and made smooth by pieces of ivory or shell in preparation for writing. Letter writers wrote with pens made of reeds (hollow stalks) with one end of the reed sharpened for writing. The "ink" used for writing was typically made from carbon soot deposits that resulted from burning wood and other materials. The soot was mixed into a solution of gum water in a metal or ceramic holder. Paul most likely used all of the mentioned materials (papyrus paper, black-soot ink, and reed pens) for the letters written during his missionary work to the Gentiles.

The Roman Empire established a formal delivery system for letters, whereby carriers on horseback or in chariots (somewhat) reliably delivered them. Normally, only government officials, the military, and the wealthy had access to this system. The typical citizen (and noncitizen) of the Roman Empire had to depend upon slaves, acquaintances, or the goodwill of travelers heading in the right direction to deliver a personal letter. This was, of course, far less reliable.[14]

---

14. See E. Randolph Richards, *Paul and First-Century Letter Writing: Secretaries, Composition and Collection* (Downers Grove, IL: InterVarsity Press, 2004) and Jerome Murphy-O'Connor, *Paul the Letter-Writer: His World, His Options, His Skills* (Collegeville, MN: The Liturgical Press, 1995), for a good introduction to Paul and his letters within the context of letters and letter writing in the ancient world.

## Paul's Use of Letter Writing

At some point during the course of his thirty years of missionary work among the Gentiles, Paul took up the practice of letter writing to keep in touch with the churches he established and address problems that arose in these communities after he departed and between his visits. It is unknown if Paul wrote letters before 50 CE, the year scholars believe Paul wrote 1 Thessalonians, the earliest of the canonical Pauline letters. It is clear, however, that Paul was a letter-writer in the second half of his thirty-year career, writing numerous letters between 50 and 60 CE. There is good reason to believe that Paul wrote more than the seven letters that appear in the canon of the New Testament. Paul refers to other (lost?) letters (see, for example, 1 Cor 5:9; 2 Cor 2:2–4), and many scholars are convinced that Philippians and 2 Corinthians are composite letters made up of material from previous correspondences between Paul and the churches in Philippi and Corinth.

### Paul the Letter Writer

In his Second Letter to the Corinthians, dated to the fall of 55 CE, Paul writes of his already widely known reputation as one whose "letters are severe and forceful" (2 Cor 10:10), and he describes his physical attributes as "weak . . . and contemptible" (2 Cor 10:10). Paul perceived that others saw a disconnect between the rhetorical power of his letters and the physical weakness of his bodily presence.

Most letter writers of this time actually dictated their letters to a secretary or a scribe, a trained and paid professional. This appears to have been the case with Romans. At the end of this letter, the scribe identifies himself in the final greeting: "I, Tertius, the writer of this letter, greet you in the Lord" (Rom 16:22). Furthermore, at the conclusion of three of his undisputed letters (1 Corinthians 16:21), Galatians 6:11), and Philemon 19)), Paul indicates that he did not write his letter himself, only signed it. Common practice with Hellenistic letters was to sign them to verify their authenticity. It is estimated that it took two to three weeks to dictate and write a letter from its beginning to its final form. It was quite an undertaking for both author and scribe.[15]

## Women as "Co-workers" in the Pauline Congregations

Paul's letters frequently mention women, most often in very favorable ways as his "co-workers" in ministry. For example, in his letter to the Philippians, Paul speaks of two women, Euodia and Syntyche, who worked side by side with him in his ministry (Phil 4:2–3).

One of the best examples of Paul's positive working relationships with women comes from his concluding remarks in Romans 16. In this chapter, Paul mentions twenty-six people by name, ten of whom are women. All of these women helped Paul in various capacities as his "co-workers": Phoebe, Prisca, Mary, Junia, Tryphaena and Tryphosa, Persis, the mother of Rufus, Julia, and Nereus's sister.

Paul viewed the roles of men and women in rather countercultural ways. In his recognition of women among his co-workers, Paul modeled for others his gospel message.

It remains unclear who delivered most of Paul's letters. In the case of the Letter to the Romans, a wealthy woman by the name of Phoebe delivered Paul's letter to the church in that city (Rom 16:1–2). As far as scholars can tell, Paul did not use the legal and established delivery system of the Roman Empire. Paul most likely relied upon some of his trusted co-workers to personally deliver his letters. Paul's close associates, such as Titus (2 Cor 12:18) and Timothy (1 Thess 3:2), are often cited as leading candidates for the delivery of Paul's letters to their intended destinations.

### The Order of Composition

Scholars are uncertain of the exact order in which the Pauline letters were written. There is little internal or external evidence to

---

15. See the Introduction to Robert Jewett, *Romans: A Commentary* (Minneapolis: Fortress Press, 2006).

help place these letters in their proper chronological sequence. Paul does not date his letters, and Christian writers of the second and third centuries CE offer no solid external evidence.

There is general agreement that the thirteen Pauline letters were written between 50 and 120 CE. The seven undisputed letters were written in the 50s, with the six remaining deutero-Pauline letters composed by the next generations of Pauline Christians, sometime between 70 and 120 CE. Internal evidence, such as concerns over the imminent (impending) return of Christ (1 Thess 4:13–18) and the eventual creation of more structured church offices and structures (1 Tim 3:1–13), helps scholars differentiate between the undisputed and later Pauline letters. Many in Paul's day wondered (and worried) about the Second Coming of Christ; this is a common theme in the undisputed letters. Attention to more organized and structured operations, such as clarifying the function and role of bishops and deacons, is more the concern of the deutero-Pauline letters, which date to a later generation of Pauline Christians.

## The Center of Paul's Thought

Identifying the "center" of Paul's thought has been a topic of debate among Pauline scholars. Nowhere in his letters does Paul offer a systematic accounting of his theology. Many (especially Protestant) scholars have identified Paul's "justification by faith" as the center of Paul's thinking and the point from which his theology flows. Others have argued that Jesus Christ himself and, therefore, Paul's Christology is his center of thought. More recently, scholars have questioned whether Paul's theological system had a single center; perhaps Paul is best understood in relation to several central motifs.

What can be said with some certainty is this: Paul was convinced that in raising the crucified Jesus from the dead, God had acted decisively in human history, offering salvation to all who professes faith in this divine act. Regardless of the occasional nature of Paul's letters, this is the fundamental conviction from which Paul lived out his call from God and probably as close as one can get to a "center" of Paul's thought.

Some consensus exists on the chronological sequencing of the seven undisputed letters. For example, almost all scholars agree that 1 Thessalonians is the earliest surviving letter of Paul (50 CE) and that the two Pauline letters written from prison (Philippians and Philemon) were composed during one of his imprisonments, perhaps one of those in Ephesus, Caesarea, or Rome. However, questions remain such as, Was Galatians written before or after 1 Corinthians? What might be the order of composition of the apparent various letter fragments that make up 2 Corinthians?

## The Formation of the Pauline Corpus

One of the more interesting historical details about Paul's letters is that, from very early on (beginning as early as the late-first century CE), they were collected and circulated together to various Christian communities. Scholars have proposed numerous theories about the origin and formation of the Pauline Corpus.[16]

One theory is that as the second half of the first century unfolded, the churches to whom Paul wrote (such as Thessalonica, Corinth, Philippi) kept the letters, preserving and copying them for their own use and circulation. Eventually, as the various Pauline Christian communities grew, expanded, and interacted, there developed a desire to collect the letters sent to the other churches. Different churches began to assemble partial collections of Paul's letters. By the early- to mid-second century CE (after the production of the Pastoral Letters), Paul's letters finally came together, forming the Pauline Corpus. This basic explanation, along with its various mutations, was dubbed the snowball or evolutionary theory.

Such snowball or evolutionary theories were successfully challenged by what became known as the big bang theories. This position argued that the Pauline Corpus was formed by the initiative of a single person or a single community or school (for example, the Pauline school). One motivating factor may have been Luke's production of the Acts of the Apostles. The circulation of Acts among the different churches intensified interest in Paul, as later generations of Christians heard of Paul's central role in the early church. Someone

---

16. See Richards, 210–223 and Murphy-O'Connor, 114–130. Both present a good overview of the different theories associated with the formation of the Pauline Corpus.

with access to one (or more) of his letters would have been motivated, after reading the Acts of the Apostles, to collect other letters that Paul wrote to the various churches he established. This theory holds that the Pauline Corpus came together very quickly, assembled by someone seeking the additional letters written by the great apostle who was now recognized as one of the key figures among the first generation of Christians.

More recently, new theories of the formation of the Pauline Corpus have taken center stage. Labeled the codex and collection theories, they offer yet another plausible explanation. The early Christians preserved and circulated the Gospels and Paul's letters using codex, that is, writing in modern "book" form versus the earlier traditional form of the scroll. This preference in format lent itself well to preserving Paul's letters together, as the codex conveniently placed Paul's letters in a single publication.[17]

## Summary: The Life and Letters of Paul

### CORE CONCEPTS

- Paul was born between 5 and 15 CE and raised in the city of Tarsus, Cilicia, as a diaspora Jew.
- For Paul, the "revelation" of the resurrected Christ (33 CE) was the turning point of his life.
- In writing his letters, Paul adapted the literary conventions of his day to fit his needs.
- The early formation of the Pauline Corpus indicates the reception of Paul already in the first century CE.

### SUPPLEMENTAL INFORMATION

- Paul had Jewish parents and a sister, but as far as scholars know, never married.

*Continued*

---

17. For a collection of contemporary essays from leading Pauline scholars on this and related matters, see Stanley E. Porter (ed.), *The Pauline Canon* (Boston, MA: Brill Academics, 2004). Porter's essay in this volume speaks directly to the various theories of the formation of the Pauline Corpus, "When and How Was the Pauline Canon Compiled? An Assessment of Theories," 95–107.

**Summary: The Life and Letters of Paul** *Continued*

- Paul was a Pharisee, although not much is known about his formal training.
- As a Pharisee, Paul had persecuted the early church and tried to destroy it.
- Paul interpreted his encounter with the risen Christ as a call to preach the "good news" of Jesus Christ to the Gentiles.
- Very little is known of the first half of Paul's thirty years of missionary outreach to the Gentiles, 35–50 CE.
- Almost all scholars agree that 1 Thessalonians (50 CE) is the earliest of the seven undisputed Pauline letters.
- Paul probably dictated several of his letters to a scribe or secretary.
- The length of the body of Paul's letters was unusually long for the conventions of the day.
- The New Testament does not record the death of Paul. Tradition holds that Emperor Nero beheaded Paul, 62–64 CE.
- The chronological order of the composition of Paul's letters remains uncertain.

## Questions for Review

1. How are Paul and first-century CE Judaism portrayed by nineteenth-century German scholarship?
2. What is meant by "covenantal nomism," and how did it affect the study of Paul's Jewish background?
3. What is the difference between a chronological and thematic approach to understanding and interpreting Paul?
4. Which source material on Paul is considered most important, and why?
5. Explain what it means to say that Paul was a diaspora Jew.
6. What is known of Paul from his autobiographical sketches?
7. In what ways do Paul's letters reveal a man educated in both Greco-Roman rhetorical style and Jewish interpretive practices?
8. When do scholars think Paul wrote the seven undisputed letters?

9. In what ways did Paul follow the standard practices of letter writing in his day?

10. What are the difficulties in determining the order of composition of Paul's letters?

## Questions for Reflection

1. What challenges to understanding and interpreting Paul do you anticipate?

2. If Paul were alive today, what might be some of the major influences affecting his life and worldview? How would these be different from those in antiquity?

3. What do you imagine was Paul's biggest challenge as he tried to live out his call and commission to preach the "good news" of Jesus to the Gentiles?

4. Which theory of the formation and editing of the Pauline Corpus do you think is the most plausible, and why?

## Recommendations for Further Reading

Furnish, Victor Paul. *The Moral Issues of Paul: Selected Issues.* 3rd ed. Nashville, TN: Abingdon Press, 2009.

As the title implies, Furnish applies the ethics of Paul to a variety of contemporary moral issues: sex, marriage and divorce, homosexuality, women in the church, and the church in the modern world. Furnish balances Paul's historical sociocultural context and contemporary moral reasoning to address these modern questions.

Roetzel, Calvin J. *The Letters of Paul: Conversations in Context.* 5th ed. Louisville, KY: Westminster John Knox Press, 2009.

This is the fifth edition of Roetzel's book, *The Letters of Paul: Conversations in Context,* originally published in 1974. It incorporates recent studies on Paul. As the subtitle implies, this book places Paul and his letters in their original historical and cultural setting, viewing the Pauline letters as conversations between Paul and his recipients.

Schnelle, Udo. *Apostle Paul: His Life and Theology.* Trans. M. Eugene Boring. Grand Rapids, MI: Baker Academic: 2003.

This work examines the life and theology of Paul and his letters, written by one of the leading German Pauline scholars. Schnelle divides his work into two parts: (1) The course of Paul's life and the development of his thought, which includes the life and letters of Paul; and (2) the basic structures of Pauline thought, which explores Paul's thinking in such areas as Christology, anthropology, and ethics. This is an excellent resource for advanced students.

Witherup, Ronald D. *101 Questions and Answers on Paul.* New York/Mahwah, NJ: Paulist Press, 2003.

Witherup uses a question-and-answer format to present many of the frequently asked questions about Paul. Covering a range of questions grouped together by seven themes (Paul's life and ministry, Paul the person, the communities and companions of Paul, Paul's letters, theology, ethics, and legacy), this book serves as a ready-reference guide in an easy-to-read format for beginning students.

Zetterholm, Magnus. *Approaches to Paul: A Student's Guide to Recent Scholarship.* Minneapolis: Fortress Press, 2009.

Zetterholm provides a roadmap of the past two hundred years of Pauline scholarship on the subject of Paul and Judaism, sorting through the paradigms and perspectives that have shaped the modern understanding of Paul, as well as offering some important insights into future directions of Pauline studies. This book offers students a historical perspective on how scholars have been researching and writing about Paul and his letters.

# CHAPTER 2

# First Thessalonians

## INTRODUCTION

This study of the seven undisputed letters of Paul begins with 1 Thessalonians because scholars generally agree that this is the earliest of Paul's surviving letters. The first section of this chapter considers the historical context of 1 Thessalonians—the setting of the letter (the author and audience, date and place of composition); Paul's arrival, stay, and departure from the city; and the message Paul preached to the Thessalonians. The second section examines what this letter reveals about Paul's theology and ethics, addressing such ideas as the belief in the imminent return of Jesus, the wrath of God, and the challenge to live a holy life.

### Earliest Pauline Letter

First Thessalonians enjoys primacy of place among the twenty-seven writings of the New Testament. Most scholars agree that the period of the New Testament writings covers roughly the years 50 CE (1 Thessalonians) to around 125 CE (the Second Letter of Peter), with the majority of the writings between 70 to 125 CE. The seven undisputed Pauline letters date back to the second generation of Christians, written in the years 50 to 60 CE. First Thessalonians ranks as the earliest piece of literature in the New Testament.

Written within twenty years of Jesus' crucifixion, 1 Thessalonians offers a glimpse into the hopes and fears of one of the earliest Christian communities. The letter makes clear that the Christians in the city of Thessalonica experienced some type of persecution ("great affliction": 1 Thess 1:6, 2:14, 3:1–5) as well as anxiety associated with the uncertain fate of their recently deceased loved ones. However, they also had great hope in the return of Jesus within their lifetime and the ongoing support of the apostle Paul.

## Lessons Learned

As valuable a resource as this letter is for understanding early Pauline Christianity, it also calls attention to some sobering realities. Paul's call and commission occurred in the early 30s CE, but 1 Thessalonians dates to 50 CE. This highlights that no records of Paul's activities and ideas that may have been written during the first-half of his thirty-year career have survived. First Thessalonians also underscores how, nearly two thousand years later, one of the deepest convictions fueling Paul's missionary zeal—the imminent return of Jesus—has still not been realized.

Further, the letter exemplifies a limitation inherent in all of Paul's letters because of their occasional nature. These letters are mainly one-way conversations. Although Paul is building on earlier conversations, he writes to specific situations and does not provide the larger context of his writing. Interpreters are left with the task of trying to reconstruct the historical and theological backgrounds of Paul's letters. It is to this reconstruction that the discussion now turns.

## HISTORICAL CONTEXT OF 1 THESSALONIANS

The writings of the New Testament give rise to basic historical questions about authorship, date and place of composition, and intended audience. Both internal and external evidence is used to answer these basic questions associated with the historical setting of Paul's letters.

Internal evidence is ascertained from the letter itself, and each letter includes some historical information. For example, Paul identifies himself, Silvanus, and Timothy in his greetings (1:1) as the authors, and often provides some brief profiles of the community or some of its members. In the case of 1 Thessalonians, both the author (Paul) and the intended destination (the city of Thessalonica) are identified. Further historical questions are raised such as whether

Paul's preaching in Thessalonica was successful and what circumstances led to Paul's expulsion from a city (Acts 17:10) where he had founded a Christian community.

Paul's letters typically do not address other historical questions such as date or place of composition. Scholars are left to answer these questions using external evidence; that is, historical information taken from source material outside the letter itself. In the case of Paul's letters, scholars most often use the Acts of the Apostles. Caution is exercised in using Acts as a reliable historical source, however, as the presentation of history in Acts is governed by Luke's theological agenda and is from a later generation.

## Outline of 1 Thessalonians[1]

| | |
|---|---|
| 1:1–10 | **Greeting and Thanksgiving**<br>Paul opens his letter with his customary greeting and thanksgiving. Co-sent by Paul, Silvanus, and Timothy, the letter offers a message of thanksgiving to the Thessalonians, that, in spite of their great affliction, they remain models of faith for fellow believers in the provinces of Macedonia and Achaia. |
| 2:1–3:13 | **Paul's History with the Thessalonians**<br>Paul recounts his successful proclamation of the gospel to the Thessalonians, offering additional |

*Continued*

---

1. Scholars debate about the literary integrity of First Thessalonians: Is this one letter or more than one letter combined into one? Earl J. Richard, *First and Second Thessalonians* (Collegeville, MN; Liturgical, 1995), 30–32, sees First Thessalonians as two originally separate letters: 2:13–4:12 and 1:1–2:12 + 4:3–5:28. Udo Schnelle, *The History and Theology of the New Testament Writings*, trans. M. Eugene Boring (London: SCM, 1998), 47–49, presents numerous twentieth-century "partition hypotheses" as to the literary integrity of First Thessalonians. Schnelle concludes: "There are no compelling arguments for any of these partition hypotheses. . . . Thus, 1 Thessalonians is a literary unity," 48–49. I too operate from the position that 1 Thessalonians was originally one letter.

| | |
|---|---|
| | **Outline of 1 Thessalonians** *Continued* |
| | thanksgiving to the Thessalonians for their imitation of the churches in Judea in withstanding hardship and persecution. Paul explains he is sending Timothy back to Thessalonica to strengthen them in their faith and encourage them in their tribulations. Paul tells them that Timothy reported back the good news of the Thessalonians' steadfast faith and love. |
| 4:1–5:25 | **Paul's Advice and Warnings**<br><br>Paul moves into the final section of the letter, asking his audience to do certain things in order to please God. He urges that they refrain from sexual immorality; that they offer mutual charity in loving one another; and that they be vigilant in preparation for the coming of Christ and the wrath of God. Paul concludes this section with a variety of exhortations, such as admonish the idle, seek what is good, rejoice always, not quench the Spirit, and do not despise prophetic utterances. |
| 5:26–28 | **Farewell**<br><br>The letter ends with Paul's directive to greet the believers in Thessalonica and to read this letter to them. |

## Author and Audience

On the question of authorship, each of Paul's letters provides internal evidence in the opening address in which he identifies himself as the author. Interestingly, the address of 1 Thessalonians identifies *three authors*: Paul, Silvanus, and Timothy. The frequent use of the third person plural *we* throughout 1 Thessalonians leaves the impression that this letter is co-sent, and perhaps coauthored, by Paul, Silvanus, and Timothy. Only three times in the letter is the first person singular *I* used, and on every occasion, Paul is speaking (see 2:18, 3:5, 5:27).

## The City of Thessalonica

Located in Greece, Thessalonica was originally founded in 315 BCE by the Macedonian General Cassander, the successor to Alexander the Great. Built as a seaport city on the Thermaic Gulf and serving as the military base for the province of Macedonia, Thessalonica developed during a flourishing period of Greek growth and expansion.

Under Roman rule, Thessalonica became the capital city of the Roman province of Macedonia in 148 BCE. In the second century BCE, the Romans built a major Roman highway, known as the Egnatian Way, facilitating trade and troop movement and exposing the citizens of Thessalonica to a vast array of social and cultural influences. During Paul's lifetime, Thessalonica had a mixed population of Romans, Greeks, and Jews. Like most cities in the Roman Empire, the religious life and practices of the people of Thessalonica were diverse, involving the worship of the Greek god Dionysius; the Egyptian deities of Isis, Osiris, and Serapis; the Phrygian god Cabirus; and the Jewish God, Yahweh.

It is not surprising that Paul established a Christian community in this trade and seaport city. The Thessalonians had strong religious sensibilities, and the layout and location of Thessalonica facilitated an easy access route to the eastern provinces and cities.

Internal evidence offers two clues about the intended audience of this letter. Both point to the Thessalonians as a community of Gentile converts. As part of the opening thanksgiving, Paul mentions "how you turned to God from idols to serve the living and true God" (1:9). Jewish law and custom strictly prohibited the worship of idols. Thus, it seems unlikely that the Thessalonians were Jewish converts. In the next section of his letter, Paul offers a second thanksgiving to the community members in the city of Thessalonica for remaining steadfast in faith despite suffering afflictions from "compatriots" (2:14). The reference to compatriots of Thessalonica probably points to the non-Jewish population of the city.

## Ascribed Authors and Recipients of Paul's Letters

In the ancient world, standard salutations were very brief, typically indicating just the name of the sender and the recipient. The address within each of Paul's letters follows this format. Note that six of the seven authentic Pauline letters are co-sent.

| Authentic Letters | | |
|---|---|---|
| Letter | Sender | Recipient |
| 1 Corinthians | Paul and Sosthenes | the church of God at Corinth |
| Romans | Paul | all those in Rome |
| 2 Corinthians | Paul and Timothy | the church of God at Corinth |
| Galatians | Paul "and those who are with me" | the assemblies of Galatia |
| Philippians | Paul and Timothy | all the saints in Christ Jesus who are at Philippi |
| 1 Thessalonians | Paul, Silvanus, and Timothy | the congregation of the Thessalonians |
| Philemon | Paul and Timothy | Philemon, Apphia, Archippus, and the church at Philemon's house |
| **Deutero-Pauline Letters** | | |
| Letter | Sender | Recipient |
| Ephesians | Paul | the saints and faithful ones in Christ Jesus |
| Colossians | Paul and Timothy | the saints and faithful believers in Christ at Colossae |
| 2 Thessalonians | Paul, Silvanus, and Timothy | the congregation of the Thessalonians |
| 1 Timothy | Paul | Timothy |
| 2 Timothy | Paul | Timothy |
| Titus | Paul | Titus |

## Date and Place of Composition

First Thessalonians offers no direct internal evidence for the date or place where Paul wrote. For this reason, scholars often turn to the external evidence provided by the Acts of the Apostles for answers. According to Luke, while Paul was on his second missionary journey (Acts 15:36–18:22), which covered much more territory than the first mission (see map on p. 63), he established communities in the province of Macedonia (the cities of Philippi, Thessalonica, and Berea). After that, Paul moved on to the province of Achaia, with a visit and speech in the city of Athens, followed by the establishment of a community in the city of Corinth. He then remained in Corinth for eighteen months (Acts 18:11).

Luke's discussion of four cities in Acts 15:36–18:22 (Thessalonica, Philippi, Athens, and Corinth) can be cross-referenced with three verses from 1 Thessalonians. First, in 1 Thessalonians 2:2, Paul writes of his suffering and mistreatment in Philippi. This may be compared with Acts 16:16–24, in which Luke writes of Paul's imprisonment in Philippi. Second, in 1 Thessalonians 3:1, Paul mentions his stay in Athens, which is consistent with the description in Acts 17:5–34 of Paul's visit and speech in Athens. Third, the opening address of 1 Thessalonians 1:1 identifies the co-senders of this letter as Paul, Silvanus (Silas), and Timothy. In Acts 18:1–11, Luke writes that upon leaving Athens, Paul moved on to the city of Corinth, where he met Timothy and Silvanus. Because Paul, Timothy, and Silvanus were together in Corinth (Acts 18:5), that city is often identified as the likely place of composition for 1 Thessalonians.

In terms of the date of the composition of 1 Thessalonians, this too can be ascertained only by inference. The details come once again from Acts 18:1–11, Luke's account of Paul's stay in Corinth. Luke mentions that Paul meets the husband-wife team of Aquila and Prisca in Corinth after their expulsion from Rome by Emperor Claudius (Acts 18:2). The Edict of Claudius, another ancient source, speaks to the expulsion of Jews, including some Christ-believing Jews, from the city of Rome, occurring in the year 49 CE.[2] Given

---

2. See, for example, Udo Schnelle, *Apostle Paul: His Life and Theology*, trans. M. Eugene Boring (Grand Rapids, MI: Baker Academic, 2005), 161–164.

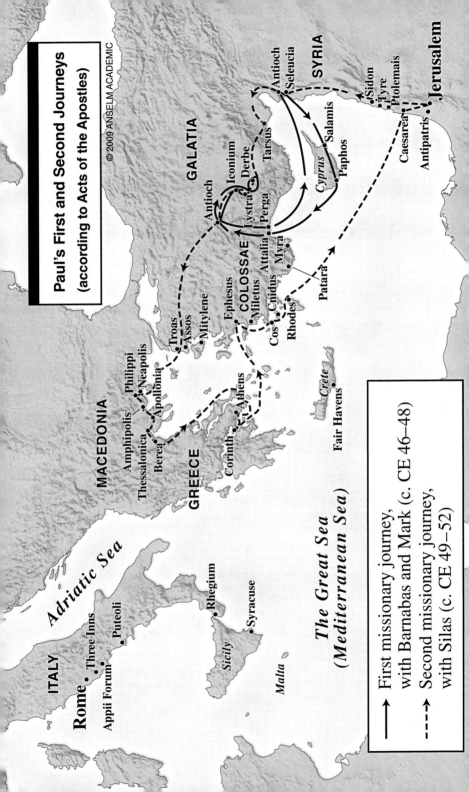

Paul's First and Second Journeys
(according to Acts of the Apostles)

© 2009 ANSELM ACADEMIC

→ First missionary journey, with Barnabas and Mark (c. CE 46–48)

---→ Second missionary journey, with Silas (c. CE 49–52)

that, according to Acts, Paul stayed in Corinth for eighteen months, and that it would have taken some time for Paul to meet Aquila and Priscilla in Corinth, most scholars infer a date of 50 CE for the composition of 1 Thessalonians.[3]

## Summary: Historical Setting for 1 Thessalonians

| | |
|---|---|
| Author | Paul, Silvanus, and Timothy |
| Audience | Gentile converts |
| Date of Composition | 50 CE |
| Place of Composition | Possibly Corinth |

## Paul's Arrival, Stay, and Departure from the City of Thessalonica

Both the letter (internal evidence, 1 Thess 2:1–12) and the Acts of the Apostles (external evidence, Acts 17:1–10) supply some details about the founding of the church in the city of Thessalonica. First Thessalonians offers some information on Paul's arrival and brief stay in Thessalonica. Luke provides information on Paul's routine arrival and sudden departure.

Luke mentions that Paul and Silas arrived in the city of Thessalonica shortly after their release from prison in Philippi (Acts 15:36–18:22). According to Luke, Paul stays in Thessalonica for three weeks ("three Sabbaths," 17:2) preaching about Jesus, the crucified and resurrected Messiah. In his letter, Paul reminds the Thessalonians of his arrival "after we [Paul, Timothy, and Silas] had suffered and been insolently treated . . . in Philippi" (1 Thess 2:2).

---

3. For an alternative date of 50 CE for 1 Thessalonians, see Richard, 1–10, esp. 7–8. Richard dates "the correspondence to the early and mid-40s from Athens and Corinth," 8.

Once in the city, Paul describes their preaching of the gospel to the Thessalonians in maternal and paternal metaphors—"as a nursing mother cares for her children" (1 Thess 2:7) and "as a father treats his children" (1 Thess 2:11). Paul emphasizes the trio's humility and sincerity in preaching to the Thessalonians, neither with "flattering speech" nor with a "pretext for greed" (1 Thess 2:5). Paul also mentions the drudgery of their daily routines, working all day and night while staying in the city (1 Thess 2:9).

Remaining details about Paul's time in Thessalonica are taken solely from Acts. Some scholars are cautious with this information, as it is derived from Luke's theological perspective with no cross-reference or verification from 1 Thessalonians. In summary, Luke reports that Paul and Silas had success in preaching to the inhabitants of Thessalonica. They were, in fact, able to convince some Jews and Greeks to join them in "the house of Jason" (Acts 17:5). However, after three weeks and the growing jealousy of some Jews (Acts 17:5), events in Thessalonica quickly turned against Paul and Silas, as well as Jason and other community members gathered at his home. False accusations of treason were leveled against them (Acts 17:7). Jason and other community members were arrested, having to pay a fine before being released (Acts 17:9). Paul and Silas escaped to Berea during the night (Acts 17:10).

## The House of Jason

Paul addresses his letter to the Thessalonians: "to the church [ekklēsia] of the Thessalonians" (1:1). The term ekklēsia literally means "congregation" and is often translated into English as church. It was common for the early Christians in a given city to gather in the homes of those who likewise professed faith in Jesus. In Acts 17, Luke writes that Jason had "welcomed" Paul and Silas into his "house" in Thessalonica. Although Paul never mentions this directly in his letter, some scholars speculate that 1 Thessalonians' intended destination was the congregation of those who gathered in the house of Jason.

© iStock photo

When preaching in cities such as Thessalonica, Corinth, and Ephesus, Paul brought his gospel message to various venues, ranging from private homes to city streets. This engraving depicts Paul preaching in Thessalonica.

## The Gospel Paul Preached to the Thessalonians

Twice in the early part of his letter, Paul writes of "the gospel of God" that he proclaimed to the Thessalonians (2:2,8,9). Once he refers to "the gospel of Christ" (3:2). Paul appears to use these two phrases interchangeably. In each, Paul uses the Greek term *euanggelion* (good news or glad tidings). Although Paul never explicitly states the exact content of the "gospel" he preached, internal evidence does shed some light.

First, Paul says "our gospel" came not only in word, but also "in power and in the holy Spirit and with much conviction" (1:5). Second, the basic content of the gospel included belief in the imminent return of Christ ("to await his Son from heaven") as well as delivery from God's "coming wrath" (1:10). The imminent Parousia (coming, presence) of Christ was a major tenet of Paul's gospel. The expectation of Christ's return combined with the accompanying divine judgment very likely created an apocalyptic-eschatological (sudden end-time) expectation among the Thessalonian Christians.

## "Satan Blocked Us"

In discussing his travel plans with the Thessalonians (1 Thess 2:17–20), Paul mentions his desire to visit them in person but notes more than once that "Satan blocked us." The Greek verb Paul uses here for Satan's action is *egkoptō*, which translated means "to block" or "to hinder."

One way of understanding how Paul thinks about Satan lies in his apocalyptic worldview. In response to his call and commission from God to proclaim the good news of the crucified and resurrected Christ to the Gentiles (Gal 1:1,15–16), Paul embarked on a divine mission until such time that Jesus returned again in the Second Coming. With the return of Jesus imminent, Satan would seek ways to disrupt God's plans. It likely made sense to Paul that Satan was trying to prevent him from sharing the good news of Jesus Christ. In four of the seven undisputed letters, Paul discusses various ways Satan attempts to disrupt him and others in an effort to thwart God's intentions: Romans 16:20; 1 Corinthians 5:5, 7:5; 2 Corinthians 2:11, 11:14, 12:7; 1 Thessalonians 2:18.

## Summary: Historical Context of 1 Thessalonians

### CORE CONCEPTS

- First Thessalonians is the earliest surviving undisputed Pauline letter.
- No internal evidence verifies the date and place of composition for 1 Thessalonians.
- Acts 17 offers some external evidence for the historical setting of 1 Thessalonians, but it is used cautiously by some scholars because it is governed by Luke's agenda.

*Continued*

---

**Summary: Historical Context of 1 Thessalonians** *Continued*

**SUPPLEMENTAL INFORMATION**

- First Thessalonians was co-sent by Paul, Silvanus, and Timothy.
- Community members in Thessalonica experienced "afflictions" and "distress."
- After some success in proclaiming the crucified and resurrected Messiah in Thessalonica, Paul and Silvanus had to quickly flee the city.
- There was a strong eschatological-apocalyptic (sudden end-time) tone to Paul's "gospel."
- According to the later witness of Acts 17, Paul established a Christian community in Thessalonica as part of his second missionary journey.
- In contrast to Acts 17, the Thessalonians were mostly Gentile converts (1 Thess 1:9–10).

# THEOLOGY AND ETHICS OF 1 THESSALONIANS

Theology and ethics are embedded within all of Paul's letters, but neither is presented in any systematic fashion. Rather, because of the occasional nature of Paul's letters, the theology and ethics in them arise out of the specific circumstances and issues within the community or in the situation of the person to whom Paul is writing.

In the case of 1 Thessalonians, three theological issues emerge: election, Parousia, and the wrath of God. The letter addresses ethical norms and behavior in light of the persecution experienced by members of the Christian congregation in Thessalonica and in anticipation of the imminent return of Christ.

## Theology

### Election

After opening the letter with a brief greeting, Paul offers a thanksgiving for the faith of the Thessalonians (1 Thess 1:2–10).

Within this thanksgiving, Paul informs the Thessalonians of how they "were chosen" by God (v. 4). The Greek word used here, *eklogē*, means, "selection, choice, election." By referring to the largely Gentile congregation in this way, Paul makes a significant claim about the community of Gentile Christ-believers at Thessalonica. Within the history of the Jewish people, the status of election by God, adherence to the Torah, and the practice of male circumcision were key ethnic and religious markers. These markers served to separate Torah-observant Jews from the "nations" (that is, the Gentiles).

## The Literacy of Paul's Audience

Literacy, the ability to read and write, was surprisingly low in the ancient world as compared to the modern Western standards of the United States and Europe. Scholars estimate the literacy rates in antiquity to be perhaps 10–15 percent of the population. Oral communication was by far the dominant mode for ancient Mediterranean people, the target audience of Paul's letters.

Most (perhaps all) of the recipients of Paul's letter to the Thessalonians could not actually read. They would have had to rely on a fellow believer to do so. Paul's use of the verb *enokidzō* (I adjure) "that this letter be read to all the brothers" indicates not only that most, if not all, of the community members were illiterate, but also it speaks to the importance that Paul attached to the letter's content.

Paul will return to using *eklogē* a few years later in his Letter to the Romans.[4]

Four times in Romans (9:11; 11:5,7,28), Paul speaks of election in the section of the letter where he discusses Jews and Gentiles in God's plan (Rom 9:1–11:36). In all four instances, Paul is speaking of God's plan of election in Israel's history, past and present. In Romans

---

4. Paul uses a variation of *eklogē* twice in his letter to the Romans: *eklektos* (chosen)— 8:33 and 16:13. In 8:33, Paul refers to the Christians in Rome as "God's chosen ones." In 16:13, Paul sent his greetings to an acquaintance in Rome, Rufus, referring to him as "chosen in the Lord."

9:11, Paul refers to "God's elective plan" with the past patriarchs and matriarchs of Abraham and Sarah, and Isaac and Rebecca. In Romans 11:5, Paul speaks of "a remnant of Israel, chosen by grace" in the present moment to be included in God's current plan of salvation with Christ. In 11:7, Paul connects Israel's past and present election: "What Israel was seeking it did not attain, but the elect attained it; the rest were hardened." And in 11:28, Paul speaks of "election" a final time, as means of uniting Jews and Gentiles: "In respect to the gospel, they are enemies on your account; but in respect to election, they are beloved because of the patriarchs."

Therefore, Paul's reference to the Gentile Christ-believers in Thessalonica as being "chosen" by God carried significant theological weight. Jewish tradition and history knew well the privileges, responsibilities, and burdens that come with the status of the "elect" among the nations. As is evident from the six-year time span between 1 Thessalonians (50 CE) and Romans (56 CE), Paul continued to develop this idea of the election of the Gentiles in God's plan of salvation.

### Parousia

Paul's firm belief in the imminent return of Jesus pervades this letter. Paul uses the term *Parousia* four times in this letter: 1 Thessalonians 2:19, 3:13, 4:15, 5:23. In addition, Paul makes two indirect references to the coming of Christ: in 1 Thessalonians 1:10 ("and to await his Son from heaven, whom he raised from the dead, Jesus"), and 1 Thessalonians 5:2 ("For you yourselves know very well that the day of the Lord will come like a thief at night"). No other Pauline letter speaks so forcefully and consistently about the coming of the Lord in the immediate future as does 1 Thessalonians. It is probably safe to say that the hope in the Parousia was part of the foundation of the gospel that Paul preached in Thessalonica. It may well have been the case that Paul's gospel equated salvation with the Parousia and did not account for some who would die before the Parousia, which led to his further elaboration on the subject.

Paul mentions the Parousia in the letter (2:1 and 3:13) and offers a fuller discussion of the events associated with Jesus' coming at the end-time in 4:13–5:11. He concludes this letter with a final reminder of the centrality of the imminent Parousia (5:23). The first two references to Jesus' "coming" appear in his extended thanksgivings.

## Parousia as a Criterion of Pauline "Authenticity"

Scholars have used a variety of criteria for determining the authenticity of Paul's letters. Broad categories, such as language, style, content, and theology, are frequently applied to the thirteen Pauline letters in the New Testament to determine authenticity. The language and theology of Parousia is one such criterion.

The theological concept of the imminent Parousia, the coming of the Lord in the near future, was part of Paul's "gospel." It is evident throughout 1 Thessalonians and is also mentioned in 1 Corinthians 15:23. The presence of Parousia language in 2 Thessalonians 2:1,8,9 is one reason why scholars debate its undisputed status. Other deutero-Pauline letters (Colossians and Ephesians) mention a future eschaton but not an imminent one. When Parousia language and theology appears elsewhere in the New Testament (James 5:7–8; 1 John 2:28; 2 Peter 1:16, 3:12), it indicates an indeterminate-future event. Later generations of Christians—the target audience of the later New Testament letters such as James, 1 John, and 2 Peter—still believed in the return of Jesus but no longer had a sense of its near-future immediacy.

There, Paul holds up the Thessalonians themselves as his reason "to boast" when Jesus returns, and he prays for them to be "blameless in holiness" in anticipation of this event. The final reference to Jesus' coming is placed in the concluding prayer (5:23), in which Paul can punctuate its importance.

Late in the letter (4:13–18), Paul expounds on the Parousia in the context of the Thessalonians' concern over their deceased loved ones. This offers the most extensive discussion on the return of Jesus in Paul's surviving letters. Paul assures the Thessalonians of the sequence of events that will unfold:

1. "the Lord himself  . . . will come down from heaven" (4:16a)
2. "the dead in Christ will rise first" (4:16b)
3. "Then we who are alive, . . . will be caught up together with them in the clouds to meet the Lord" (4:17)

Afterward, Paul adds a final warning about remaining vigilant for Jesus' coming (5:1-3), using metaphors to capture the tension between secrecy ("the day of the Lord will come like a thief at night," 5:2) and urgency ("like labor pains upon a pregnant woman," 5:3) as it relates to the Parousia.[5]

### The Wrath of God

The wrath accompanying the Lord's return is also discussed in 1 Thessalonians.[6] Paul speaks of the wrath at three points in his letter, each time connecting it to events associated with the Parousia: 1 Thessalonians 1:10 ("to await his Son from heaven, whom he raised from the dead, Jesus, who delivers us from the coming wrath"); 1 Thessalonians 2:16b ("the wrath of God has finally begun to come upon them"); and 1 Thessalonians 5:9 ("For God did not destine us for wrath, but to gain salvation through our Lord Jesus Christ").

In all three instances, the wrath of God is closely connected to the judgment of God. In the Parousia, the unbelievers and those who caused the "great affliction" upon the Thessalonians will receive the wrath of God. However, the wrath is also connected to God's mercy, as those who believe in Christ will be "delivered" and taken to heaven.

## Ethics

### Imitation of Paul and His Co-workers in Tribulation

Internal evidence from the letter indicates that members of the Thessalonian congregation experienced some type of tribulation (1:6, 3:4) and distress (3:7) in their lives. The manner in which Paul speaks to these afflictions suggests different types of trouble for the Thessalonians.

In the letter's first thanksgiving, Paul addresses up front one of the pressing matters within the Thessalonian community: the "great affliction" that has accompanied both the receiving and the living out

---

5. For an extended discussion of the Parousia in Paul's two letters to the Thessalonians, see James D. G. Dunn, *The Theology of Paul the Apostle* (Grand Rapids, MI: Eerdmans, 1998), 298–315.

6. See Schnelle, *Apostle Paul*, 189: "The content of the Pauline gospel as found in 1 Thessalonians can be precisely described: God's eschatological act of salvation in Jesus Christ, the risen one who will return in the near future to save believers from the divine wrath erupting as part of the final events."

of Paul's gospel by the Thessalonians. Paul places these tribulations in perspective so as to prevent the Thessalonians from being disturbed. He notes that believers are destined for trouble and affliction (3:3) and that this was predicted (3:4). Reports from Timothy of the faith and love among community members offered Paul hope for the Thessalonians' ability to survive this threat (3:6–8).

Some of the trouble and tribulation was likely associated with the community members in Thessalonica turning "to God from idols" (1 Thess 1:9). This would have had significant cultural and social ramifications, affecting day-to-day living. No longer participating in the religious customs and ceremonies of the city (for example, offering sacrifice to the local gods, who were thought to protect and bless the city) would have been perceived as antisocial, if not seditious.

Paul praises the Thessalonians for their endurance in faith despite these tribulations. For Paul, the congregation's endurance lies in imitation: "You became imitators of us and of the Lord" (1:6). The Thessalonians' imitation of how Jesus, Paul, Silvanus, and Timothy coped with the tribulations in their lives probably became the key to their survival. Their imitation was so successful that the Christian community in Thessalonica became "a model for all the believers in Macedonia and in Achaia" (1:7). Paul may well be referring to the Christian congregation in Philippi (Macedonia) and Corinth (Achaia). This widespread recognition may point to the depth of the tribulations experienced by the recipients of Paul's letter.

### Live in Holiness

Closely connected to his call for the Thessalonians to be imitators of him and his co-workers in times of tribulation are Paul's expectations that the Thessalonians live by high ethical standards, which, in Thessalonica, may have slipped because some had had their faith shaken. Paul grounds his position in a divine imperative: "This is the will of God, your holiness" (4:3).

Paul offers two concrete ways to live a life of holiness: avoid sexual immorality and offer acts of charity to each other. He presents appropriate sexual behavior in the context of betrothal and marriage. A man ought not seek a wife "in lustful passion" or to "exploit a brother" (4:5–6). Paul cites the nonbelieving Gentiles in their midst as contrasting models of moral behavior for Christ-believing Gentiles.

In his advice to the Thessalonians on sexual morality, Paul mentions two key phrases that touch on ancient marriage strategies: acquiring a wife (4:4) and not exploiting a brother (4:6). Marriages in antiquity were typically arranged, usually by the eldest available male relative (father, uncle, elder brother, etc.). Marriage was less a commitment between two individuals than an alignment between families to preserve, or strengthen, wealth and social status. Trust and shared benefits between the adjoined families was an important factor in successful marriage arrangements. Paul's directive to the Thessalonians to seek a wife honorably without taking advantage of a brother speaks to Paul's marital/marriage ethics as he thought it ought to be lived out, even in Gentile congregations. Paul will expound on this very topic in his later letter to the Corinthians (1 Cor 7).

In terms of charity (that is, goodwill and support to others), Paul offers a high compliment to the Thessalonians, noting their well-founded reputation in this regard throughout Macedonia (4:9–10). Nonetheless, Paul urges them to continue in their charity so as to live a simple and peaceful life. Paul concludes his discussion on holiness by emphasizing two motivations for living a lifestyle of sexual morality and mutual charity: the opportunity to show proper behavior to "outsiders" and the ability to be independent of others (4:12). Paul gives a glimpse here of the perhaps intentional isolation of the community members within the larger social structures of the city of Thessalonica.

In his concluding prayer of petition, Paul asks God to make the Thessalonians "perfectly holy" (5:23). As the prayer unfolds, it becomes clear why Paul emphasizes the moral imperative for holiness—so that the members of the Gentile congregation in Thessalonica will be "blameless" at the Second Coming of Christ (5:24). Paul's apocalyptic worldview is evident throughout the theology and ethics embedded within the letter.

### Love One Another

The language of love permeates this letter (1 Thess 1:3, 3:6,12, 4:9, 5:8, 13). In each case, Paul uses the Greek term *agapē* (divine love). Twice the term is associated with the three virtues of faith, hope, and love (1:3, 5:8) and once with the twin virtues of faith and love (3:6). In the three remaining instances, Paul uses love as a moral imperative, with each mention of the call to love one another adding a new layer of challenge.

In the first case, Paul simply discusses love in the context of a prayer of petition that the Lord "make you increase and abound in love for one another and for all, just as we have for you" (3:12). The second mention of love as a moral imperative comes from Paul's belief that this is a divine directive: "for you yourselves have been taught by God to love one another" (4:9). The third instance of love as a moral imperative is the most challenging—to love those "who admonish you, and to show esteem for them with special love on account of their work" (5:12–13). Paul encourages the Thessalonians to achieve this high standard, both because they have a model in himself, Silas, and Timothy and because it is a divine directive.

## The Three Virtues of Faith, Hope, and Love

Twice in his letter to the Thessalonians, Paul speaks of the three virtues of faith, hope, and love:

> calling to mind your work of faith and labor of love and endurance in hope (1:3)

> let us be sober, putting on the breastplate of faith and love and the helmet that is hope for salvation (5:8)

Paul uses varying formats and metaphors to present these virtues. In his Letter to the Galatians, Paul introduces another configuration of these virtues:

> For through the Spirit, by faith, we await the hope of righteousness. For in Christ Jesus, neither circumcision nor uncircumcision counts for anything, but only faith working through love. (5:5–6)

In his First Letter to the Corinthians, Paul offers his most succinct presentation of these three virtues:

> So faith, hope, love remain, these three; but the greatest of these is love. (13:13)

## Summary: Theology and Ethics in 1 Thessalonians

### CORE CONCEPTS

- Paul's claim that the Thessalonians are God's "chosen" (elect) carried significant theological weight.
- The imminent return of Jesus and the accompanying wrath of God form the theological foundation of 1 Thessalonians.
- The call to live a holy life is the ethical imperative of 1 Thessalonians.

### SUPPLEMENTAL INFORMATION

- Paul does not present his theology and ethics in a systematic way in 1 Thessalonians.
- Paul makes a passing reference to Christians as God's "selection, choice, election."
- Paul's belief in the imminent return of Jesus is a recurring topic in this letter.
- God's wrath at the end-time involves both judgment and mercy.
- For Paul, "imitation" is key to surviving tribulation and distress.
- Paul holds the Christians in Thessalonica to high ethical standards.

## Questions for Review

1. What sources are used to determine the historical setting of 1 Thessalonians?
2. In what ways did Paul experience success in his missionary work in the city of Thessalonica?
3. What elements comprised "the gospel of God" that Paul preached to the Thessalonians?
4. What is the significance of Paul's reference to the Thessalonians as God's "selection, choice, election"?
5. What does Paul tell the Thessalonians about the end-time in 4:13–5:11?

6. What might have been some of the Thessalonians' great tribulations?

7. What metaphors does Paul use to describe his relationship with the Thessalonians?

8. How did Paul think the Thessalonians ought to behave toward each other in their congregation?

9. Why is Acts 15:36–18:22 important to understanding 1 Thessalonians? What cautions need to be considered in using Acts as a source?

10. According to Luke, why did Paul and Silas (Silvanus) flee Thessalonica?

## Questions for Reflection

1. What obstacles do you think the Gentile Christ-believers in Thessalonica experienced?

2. Describe Timothy's role in his work with the Thessalonians. Where do you think Timothy was challenged in his work?

3. How might you explain that Paul's firm belief in the *imminent* return of Jesus in his lifetime did not, in fact, occur?

4. How might people of faith today live by Paul's moral imperative to live "blamelessly" and in holiness?

## Recommendations for Further Reading

Donfried, Karl Paul. *Paul, Thessalonica and Early Christianity*. New York and London: T & T Clark, 2002.

Donfried discusses the major Pauline themes as well as the religious and cultural context of early Christianity that inform Paul's First Letter to the Thessalonians. This book offers substantial information for students.

Gaventa, Beverly Roberts. *First and Second Thessalonians*. Interpretation. Louisville, KY: Westminster John Knox Press, 1998.

In this short and readable commentary, Gaventa offers the reader a modern interpretation of 1 and 2 Thessalonians. She presents interesting "Reflections" scattered throughout her commentary on areas such as "Maternal Imagery in the Letters of Paul" and "Preaching and Teaching Eschatology."

Green, Gene L. *The Letters to the Thessalonians*. Grand Rapids, MI: Eerdmans, 2002.

Green offers extended commentary on the major historical and theological issues associated with the two letters. His introduction is especially informative for beginning students of Paul who would benefit from background on the geography of the region, as well as the social, political, and religious environment of the city of Thessalonica.

Richard, Earl J. *First and Second Thessalonians*. Sacra Pagina 11. Collegeville, MN: The Liturgical Press, 1995.

Similar to each of the commentaries in the Sacra Pagina series, Richard offers an extended introduction to Paul's letters to the Thessalonians, covering areas such as "New Views on the Pauline Mission and 1 Thessalonians" and "Circumstances of Mission and Correspondence according to Acts." Richard's attention to the language and rhetoric of these two letters helps students better understand the nuances of Paul and his followers.

Wright, N. T. *Paul for Everyone: Galatians and Thessalonians*. Louisville, KY: Westminster John Knox Press, 2004.

As the title of this text implies, Wright presents the letter to the Galatians and the two letters to the Thessalonians in a passage-by-passage commentary providing historical background and context helpful for modern readers of the New Testament. This book is short and easy to read, even for beginners in Pauline studies.

# CHAPTER 3

# First Corinthians

## INTRODUCTION

Chapters 2–8 in part 1 of this book examine the seven undisputed letters of Paul according to their likely order of composition. Although scholars generally agree that 1 Thessalonians is the earliest surviving letter of Paul, they debate whether Galatians or 1 Corinthians came next.[1] This book presents 1 Corinthians as the next surviving letter. The opening section of this chapter discusses the historical context of 1 Corinthians: the setting of the letter (author, audience, date, and place of composition); Paul's arrival, stay, and departure from Corinth; and the division within the community. The second closing section of the chapter investigates the theology and ethics of Paul as reflected in 1 Corinthians, with topics ranging from the unity of the church in Christ and the gifts of the Holy Spirit to practical moral advice in areas such as marriage and lawsuits among community members.

---

1. The debate centers on the dating of Galatians. Scholars who date Galatians early—written before 1 Corinthians—favor the *south Galatian theory*, which argues that Paul wrote to the churches in the southern region of Galatia, in the districts of Lycaonia, Pisidia, and Isauria. He established these churches on his first missionary trip (Acts 13–14). Those who support the *north Galatian theory* hold that internal evidence from the letter indicates that Paul addressed it to those in the northern region of Galatia. For example, Paul's reference to the ethnic name *Galatians* in 3:1 more aptly fits the inhabitants of the north. This theory holds that Paul established the churches of northern Galatia on his second missionary journey (Acts 15:36–18:22) and wrote his letter during his trip through Macedonia (Acts 20:1–3), on his third missionary journey. For more details on each theory, see Udo Schnelle, *Apostle Paul: His Life and Theology*. Trans. M. Eugene Boring (Grand Rapids, MI: Baker Academic, 2005), 266–271.

## Snapshot of Some of the Earliest Christian Congregations

Of the seven undisputed letters of Paul, 1 Corinthians provides readers with a rich opportunity to see the many social, political, and religious dimensions of the early Christian communities. The circumstances in Corinth that prompted Paul's letter reflect a whole host of problems that arose after he departed from the city. Some of these problems were internal, for example, the development of factions within the congregation (see 1 Cor 1–4). Others were external, such as the question of how community members should interact with non-Christians in matters such as eating meat that has been offered to idols or whether believers should be involved in litigation in courts (see 1 Cor 6–8). These internal and external problems offer a good sampling of the societal and cultural challenges faced by these early Christ-believers. In addition, 1 Corinthians offers some of the most extensive theological treatments on topics ranging from the proper use of the gifts of the Holy Spirit (see 1 Cor 12) to the resurrection from the dead (see 1 Cor 15). This letter illustrates well the struggles of early believers to define their religious identities amid numerous questions and challenges not anticipated or answered by the earlier Jesus tradition.

## Communication Channels

First Corinthians provides valuable "inside information" about how Paul and the Christian church in Corinth communicated with each other. First, it mentions prior letters sent between Paul and the Corinthians. Paul indicates that he wrote a previous letter to them ("I wrote to you in my letter not to associate with immoral people," 5:9), and the Corinthians themselves wrote to Paul ("Now in regard to the matters about which you wrote . . . ," 7:1). These letters, unfortunately, have been lost. In any case, it is clear that 1 Corinthians is not the first letter between Paul and Corinthians. Second, the opening and closing of the letter also recall personal envoys between Paul and some members of the congregation in Corinth:

> For it has been reported to me about you, my brothers, by Chloe's people, that there are rivalries among you. (1:11)

I rejoice in the arrival of Stephanas, Fortunatus, and Achaicus, because they made up for your absence, for they refreshed my spirit as well as yours. So give recognition to such people. (16:17–18)

These delegations kept Paul updated and informed of developments within the Corinthian community since his departure.

## HISTORICAL CONTEXT OF 1 CORINTHIANS

Establishing the setting for Paul's letters involves answering questions about each letter's authorship, date, place of composition, and intended audience. Internal clues from the letter, as well as some external information from the Acts of the Apostles, help in ascertaining the historical setting of 1 Corinthians.

### Outline of 1 Corinthians[2]

| 1:1–9 | **Greeting and Thanksgiving** |
|---|---|
|  | The letter opens with a greeting from Paul and Sosthenes. A brief thanksgiving follows, with Paul highlighting the abundance of discourse, knowledge, and spiritual gifts bestowed upon the church in Corinth. |

*Continued*

2. Notable scholars from the last century (for example, Johannes Weiss and Walter Schmithals) argued for 1 Corinthians being a composite letter. In his 1910 commentary, Weiss contended that a later editor compiled two letters from Paul, making the canonical 1 Corinthians. Schmithals, who spent more than thirty years studying the Corinthian letters, eventually concluded by the 1980s that 1 Corinthians was a composite of five original letters Paul sent to Corinth. For a longer discussion of these and other partition theories of 1 Corinthians, see Raymond F. Collins, *First Corinthians*, SP 7. (Collegeville, MN; Liturgical, 1999), 10–14. Most scholars today see 1 Corinthians as a single letter originally composed by Paul and agree with Collins's position on the literary integrity of 1 Corinthians: "No manuscript evidence exists to suggest that 1 Corinthians once existed in a form other than that in which it exists today," 12.

*Continued*

**Outline of 1 Corinthians** *Continued*

| | |
|---|---|
| 16:1–24 | **Concluding Matters and Final Greeting** |
| | Paul ends his letter with an appeal for his collection for the poor in Jerusalem, details of his upcoming travel plans, and gives list of greetings to and from mutual acquaintances. A final exhortation to carry out all actions with love summarizes well Paul's unifying message to the divided Corinthian church. |

## Author and Audience

Like 1 Thessalonians, which identifies three co-senders (Paul, Silvanus, and Timothy), 1 Corinthians lists two co-senders in the address: Paul and Sosthenes. As discussed in chapter 2, the frequent use of the third person plural *we* throughout 1 Thessalonians leaves the impression that this letter was co-sent, and perhaps co-authored, by Paul, Silvanus, and Timothy. Only three times in the letter does the first person singular *I* appear, and on every occasion, Paul is the speaker (see 2:18, 3:5, and 5:27). First Corinthians differs in this regard. The consistent use of the first person singular *I* (eighty-six times) throughout the letter clearly indicates that Paul is the principal author.

### The City of Corinth[3]

Before Paul's arrival, Corinth had flourished for centuries as a Greek city-state before being destroyed in 146 BCE by the Roman Consul Lucius Mummius. It lay in ruins for nearly a century until

*Continued*

---

3. See Bruce W. Winter, *After Paul Left Corinth: The Influence of Secular Ethics and Social Change* (Grand Rapids, MI; Eerdmans, 2001), 7–25, for a good background discussion on the culture and society of Corinth. See also Calvin J. Roetzel, *The Letters of Paul: Conversations in Context*, 5th ed. (Louisville, KY: Westminster John Knox, 2009), 30–46, for an overview of Hellenistic religion and philosophy.

> **The City of Corinth** *Continued*
>
> Julius Caesar refounded the city in 44 BCE. With an ideal location between the two harbors of Cenchrea and Lechaeum, and having been rebuilt in a Roman architectural style, the city soon emerged as a major center for commerce and trade. In 27 BCE, Corinth was named the capital of the region of Achaia.
>
> During his time in Corinth, Paul likely interacted with a diverse group of Greek- and Latin-speaking people, Jews and Gentiles, and Greeks and Romans. Similar to the city of Thessalonica, Corinth was home to numerous polytheistic religious practices. It was a major center for the cult of the Egyptian gods Isis and Osiris and of Asclepius, the Greek god of healing. Altars and shrines dedicated to gods such as Poseidon, Apollo, and Hermes were also commonplace. Corinth also had a Jewish synagogue, dedicated to the prayer, study, and worship of Yahweh. For a monotheist, living in a polytheistic city such as Corinth posed numerous challenges. In 1 Corinthians 8–10, Paul addresses one such challenge, namely the eating of meat that has been offered to a Greco-Roman god.

The letter is addressed to the church in Corinth and provides a rather clear profile of the believers there. First, these believers were predominantly Gentile. In discussing spiritual gifts, Paul writes: "You know how, when you were pagans, you were constantly attracted and led away to mute idols" (1 Cor 12:2, see also 8:10). Despite its largely Gentile population, this community did have a significant presence of Jewish Christ-believers. Paul's frequent references to Jewish/Gentile relations throughout the letter leave the impression of mixed community (see, for example, 1 Cor 1:22–24, 7:18, 9:20, 10:32).[4]

In addition to the mixed ethnic congregation, the letter also suggests that members came from different economic and social backgrounds. The majority of members were from the lower classes, neither "powerful" nor of "noble birth" (1:26), and some even slaves (7:21). However, the congregation of the Corinthians also included wealthy members, some of whom were homeowners, with enough

---

4. The report from Luke in Acts 18 about "synagogue officials" (Crispus, 18:8 and Sosthenes, 18:17) could also point to a Jewish presence in the church in Corinth.

means to support the poor in Jerusalem (1 Cor 1:16; 11:22a; 16:2,15). Although the letter contains no information about the total number of believers, scholars estimate the size of the church in Corinth to be "relatively small," perhaps around one hundred people.[5]

## Date and Place of Composition

As the letter draws to a close, Paul mentions that he wrote it from the city of Ephesus in a discussion of his future travel plans to pass through Macedonia and spend some extended time with them (1Cor 16:5–9). Unfortunately, the letter offers no clues to the date of Paul's composition of 1 Corinthians. Paul's reference to staying in Ephesus until Pentecost, however, does indicate that this letter may have been composed in the springtime, as the Jewish Feast of Pentecost is an annual spring celebration.

### More Than a Simple Thanksgiving

After greeting the Corinthians, Paul expresses thanksgiving (1:4–9). There is more to Paul's statement of thanksgiving to the Corinthians than first meets the eye. The thanksgiving signals some of Paul's major concerns about the church in Corinth: overreliance on human wisdom, the return of Christ, and factions in the congregation. First, he points out that the riches in discourse and knowledge Corinthians enjoy are given to them in Christ Jesus. Christ is the source of their enrichment, not human wisdom. Second, the abundance of spiritual gifts among the church members is not an end in itself. Gifts of the Holy Spirit are a means to serve the community until the return of Christ. Third, God called the Corinthians to relationship with his Son, united in Christ, not divided into groups with allegiances to Paul, Apollos, or Cephas.

In trying to date 1 Thessalonians, scholars commonly conclude that Paul wrote it from the city of Corinth in 50 CE. Given Luke's discussion in Acts 18 of Paul's stay in Corinth, some conjecture is

5. Collins, 97; Schnelle, *Apostle Paul*, 194.

possible regarding the date of 1 Corinthians. According to Luke, Paul remained there for eighteen months (see Acts 18:11). This dates Paul's departure from Corinth at 51 CE, most likely in the summer of that year given that travel was often severely hampered in the winter. In Acts 18:18–23, Luke details Paul's travels between his extended stays in Corinth (eighteen months) and Ephesus (twenty-seven months). These trips possibly took place from the summer of 51 to the spring of 52, with Paul's arrival in Ephesus (Acts 19:1) in the spring of 52. According to Luke, Paul then remained in Ephesus for almost three years (Acts 19:8,10, 20:31). Assuming that Paul wrote 1 Corinthians toward the end of his stay in Ephesus and near the Feast of Pentecost, this would date 1 Corinthians to the spring of 55 CE.

## Summary: Historical Setting for 1 Corinthians

| | |
|---|---|
| Author | Paul (along with Sosthenes) |
| Audience | Gentile-Jewish mix, mostly poor, some rich |
| Date of Composition | Spring 55 CE |
| Place of Composition | Possibly Ephesus |

## Paul's Arrival, Stay, and Departure from Corinth

As is often the case, Paul had no need in the letter itself to address such historical issues as his arrival, stay, and departure from Corinth. Scholars, therefore, are left to rely upon Acts from which to create a hypothesized scenario of Paul's time in Corinth.

In Acts 18:1–2, Luke reports that Paul arrived in Corinth after leaving Athens. In Luke's chronology, Paul's arrival in Corinth marked the final stop on his second missionary journey (Acts 15:36–18:22). Although Luke provides no exact date, he does mention Paul's early encounter with Aquila and Priscilla, who were expelled from the city of Rome because of the edict of the Emperor Claudius. This edict is commonly dated to the year 49 CE. Luke's note that Aquila and Prisca "had recently come from Italy" (v. 2) before Paul met them suggests that Paul arrived in Corinth sometime in 49–50 CE. This date is reinforced by Luke's reference to the Jews' appeal to Gallio to expel Paul from Corinth (Acts 18:12–16). Archeological evidence confirms that Gallio served as the proconsul of Achaia in the years 51–52 CE.[6]

In Acts 18:11, Luke provides the only reference to the duration of Paul's stay in Corinth, one and half years. The letter itself does offer some information about the gospel Paul preached to the Corinthians during his eighteen-month stay: "When I came . . . proclaiming the mystery of God, I did not come with sublimity of words or of wisdom" (1 Cor 2:1). This "mystery of God" centered upon Jesus and the cross: "For I resolved to know nothing while I was with you except Jesus Christ, and him crucified" (1 Cor 2:2, see also 1 Cor 1:18–25).

According to Luke (Acts 18:5–10), Paul's gospel message that Jesus was the crucified Messiah met with a mixed response in Corinth. Although "many Jews" opposed Paul, some Jewish leaders (Crispus and Sosthenes) embraced Paul and his message. Paul found more success among the "God-fearing" Gentiles. Luke cites Titus Justus and his entire household as well as many Corinthians who came to believe in Paul's gospel and were baptized.

Jewish opposition to Paul's presence in Corinth was not enough to force him to leave the city as quickly as he left Thessalonica (Acts 17:9–10). In fact, Luke reports that Paul's departure was rather uneventful (Acts 18:18a).

## Who Was Sosthenes?

Beyond being the co-sender of 1 Corinthians, what is known of Sosthenes? The New Testament includes only one other reference to him, in Acts 18:17.

*Continued*

---

6. For a discussion of the letter fragments discovered at Delphi and the date of Gallio's term of office, see Jerome Murphy-O'Connor, *St. Paul's Corinth: Texts and Archaeology*, 3rd ed. (Collegeville, MN: The Liturgical Press, 2002), 161–167.

In the greeting of 1 Corinthians, Paul refers to him as "Sosthenes our brother." Such familial language of *brother* and *sister* is used a total of twenty-one times throughout this letter. The designation as a *brother* suggests that Sosthenes was someone known and trusted by both Paul and the church in Corinth. Albeit a less reliable written source, Acts 18 narrates Paul's visit and eighteen-month stay in the city of Corinth. In Acts 18:17, Luke refers to a Sosthenes as "the synagogue official" who the Jews "beat . . . in full view of the tribunal" in retaliation for Gallio's (the proconsul of Achaia) refusal to hear their complaints against Paul.

From this limited information, and assuming this is the same Sosthenes as mentioned in 1 Corinthians, it can be surmised that Sosthenes was a Jew who lived in Corinth and held some authority and status within the local Jewish synagogue. He was persecuted for his beliefs and was present with Paul at the writing of this letter to the Corinthians.

## Divisions within the Community

Internal evidence from 1 Corinthians indicates that serious problems existed among the believers in Corinth. They may well have existed before Paul's departure, but the problem apparently became more acute after he left. These encompassed a range of issues, including the unity of the church (1 Cor 1), believers' moral conduct and sexual practices (1 Cor 5–7), questions on how to live as a Christian in Roman Corinth (1 Cor 8:1–10:33), theological debates on the purpose and tradition of the Lord's supper (11:2–34), and the meaning of the resurrection of the dead (15:1–58). Disagreements among community members on how best to handle these problems likely contributed to the factions that developed within the congregation and prompted Paul's writing of this letter (1:10–17).[7] Simply put, the Corinthians had many problems. In this letter, Paul tried to address them one by one, beginning with the most serious: the problem of church unity.

---

7. Scholarly theories and attempts to reconstruct the basis of these communal factions abound. See, for example, Winter, 25–28; Collins, 16–17; Schnelle, *New Testament Writings*, 66–70.

## The Image of the Athlete

As part of his concluding comments on Christian freedom, Paul offers images of the runner and boxer and their drive and discipline in order to emphasize the discipline he exercises in order to live according to the gospel he preaches (1 Cor 9:24–27).

Ancient literature used the image of the athlete, also known as the *agōn* motif, as a metaphor for the struggle for truth. Paul rarely uses athletic images and languages in his surviving letters; in fact, the only other athletic reference—to a runner—appears in Philippians 2:16, 3:13–14.

Paul might have relied on athletic images in his letter to the Corinthians because of the well-known Isthmian Games held every two years in April/May on the outskirts of the city of Corinth. Ranked second in importance only to the Olympic Games, these athletic competitions were popular and festive and were seen as an opportunity to celebrate Roman culture and tradition. It is possible that the Isthmian Games took place during Paul's stay in Corinth. Paul contrasts the perishable pine-wreath crown given to the victors of the Isthmian Games with the imperishable crown he urges believers to pursue.[8]

© Vanni Archive/CORBIS

Ancient engraving of a champion of the Isthmian Games, held during the time of Paul on the outskirts of Corinth

---

8. For a discussion on the Isthmian Games, see Murphy-O'Connor, 12–15.

After his departure from the city and before the writing of 1 Corinthians, Paul and Corinthian community members corresponded in both oral and written form (1 Cor 1:11, 5:9, 7:1, 16:17–18). It is likely that some (perhaps many) of their problems were mentioned already in these letters. Much of the content of 1 Corinthians indicates the types of problems that led to the divisions of the community.[9]

- The problem of disunity (1:10–4:21)
- Not living the Christian ethical life (5:1–7:40)
- Eating meat offered to idols (8:1–11:1)
- Inappropriate conduct in worship (11:2–34)
- Proper use of spiritual gifts (12:1–14:40)
- Defending the premise that there will be a future resurrection of the dead (15:1–58)

## First Corinthians and the Early Church Fathers[10]

Toward the end of the first century CE, the congregation in Rome wrote a letter to the congregation in Corinth, later attributed to Clement, Bishop of Rome, with the title, *The First Letter of Clement to the Corinthians*. As a way of confronting ongoing divisions within the community, the letter mentions the issues addressed by Paul in 1 Corinthians 1–4:

Take up the epistle of the blessed Apostle Paul. What did he first write to you in the beginning of the gospel? Truly,

*Continued*

9. For two commentaries on 1 Corinthians that are structured based on the rhetorical design of this letter, see Collins, *First Corinthians* and Ben Witherington III, *Conflict and Community in Corinth: A Socio-Rhetorical Commentary on 1 and 2 Corinthians* (Grand Rapids, MI: Eerdmans, 1995).

10. See Wilhelm Pratscher, *The Apostolic Fathers: An Introduction* (Waco, TX: Baylor University Press, 2010), 47–70, for the historical, literary, and theological background to *The First Epistle of Clement*.

he wrote to you in the Spirit about himself, and Cephas, and Apollos, because even then parties had split into factions. (*1 Clement* 47:1–3)[11]

Another early church father, Ignatius of Antioch, wrote a series of seven letters before his martyrdom in Rome (105–115 CE).[12] In four of these letters, Ignatius draws directly from Paul's First Letter to the Corinthians:

### Ignatius's Letters Parallel Paul's Letters

| Ignatian Passages | Pauline Passages |
|---|---|
| Romans 5:1 | 1 Corinthians 4:4 |
| Ephesians 18:1 | 1 Corinthians 1:19–20 |
| Ephesians 16:1 and Philadelphians 3:3 | 1 Corinthians 6:9–10 |
| Magnesians 10:21 | Corinthians 5:9a |

The early church fathers testify to the legacy of Paul and the early impact made by the First Letter to the Corinthians in Christian tradition.

## Summary: Historical Context of 1 Corinthians

### CORE CONCEPTS

- First Corinthians provides many details about the struggles of some of the early Christians in the city of Corinth.

*Continued*

---

11. English translation from Michael W. Holmes, *The Apostolic Fathers in English* (3rd ed.; Grand Rapids, MI: Baker Academic, 2006), 64.

12. The seven letters include *To the Ephesians, To the Magnesians, To the Trallians, To the Romans, To the Philadelphians, To the Smyrnaeans,* and *To Polycarp, Bishop of Smyrna.*

**Summary: Historical Context of 1 Corinthians** *Continued*

- Internal evidence suggests that the Corinthian believers were a mixed ethnic congregation with different economic and social backgrounds.
- The later witness of Acts 18 provides some information to offer a conjecture for the historical setting of 1 Corinthians.

**SUPPLEMENTAL INFORMATION**

- First Corinthians was co-sent by Sosthenes, but the primary author is Paul, who commonly speaks in the first person *I*.
- The congregation in Corinth comprised perhaps around one hundred believers consisting of mostly Gentile converts.
- Paul apparently wrote 1 Corinthians from Ephesus.
- The congregation in Corinth developed factions. They may well have existed before Paul's departure, but the problem apparently became more acute after his departure.
- According to Luke, Paul established a Christian community in Corinth at the end of his second missionary journey.
- Luke reports that Paul spent eighteen months in Corinth.

# THEOLOGY AND ETHICS OF 1 CORINTHIANS

The theology and ethics reflected in 1 Corinthians are closely connected to the Corinthians problems (for example, women praying and prophesying unveiled) and questions (such as, should single believers be allowed to marry?). Differing attempts to address these problems and questions fostered divisions and factions within the congregation. Paul wrote 1 Corinthians in an attempt to heal these divisions.[13]

---

13. Winter, 27, argues that the problems that arose in Corinth after "Paul's' departure did so partly because the Christians were 'cosmopolitans,' i.e., citizens of this world, and, in particular, citizens or residents of Roman Corinth. They had grown up in, and imbibed that culture before they became Christians. They reacted to some issues that arose after Paul left on the basis of the learnt conventions and cultural mores of Corinthian *Romanitas*."

# Theology

## The Unity of the Church in Christ

After his greeting and thanksgiving, Paul immediately addresses the most pressing matter—a lack of unity of mind and purpose in the Corinthian community. News of this problem reached Paul by way of reports from Chloe's people (1 Cor 1:11). Paul indicates that the believers formed "rivalries" based on their baptismal initiation, referring to the Corinthian slogan, "I belong to . . ." (1 Cor 1:12) as the source of the divisions. Individual Corinthians were pledging their allegiance to the one by whom they were baptized—whether Paul, Apollos, or Cephas (Peter). Paul's initial appeal to unity in the opening verses of this letter centers on Jesus Christ. In fact, 1 Cor 1:17–18 can be considered the theme of Paul's extended discussion on the unity of the church in Christ (1 Cor 1–4):

For Paul, the tensions in the church in Corinth had many causes, including theology (resurrection), spiritual gifts, and (as Paul would learn later and address in 2 Corinthians 10–13) authority. It may also be the case that tensions were partly rooted in a misunderstanding of the role of baptism. The majority of these Corinthians had Gentile backgrounds; thus, the practices and beliefs of the numerous polytheistic religious cults may have influenced how they lived out their faith as Christ-believers. Initiation rites of these ancient Greek and Roman religious cults comprised a central component of one's religious identity and practice.

The Christ-believers in Corinth would have found it natural to place an equally high value on their rite of initiation (baptism) into Christianity. In doing so, authority of the leaders in the community who baptized would have been granted by the believer. Those baptized (and presumably converted) by these leaders were naturally loyal to them. Paul offers a useful metaphor of planting, watering, and growing seeds in God's fields to highlight the problem of factions forming around the leaders of the congregation in Corinth (1 Cor 3:5–9).

Baptism served to initiate and incorporate one into the community (1 Cor 6:11). For Paul, the person who administered baptism does not matter. However, for others in Corinth, baptism loyalties fostered divided alliances within the community. According to Paul, this sad development diffused—and could potentially empty—the power of the cross of Christ.

### Divine Wisdom and the Power of the Cross

For Paul, another tension in the church in Corinth, leading to divisions within the community, was the confusing of human wisdom with divine wisdom. The Corinthian Christians likely knew well the teachings of the rhetorical schools (for example, the Cynic movement), which taught that the search for wisdom and knowledge led to power. Paul acknowledged up front that the Corinthians excelled in this area, "enriched in every way, with all discourse and all knowledge" (1 Cor 1:5).[14]

Paul recognized that preaching "Christ crucified" did not, at face value, make sense to Jews or Gentiles in Corinth. Rather, his gospel message offered "a stumbling block to Jews and foolishness to Gentiles" (1 Cor 1:23). According to Paul, an overreliance on human wisdom and the subordination of love to knowledge posed a real danger. First, it minimized the importance and role of faith, which is essential for understanding the presence of God's power in the cross of Christ (1 Cor 2:5). Second, it failed to recognize that God's wisdom is revealed to us not by human wisdom or knowledge but "through the Spirit" (1 Cor 2:10). Third, an individual's wisdom ran the risk of being prioritized over the community's unity.

## First Corinthian Slogans

Throughout the letter, Paul raises a variety of slogans used by the Corinthian Christians. For example:

- I belong to . . . (Paul, Apollos, Cephas, Christ) (1:12)
- Everything is lawful for me. (6:12)
- Food for the stomach and the stomach for food. (6:13)
- It is a good thing for a man not to touch a woman. (7:1)
- It is a good thing for a person to remain as he is. (7:26)

*Continued*

---

14. The Corinthians may even have had a model of human wisdom in Apollos, one of their community leaders. Luke describes him as "an eloquent speaker," an "authority on scriptures" (Acts 18:24), who spent time in Corinth (Acts 19:1) and whom Paul credited with influencing the Corinthians (1 Cor 1:12, 3:5–6,21–22, 4:6).

## Gifts of the Holy Spirit and Christian Love

Just as he acknowledged the "riches" of the Corinthians (discourse and knowledge) in his opening remarks, Paul identifies spiritual gifts as a strength of the church in Corinth (1 Cor 1:7). Paul's praise early in the letter prepares for addressing a correlative problem: the exercise of the Spirit's gifts had created some significant problems (1 Cor. 12:1–14:40). The Corinthians apparently had questions on this topic and sought Paul's advice ("Now in regard to spiritual gifts, brothers, I do not want you to be unaware" [1 Cor 12:1]).

Paul begins by listing the gifts of the Spirit (1 Cor 12:8–11)—wisdom, knowledge, faith, healing, mighty deed, prophecy, discernment of spirits, speaking in tongues, and interpreting tongues. He employs the metaphor of a body with its many parts working together to demonstrate how the various and different gifts of the Spirit work together to unify the church and serve the congregation as a whole (12:12–26). In this way, the Christian community is to function as the "Christ's body, and individually parts of it" (12:27). For Paul, the gifts within the body of Christ are hierarchically ordered in accordance to their functions: "first, apostles; second, prophets; third, teachers; then, mighty deeds; then gifts of healing, assistance, administration, and varieties of tongues" (12:28).

Paul's emphasis on the variety and number of spiritual gifts was motivated by the Corinthians' apparent preference for ecstatic tongues with a simultaneous devaluing of prophecy (1 Cor 14:1–5). He tempers the Corinthians' enthusiasm for speaking in tongues by pointing out that "whoever speaks in tongues builds himself up, but who prophesies builds up the church" (14:4). Paul is relentless that gifts of the Spirit, especially prophecy, be directed to unite the church: "Thus, tongues are a sign not for those who believe but for unbelievers, whereas prophecy is not for unbelievers but for those who believe" (14:22).

In his extended discussion on the proper use of the gifts of the Spirit, Paul stops midway and makes an important transitional statement: "Strive eagerly for the greatest spiritual gifts. But I shall show you a still more excellent way" (1 Cor 12:31). Here, Paul details the supremacy of Christian love (*agapē*), subordinating even spiritual gifts (tongues, prophecy, knowledge, and faith) to the actions of *agapē*, which the Corinthian Christians are called to embrace and live (1 Cor 13). This "more excellent way" (1 Cor 12:31b) endures beyond prophecy and tongues and is key to exercising the gifts of the Spirit and uniting the church.

In his letter to the Thessalonians, Paul associated the virtue of love (*agapē*) with faith and hope (1 Thess 1:3, 5:8). He does so again in 1 Corinthians, but now orders these virtues: "So faith, hope, love remain, these three; but the greatest of these is love" (1 Cor 13:13). In a concluding remark, Paul succinctly reminds the Corinthians of the importance of Christian love for healing the divisions in Corinth: "Your every act should be done with love" (1 Cor 16:14). In the nearly five years between the writing of 1 Thessalonians and 1 Corinthians, Paul's theology of the three virtues emerges.

## The Resurrection and the Parousia

Paul's treatment of the Resurrection and the imminent return of Christ are prompted by yet another significant misunderstanding on the part of some Corinthians, this time about the Resurrection of Christ and future resurrection of the dead when Christ returns. Paul discusses the Resurrection using a threefold approach. He begins with a summary of the gospel he originally preached in Corinth (1 Cor 15:1–11). It amounts to a recapping

For Paul, belief in the bodily resurrection of Christ was central to Christian identity and inextricably linked to events associated with the end-time.

of the kerygma (oral preaching) about the Resurrection of Jesus, which clearly testifies both to the scriptural tradition and to the list of eyewitnesses to Jesus' Resurrection. Paul then takes up the most serious charge that some deny the resurrection of the dead (1 Cor 15:12). Refuting this denial of the resurrection of the dead in 15:12–34 allows Paul to defend the absolute necessity of the bodily Resurrection of Christ. Not only "your faith is vain" (15:17) if Christ did not physically rise from the dead, but also there is no hope for the general resurrection of the dead upon Christ's return. In this context, Paul lays out the order of events associated with the eschaton (end time): the Resurrection of Christ, his return, the resurrection of believers, and then the handing over of the kingdom to God (15:23–24).

Paul concludes his discussion on the resurrection with some theological reflections on the resurrected body (1 Cor 15:36–49) and the transformation associated with the resurrection event (15:50–58). He does so to address questions the Corinthians have about resurrection: "How are the dead raised? With what kind of body will they come back?" (15:35). To answer these questions, Paul uses the analogies of a seed and the first man, Adam, from the Old Testament Book of Genesis (see Genesis 2:7). The dead are raised just as a seed is transformed into a plant during the growing process. Similarly, the resurrected body will no longer have natural earthly properties like Adam (the first man), but upon resurrection, will be endowed with heavenly properties like Christ (the second man).

## Jesus' Post-Resurrection Appearances

Early in his discussion on the Resurrection (1 Cor 15:1–58), Paul tells the Corinthians of a tradition "handed on" to him about Jesus' post-Resurrection appearances (15:3–8).

Paul's account dating to 55 CE, is the New Testament's earliest written attestation to Jesus' post-Resurrection appearances. All four New Testament Gospels contain accounts of Jesus' post-Resurrection appearances, but these narratives were written later, between 70–100 CE (Mark, 70 CE; Matthew, 80 CE; Luke, 85–90 CE; and John, 100 CE). A comparison of Paul's account and the Gospels' accounts of the post-Resurrection appearances reveals two curiosities. First, in all four Gospels, Mary Magdalene is the first to experience a post-resurrection appearance by Jesus. Yet the appearance to Mary Magdalene is not part of Paul's early-received tradition. Second, Paul's tradition about Jesus' appearances to James and to the "over five hundred brothers" is not mentioned at all in the Gospel narratives.

The final post-Resurrection appearance mentioned is to Paul himself: "Last of all, as to one born abnormally, he appeared to me" (1 Cor 15:8). Paul added the account of this appearance to the tradition that had been handed on to him. This would have given Paul credibility as an apostle, as well as give his announcement of the gospel message authority.

The Resurrection event will remove "the sting of death" and instantly transform corruptible and mortal earthly bodies into incorruptible and immortal heavenly bodies (see 1 Cor 15:50–55). Paul finishes his thought by focusing once again on the resurrected Christ. God won this victory over sin and death through Christ (15:57). Thus, all labor and work in the church in Corinth must be directed to the Lord (15:58).

# Ethics

Beginning in 1 Corinthians 7, Paul takes up six matters about which the congregation in Corinth had sought his advice. Many of these touch on ethical behavior: marriage and celibacy (7:1–24); virgins (7:25–40); eating meat that has been sacrificed to idols (8:1–11:1); spiritual gifts (12:1–14:40); the collection for the poor saints in Judea (16:1–4); and his co-worker Apollos (16:12).[15] The community sought Paul's input because these matters posed significant ethical challenges in the day-to-day living of the Christian faith in Roman Corinth. Paul's remarks on sexual morality, legal disputes, marriage, sacrificial meat, and misconduct at liturgies warrant further discussion.

## Sexual Morality and Litigation

Immediately following his extended discussion on the need for unity in the community of believers (1 Cor 1:10–4:21) and before answering specific questions from the Corinthians, Paul addresses the pressing rumor of the day of a man sleeping with his father's wife (1 Cor 5:1). It is likely that the father's wife is the man's stepmother. Given the relatively small size of the Corinthian congregation, this situation was likely common knowledge within the community. Paul's firm condemnation of this man and his sexual misconduct (5:2–5) provided him with the opening to appeal for a broader disassociation from all types of immoral people and their behavior (5:9–13), as well as to focus on a particular sexual sin among the Corinthian men: relations with prostitutes (1 Cor 6:12–20). Paul argues that the Corinthian slogan "Everything is lawful" (6:12), cannot be used to justify sexual

---

15. Paul's response to each topic begins with the introductory formula: "Now in regard to . . ." (*peri de*), indicating that he is addressing concerns brought to him by the Corinthians.

immorality. The unity of the church could easily have been impacted by different views on how to respond—if at all—to this problem.

Regarding another immoral behavior, Paul cites the example of lawsuits among community believers (1 Cor 6:1–11). Naturally involving Roman courts to settle legal disputes between believers also threatened the unity of a Christian community united in Christ and grounded in love. For Paul, "the holy ones" (6:1), the community leaders, were solely qualified to judge cases between fellow Christ-believers. In a series of rhetorical questions (6:2–7), Paul tries to shame the Corinthians, asking, for example, "Can it be that there is not one among you wise enough to be able to settle a case between brothers?" (6:5).

## Paul's Eschatological Worldview

A good example of Paul's eschatological (end-time) worldview can be found in 1 Corinthians 7:29. Paul saw all around him signs of the imminent return of Christ (the Parousia), which would usher in the new age (7:31: "For the world in its present form is passing away"). This was likely part of the message Paul preached to the community during his time in Corinth. However, this perspective raised some very real practical questions for the Corinthians, not the least of which were, How should they live in this eschatological tension? How should they carry on with their lives waiting for the Second Coming of Christ?

Paul's recommendation in response to these questions is telling: "Everyone should remain in the state in which he was called" (7:20). This was Paul's advice whether a person was married or single, circumcised or uncircumcised, even slave or free (7:17).

### Married Couples, Singles, and Widows

Marriage and sexuality are the first issues that Paul formally addresses in his responses to Corinthians' questions. This likely indicates its importance for both Paul and the Corinthians. Paul offers advice to the married (7:1–16), the unmarried (7:25–38), and the widowed (7:39–40).

Paul begins by affirming the importance and legitimacy of marriage. Husbands and wives are bound to each other with mutual love, including conjugal love. Here, Paul reveals his own (preferred) celibate state (7:7)[16] but stops short of advocating celibacy within marriage. This specific advice, combined with the Corinthian slogan in 7:1 ("It is a good thing for a man not to touch a woman"), suggests

## On Being Made Holy

First Corinthians 7 opens with the line: "Now in regard to the matters about which you wrote. . . ." The Corinthians had asked Paul about the problem of being married to an "unbeliever." This was apparently a source of marital distress for some (perhaps many) couples. Not surprisingly, Paul strongly encouraged married couples against divorce, especially when the unbelieving spouse accepts (tolerates) the conversion of the other. However, then Paul offers a puzzling rationale: "For the unbelieving husband is made holy through his wife, and the unbelieving wife is made holy through the brother. Otherwise your children would be unclean, whereas in fact they are holy" (1 Cor 7:14).

Paul's position—that the faith of one can sanctify or make holy another—seems quite unusual given his otherwise consistent stance that one must make a personal faith commitment in order to be saved, to be made clean and holy. Many Pauline scholars have attempted to harmonize Paul's position with his overall theology and ethics. There has been reluctance in modern studies to let Paul's inconsistency speak for itself. It may simply be the case that as Paul reflected upon the very real practical problems facing these couples in Corinth; he opted for a more pastoral response. However, there could be a connection to fellowship with demons via idol food and being made holy through fellowship (through marriage) with a believer.[17]

---

16. Paul sees celibacy as "a particular gift" that not all people possess (see 1 Cor 7:7).

17. For a good overview of the history of interpretation and cultural background of 1 Cor 7:12–16, see Margaret Y. MacDonald and Leif E. Vaage, "Unclean but Holy Children: Paul's Everyday Quandary in 1 Corinthians 7:14c," *Catholic Biblical Quarterly* 73 (2011): 526–546.

that some Corinthians were promoting (or even living) celibate marriages, regarding any form of sexual relations as a violation of the dynamic working of the Spirit in their lives. Paul discouraged such renunciations most likely for practical, pastoral reasons. His general prohibition against divorce (7:11) is likely rooted in similar concerns for the well-being of the community's marital matters. Paul's prohibition against divorce qualified. If an unbeliever wishes to divorce a believer, that is acceptable to Paul (see 1 Cor 7:15). This is the so-called "Pauline exception" for divorce.

To the unmarried (singles and widows), Paul offers again the Corinthian slogan, "It is a good thing . . . ," but completes it with his own ending: "It is a good thing for a person to remain as he is" (1 Cor 7:26). Paul sees the single state of the unmarried or widowed as a preferred state, because unmarried men and women, virgins and widows, can devote their energies to the Lord (7:34). As, according to Paul, "time is running out" (7:29), so one's energy is well spent in preparations for the return of Christ. Paul nicely summarizes his position in his comments on the subject in 7:39–40, where he shows a clear preference for believing widows to remain focused on their duties as Christians.

### Meat Sacrificed to Idols

Paul devoted considerable space in his letter on the topic of "meat sacrificed to idols" (three full chapters, 1 Cor 8:1–11:1), suggesting that members of the Corinthian church had significant differences about what the believer is allowed to eat. Paul's detailed response reflects a major moral dilemma faced by the Corinthians. Professing faith in one God prohibited the consumption of this "defiled" meat, as fellow believers (and Judaic Christians in general) could interpret it as blasphemy. Yet refusing to eat this meat represented a serious violation of social and cultural norms in Corinth, possibly even scandalizing nonbelievers.

This problem allows Paul to speak to the power and responsibility of Christian knowledge and freedom. As a believer, the Corinthian Christian had a certain "liberty" in the knowledge of his faith that nonbelievers (the weak) did not enjoy (1 Cor 8:8). Yet Paul cautioned the congregation to avoid causing scandal with their new-found freedom in Christ. Paul offers his own personal stance that if food caused someone to sin, then Paul would abstain from eating meat in order not to lead that person to sin (8:13). Once again, just as with his advice to the married and single, Paul's final words on this topic provide a good summary of his position: do all things for the glory of God and avoid offending fellow believers (10:31–33).

## Misconduct at Christian Worship

Another serious breach of ethical behavior by the Corinthians occurred in the context of their worship experience. Similar to many of the problems in the church in Corinth, the root of the difficulties lay in the divisions (in regard to both theology and authority) within the congregation.

The first issue Paul confronts is what Corinthian men and women were wearing on their heads while praying or prophesying. Men were covering their heads and women were not (1 Cor 11:4–5). Paul believed that while this may have been acceptable practice in pagan cult-worship rituals, it created gender-confusion in a Christian worship assembly. Paul argues that Christian worship must model the hierarchical structure of the cosmos: God,

### Speaking in Tongues

Some members of the Corinthian community possessed the gift of speaking in tongues or "ecstatic speech" (in Greek, *glossolalia*). Paul devotes an entire chapter of his letter (1 Corinthians 14) to this topic and begins by defining the phenomenon (1 Cor 14:2,5).

Paul explained that ecstatic speech, the utterances of strange and indiscernible sounds from a believer, was a private experience between that believer and God. He refers to it as "utter unintelligible speech" (1 Cor 14:9). While it provided evidence of the Spirit's presence in the community, speaking in tongues did little to build up the body of the church unless the unintelligible sounds were interpreted for the wider group. Because it was so sensational and because some Corinthians considered it the highest of the spiritual gifts, it seems likely that the experience of *glossolalia* by only some believers was another source of division within this community.

Christ, man, woman (11:7–12).[18] Women praying and prophesying with unveiled heads may have been practiced within the Corinthian church, given that Paul anticipates a negative reaction to his instructions (1 Cor 11:16).

As he transitions to the more grievous offense occurring in the church in Corinth, Paul states, "I do not praise the fact that your meetings are doing more harm than good" (11:17). The "harm" to which Paul refers is occurring at liturgies (the eating of the Lord's supper). The Corinthians had been gathering in smaller groups rather than sharing the liturgy together. Believers were apparently dining within their own socioeconomic groups, further exasperating the already existing divisions within the congregation. In addition to eating separately, some are also getting "drunk" at the celebrations (11:21). Reminding the Corinthians of the received tradition on the Lord's supper that Paul brought to the community (11:23–25), he condemns this behavior as "unworthy" of the Christian conduct. He even attributes that some in the community are "ill and infirm and . . . dying" because of this misconduct at liturgy (11:30). Paul offers a twofold solution to this problem: wait for one another to share the Lord's supper together and eat a meal at home before coming to celebrate the liturgy (11:33–34a). The rituals associated with celebrating the Lord's supper involved repeating the words of Christ and did not include eating an actual meal. The point was not to satisfy hunger but to do "in remembrance of me" (11:24,25).

Paul chooses not to address in writing the additional misconduct at these liturgical assemblies. Concluding his remarks on this subject, Paul says, "The other matters I shall set in order when I come" (11:34b).

---

18. Some scholars argue that the position on women not having any authority over a man or speaking in church may be a possible non-Pauline interpolation of 1 Corinthians 14, as elsewhere Paul seems to have no problem with women having authority in the church (for example, Phoebe in Romans 16:1–2).

## Summary: Theology and Ethics in 1 Corinthians

### CORE CONCEPTS

- Paul wrote 1 Corinthians to address numerous divisions and points of dispute in the church at Corinth.
- The unity of the Corinthian church in Christ grounds Paul's theology and ethics in this letter.
- Christian love (*agapē*) is the ethical imperative of 1 Corinthians.

### SUPPLEMENTAL INFORMATION

- Paul was concerned that the Corinthians would value human wisdom over church unity.
- Some in the Corinthian church viewed speaking in tongues as an important gift of the Spirit.
- Paul adamantly defended the bodily Resurrection of Christ.
- Paul encouraged marital love and sexual relations within marriage.
- Believers settling cases against each other in Roman courts and Corinthian men involved with prostitutes were two of the pressing moral problems that Paul addressed.
- Paul suggested carefully balancing the power of Christian freedom with knowledge as the best way of handling problems in the congregation, such as eating meat sacrificed to idols.
- In Paul's view, serious misconduct was occurring at the Corinthian church's gatherings for prayer and worship.

## Questions for Review

1. What can be learned from 1 Corinthians about its historical setting?
2. How does the later source, Acts 18, contribute to understanding 1 Corinthians?
3. What demographics are known about the believers in the church at Corinth?

4. What were some of the problems in Corinth that Paul encountered?

5. How did baptism become a source of division and competing constructions of authority in the Corinthian church?

6. What does Paul list as the gifts of the Spirit, and what does he say about the gift of speaking in tongues? For Paul, what is more important—the expression of a gift or that gift's usefulness for the whole body of Christ?

7. What analogies does Paul use to describe the resurrected body?

8. What advice does Paul offer to married couples?

9. Why did eating meat that had been sacrificed to gods pose a serious moral dilemma for the Corinthian Christians? What were the different perspectives about this within the Corinthian church?

10. What behaviors at Corinthian worship celebrations upset Paul?

## Questions for Reflection

1. How might Christian worship look today if it included a communal meal, as was common in the earliest churches, including Corinth?

2. Paul and the Christians in Corinth corresponded with each other after Paul's departure (1:11, 5:9, 7:1, 16:17–18). How might this have led to some of the difficulties in the church in Corinth?

3. In 1 Corinthians, Paul's emerging theology surfaces in areas such as the power of the cross, the gifts of the Holy Spirit, Christian love, the Resurrection, and the Parousia. How do you imagine the Corinthians processed all this theology?

4. Which ethical standards suggested by Paul do you think most challenged the Corinthian Christians?

## Recommendations for Further Reading

Adams, Edward, and David G. Horrell, eds. *Christianity at Corinth: The Quest for the Pauline Church.* Louisville, KY: Westminster John Knox Press, 2004.

Adams and Horrell have compiled into this single work some of the best scholarly studies written on Paul and his letters to the Corinthians over the past century. Divided into two parts ("Extracts from the History of Scholarship on Christianity at Corinth" and "Methodological

Reflections"), this book offers the research and insights from scholars ranging from C. K. Barrett and Nils A. Dahl to Elisabeth Schüssler Fiorenza and Margaret Y. MacDonald.

Grant, Robert M. *Paul in the Roman World: The Conflict at Corinth.* Louisville, KY: Westminster John Knox Press, 2001.

Grant provides a short overview of the religious, political, and cultural dimensions of the city of Corinth during Paul's lifetime. The book is divided into three parts: Part 1 (business and politics) covers Paul's journey to Corinth and the realities of city life that Paul encountered. Part 2 (religion and ritual) discusses the religious practices of the Corinthians, including the liturgical experiences at Corinth. Part 3 (Paul on sexuality) addresses the expected sexual ethics and the marital problems encountered in the community.

Murphy-O'Connor, Jerome. *St. Paul's Corinth: Texts and Archaeology.* Third Revised and Expanded Edition. Collegeville, MN: Liturgical Press, 2002.

In part 1, Murphy-O'Connor offers more than thirty Greek and Latin texts about ancient Corinth, covering a three-hundred-year period (100 BCE–200 CE). Part 2 details textual evidence of two events associated with Paul's stay in Corinth: the Edict of Claudius and the term of the office of the proconsul Gallio. Part 3 presents archeological insights into the houses, temples, and shops in Corinth that affected Paul and his missionary work.

Winter, Bruce W. *After Paul Left Corinth: The Influence of Secular Ethics and Social Change.* Grand Rapids, MI: Eerdmans, 2001.

As the subtitle suggests, Winter explores the impact of the secular culture on the early Christian community in Corinth. Divided into two parts (the influence of secular ethics and the influence of social changes), Winter argues that these influences account for many of the problems that arose in this community after Paul's departure. Relying upon many secondary sources, Winter offers many new and original insights into the city of Corinth after Paul left.

Witherington, Ben, III. *Conflict and Community in Corinth: A Socio-Rhetorical Commentary on 1 and 2 Corinthians.* Grand Rapids, MI: Eerdmans, 1995.

As the subtitle implies, Witherington approaches his commentary on the Corinthian correspondences from the rhetorical structure used to construct these two letters. For each rhetorical unit, Witherington provides "A Closer Look" section that explores in some depth the social and cultural customs of the ancient world, such as "Dining in Roman Corinth," "Pagan Views of Salvation," and "Head-Coverings and Religion in Roman Cities."

# CHAPTER 4

# Second Corinthians

## INTRODUCTION

Proceeding with a chronological treatment of Paul's undisputed letters, the text now examines 2 Corinthians. The first section of this chapter focuses on the historical context of 2 Corinthians: the setting of the letter; events that transpired between the writing of 1 and 2 Corinthians; and the question of whether 2 Corinthians is a single or composite letter. The second section investigates the theology and ethics of Paul in 2 Corinthians, covering topics from Paul's defense of his apostleship to the collection for the poor in Jerusalem as a moral duty.

### A Personal Letter

As seen in the discussions of 1 Thessalonians and 1 Corinthians, Paul shows a personal side to the early Christian congregations.[1] Although all of the surviving Pauline letters contain a personal element, 2 Corinthians is commonly referred to as Paul's most personal letter. Paul expresses an array of emotions, ranging from serious depression (2 Cor 1:8) and anxiety (2 Cor 2:13) to genuine joy (2 Cor 7:4) and self-satisfaction (2 Cor 12:12).[2]

---

1. For example, Paul expresses his deep affection for the Thessalonians: "We were gentle among you as a nursing mother cares for her children" (1 Thess 2:7). Paul is also willing to convey his anger and frustration at the Corinthians: "I say this to shame you. Can it be that there is not one among you wise enough to be able to settle a case between brothers?" (1 Cor 6:5).

2. Paul even mentions a now-lost letter, the so-called letter of tears (2 Cor 2:4), that he sent to the community at Corinth between the writing of 1 and 2 Corinthians.

## An Apologetic Letter

As with 1 Thessalonians and 1 Corinthians, Paul wrote 2 Corinthians for a very specific purpose. In the case of 2 Corinthians, the purpose is clear: to defend himself and his ministry on numerous fronts. Paul has to answer to charges and accusations leveled by intruders (the "superapostles" among others, see 2 Cor 11:5) who have made their way into the Corinthian congregation since Paul left, and he has to win back those believers in Corinth who no longer see him as their authoritative voice and leader. In this sense, 2 Corinthians is best understood as an apologetic letter.

Whereas 1 Corinthians was intended to reconcile the Corinthians with themselves, uniting the factions in the community and bringing them together as one in Christ, Paul writes 2 Corinthians in the hope of reconciliation between himself and the Corinthians. In essence, the authority that Paul *assumed* in 1 Corinthians he must now *defend* in 2 Corinthians. The problems in Corinth proved to be more vexing than Paul understood them to be when he wrote 1 Corinthians. If Paul can successfully defend himself and win back the trust and support of the Corinthian congregation, it would facilitate a reconciliation between Paul and the Corinthians and give them all the more reason to "boast" of each other "on the day of our Lord Jesus" (2 Cor 1:14). Paul's desire to heal the rift that developed between him and the Corinthians was consistent with his message as a whole: his missionary work is a "ministry of reconciliation" (2 Cor 5:18), and he and Timothy are "ambassadors for Christ" (2 Cor 5:20).

# HISTORICAL CONTEXT OF 2 CORINTHIANS

Second Corinthians, like 1 Thessalonians and 1 Corinthians, provides some historical information that helps address the questions of authorship, date and place of composition, and intended audience. The Acts of the Apostles once again serves as an external source, despite the limitations of its historical reliability.[3]

---

3. Although Luke's discussion of Paul's missionary work in Thessalonica and Corinth in Acts 17–18 offers supplemental details for 1 Thessalonians and 1 Corinthians, Acts 20 too supplies some (albeit more limited) details for 2 Corinthians.

## Outline of 2 Corinthians

| 1:1–11 | **Greeting and Thanksgiving** |
|---|---|
| | The letter opens with a greeting from Paul and Timothy to the church in Corinth, which is extended to "all the holy ones throughout Achaia" (1:1). The short thanksgiving is filled with the language of encouragement and affliction. Paul offers his gratitude to God who rescues us (presumably himself and Timothy) from a terrible affliction that nearly took their lives in the province of Asia Minor. |
| 1:12–2:13 | **The Crisis Causing the Delayed Visit to Corinth** |
| | Paul begins the body of his letter by explaining why he is in the region of Macedonia, not in the city of Corinth as previously planned: some people in Corinth deeply pained Paul. The experience prompted Paul to write a letter of response (now lost) with many tears. Rather than follow up with a visit to Corinth, Paul decided to go to Troas in search of Titus. Not finding him, Paul quickly traveled on to Macedonia. |
| 2:14–7:4 | **Paul's Ministry** |
| | In an abrupt change in focus, Paul next addresses his missionary work, characterizing it as a ministry of a new covenant (of the spirit written on the heart); this covenant surpasses Israel's covenant (of the letter, written on stone). Paul writes of the role that hardships endured for the sake of the good news plays in this new covenant and of the future reward that awaits all believers upon the return of Christ. Paul concludes this section by further defining his missionary work as a ministry of reconciliation, which models the world's reconciliation to God through Christ, and by appealing to all believers with a call to live a holy life. |

*Continued*

| 7:5–16 | **The Arrival of Titus in Macedonia: Crisis Resolved** |
|---|---|
| | Paul returns to the earlier topic of his delayed visit to Corinth (2 Cor 1:12–2:13), reporting that he and Timothy found Titus in Macedonia. Titus brought the news that the Corinthians had responded well to his letter sent in tears, resulting in yearning, lament, and zeal for Paul. Although Paul's letter "saddened [the Corinthians] into repentance" (7:9), it served to reconcile Paul and the church in Corinth. |
| 8:1–9:15 | **The Collection** |
| | Paul moves on to a new subject, urging the Corinthians to follow the lead of the churches in Macedonia, who eagerly participate in the collection of money for the poor in Jerusalem. In doing so, they would fulfill the commitment they had made last year as to their promised gift. Paul is grateful that Titus takes the lead on this project and reminds the Corinthians that "God loves a cheerful giver" (9:7). |
| 10:1–13:10 | **Paul's Self-defense** |
| | Paul now launches into another new topic: a defense of himself as an apostle. His opponents (the so-called superapostles) have fundamentally questioned his authority as a legitimate apostle on numerous fronts (for example, because Paul boasts about his authority and yet has a weak bodily presence and is a poor speaker/preacher). Paul responds that his opponents preach a different gospel, which causes division. To defend himself, Paul offers numerous examples of his authority and authenticity as a true apostle, ranging from his personal sufferings to his miracle working. The letter concludes with an expression of Paul's sincere concern for the church in Corinth and an appeal to Corinthians to live a holy life. |

*Continued*

---

**Outline of 2 Corinthians** *Continued*

| 13:11–13 | **Final Exhortation and Blessing** |
|---|---|
| | Paul concludes his letter with a short list of exhortations he expects the Corinthians to obey, along with a final blessing set in a Trinitarian formula. |

## Author and Audience

First Corinthians lists Paul and Sosthenes as the two co-senders. Second Corinthians likewise lists two co-senders, this time, Paul and Timothy. Although Paul frequently uses the first person plural *we* in the letter in reference to Timothy and himself, Paul comes across as the main author. Paul's description of Timothy as "our brother" (1:1) points to the Corinthians' familiarity with him: Timothy, along with

### Paul's Language of Encouragement

Paul uses the term *paraklēsis* (encouragement, comfort) and its various derivations twenty-eight times in 2 Corinthians. The derivations are particularly prominent in Paul's thanksgiving (1:3–11), appearing ten times. Paul associates *paraklēsis* with *affliction* and *suffering* in the first half of the thanksgiving (1:3–7). For example, Paul explains that God encourages those who suffer affliction so that they are able to encourage others who are afflicted. Affliction and suffering become an important point of contact between the Corinthians and Paul. His suffering is the main focus of the second half of the thanksgiving (1:8–11), which serves to remind the Corinthians of the power of prayer and of the God who raises the dead. For example, Paul notes that he and Timothy suffered much and feared death while in Asia, but that they placed their trust in the God who raises the dead and God rescued them. Paul also credits the prayers of many for helping him and Timothy.

Paul and Silvanus, was part of the missionary team that had preached the gospel to the Corinthians (2 Cor 1:19; Acts 18:5).

The intended audience of 2 Corinthians remains the same as in 1 Corinthians: "the church of God that is in Corinth," with Paul extending the audience to include "all the holy ones throughout Achaia," the province of which Corinth was the capital (2 Cor 1:1). It seems likely that Paul's extension of this letter beyond the city limits of Corinth reflects the degree to which Paul's Christian opponents had affected believers in Corinth and in the larger region of Achaia.[4] The Corinthian congregation, as noted in chapter 3, had a mixed ethnic makeup, perhaps numbering around one hundred (predominantly Gentile, with some significant Jewish presence), with varying economic and social backgrounds (largely of the lower classes but with some wealthier believers).

## Date and Place of Composition[5]

In 2 Corinthians, Paul provides a significant amount of information about his travels, visits, and communications through letters and messengers to the Corinthians. These details will be considered more fully later. Two clues indicate a possible place and date of composition. First, Paul tells the Corinthians that, rather than visiting them in Corinth as originally planned (1 Cor 16:5–9), he went to Troas and then Macedonia in search of Titus (2 Cor 2:12–13), finally finding Titus in Macedonia (2 Cor 7:5–7, 8:1-5, 9:3–4). (Macedonia is the region that includes the churches of Thessalonica and Philippi.) These references suggest that he and Timothy, along with Titus, spent some time in Macedonia preaching the gospel. Acts 20:1–4 mentions Paul's presence in Macedonia, where he "provided many words of encouragement for them" (20:2).

---

4. The question of Paul's Christian opponents will be discussed later in the chapter.

5. The various partition hypotheses for 2 Corinthians suggest numerous dates and places of composition for this canonical letter. The question of the literary integrity of 2 Corinthians will be discussed later in this chapter. The position taken in this book is that 2 Corinthians is a single letter, written over a short period. In support of this position, see Udo Schnelle, *Apostle Paul: His Life and Theology* (trans. M. Eugene Boring; Grand Rapids, MN: Baker Academic, 2005), 237–345; Jan Lambrecht, SJ, *Second Corinthians* (SP 8; Collegeville, MN: Liturgical, 1999), 7–9.

## The Sufferings of Paul

Second Corinthians bears testimony to the sufferings of Paul more so than any other Pauline letter. In four separate contexts, Paul speaks of his torments: 1:3–11, 4:8–9, 6:4–10, 11:23–29. As the letter unfolds, Paul becomes increasingly more specific about what he has endured for the gospel he preached:

- Afflictions that came to us in the province of Asia. (1:8)
- We were afflicted in every way, but not constrained; perplexed, but not driven to despair; persecuted, but not abandoned; struck down, but not destroyed. (4:8–9)
- In everything we commend ourselves as ministers of God, through much endurance, in afflictions, hardships, constraints, beatings, imprisonments, riots, labors, vigils, fasts. (6:4–5)
- Five times at the hands of the Jews I received forty lashes minus one. Three times I was beaten with rods, once I was stoned, three times I was shipwrecked, I passed a night and a day on the deep. (11:24–25)

Paul's numerous and recurring hardships offer a bond of empathy between the apostle and the Corinthians, who likewise have faced hardship—due in no small part to their disagreements with one another and with Paul himself.

A second clue to a possible date of composition stems from his discussion of the collection for the poor in Jerusalem (2 Cor 8:10–11). While giving advice about the collection, Paul mentions that the Corinthians began to act last year. Given that 1 Corinthians was probably written in the spring of 55 CE and given that the Macedonians celebrated a new year each fall, Paul's reference to "last year" suggests that 2 Corinthians could have been written as early as the fall of 55 CE, possibly as late as the fall of 57 CE.

> ### Summary: Historical Setting for 2 Corinthians

| Author | Paul (co-sent by Timothy) |
|---|---|
| Audience | Corinthian congregation |
| Date of Composition | Fall 55–57 CE |
| Place of Composition | Region of Macedonia |

## What Led to the Writing of 2 Corinthians?

Details from this letter allow for only a sketchy reconstruction of the events that transpired between the writing of 1 and 2 Corinthians. This reconstruction begins, however, with Paul's concluding remarks from 1 Corinthians:

> I shall come to you after I pass through Macedonia . . . and perhaps I shall stay or even spend the winter with you. . . . For I do not wish to see you now just in passing, but I hope to spend some time with you, if the Lord permits. I shall stay in Ephesus until Pentecost. (16:5–8)

At some point between making these original travel plans and writing 2 Corinthians, Paul made a brief second trip from Ephesus to Corinth (2 Cor 12:14, 13:1). That visit did not go as planned. It involved "painful circumstances" (2 Cor 2:1) for Paul although the letter provides no details about this crisis. Clearly, however, Paul was offended (perhaps humiliated) by some in the congregation, which prompted him to quickly return to Ephesus and write a letter to the Corinthians "with many tears" (2 Cor 2:4). Titus delivered this tearful letter to the Corinthians (2 Cor 7:5–9). That Paul mentions this crisis and its resolution in two places in 2 Corinthians (2 Cor 2:3–11, 7:5–12) indicates the importance in his mind of these relatively recent events.

After this contentious and humiliating visit to Corinth, Paul (and presumably, Timothy) faced some type of life-threatening situation in

Asia (2 Cor 1:8). Soon after this incident, Paul searched for Titus in Troas. Not finding him there, Paul moved on to Macedonia, where he found Titus upon returning from Corinth (2 Cor 7:5–12). It is at this point that Paul learns from Titus that his tearful letter had its desired effect: the congregation sought to reconcile with Paul.

While in Macedonia, Paul decided to write 2 Corinthians, in which he announces that he intends to visit Corinth once again (2 Cor 12:14, 13:1). One of Paul's main motives for writing this second letter to the community at Corinth (or most of them, in any case) related to his decision to take on his opponents—the "super-apostles . . . who masquerade as apostles of Christ" (11:5,13). These superapostles in the church in Corinth discredited Paul and preached a different gospel (11:3–5).

## Paul's Opponents in Corinth[6]

One of the main problems Paul addressed in 1 Corinthians was the problem of factions within the church. Whether 1 Corinthians healed these divisions is not known. It is known, however, that a new problem developed: others present in the congregation opposed Paul and his gospel, and Paul was not present to defend himself.

Second Corinthians 10–13 offers some insight into these Christian opponents and their message as well as Paul's defense

*Continued*

6. See Ben Witherington III, *Conflict and Community in Corinth: A Socio-Rhetorical Commentary on 1 and 2 Corinthians* (Grand Rapids, MI: Eerdmans, 1995), 345–350, for a good overview of the possible opponents of Paul in Corinth. Witherington rightly cautions: "It is important that we neither underestimate nor overestimate Paul's Corinthian opponents," 345. See also Lambrecht, 6–7, who presents the various scholarly profiles of Paul's opponents: (1) the "Judaizers" Paul fought in Galatia; (2) Jewish Christian Gnostics; (3) Hellenistic Jewish Christians; (4) apostles from Jerusalem; (5) Christian "hybrists" who opposed Paul based on Hellenistic social conventions. Schnelle, 261, offer his own profile of Paul's opponents: "early Christian itinerant missionaries of Jewish-Hellenistic origin who charged Paul with lacking spiritual power and who wanted to legitimate themselves as authentic apostles and bearers of the Spirit."

strategies. The opponents were apparently Jewish Christians (11:22) who came to Corinth with "letters of recommendation" (3:1), possibly from Peter, to verify their authority and status. Knowledgeable and well trained in speech (11:6), they appealed to their experiences of visions (12:1–4) and performing miracles (12:12), prompting Paul to sarcastically refer to them as the superapostles (11:5, 12:11). They accused Paul of asserting too much authority (10:8), noting the contrast between his "severe and forceful" letters and his weak bodily presence and poor speech (10:10). What kind of an apostle is a poor preacher who cannot miraculously heal himself, they appear to have wondered.

Paul defended himself, asserting that these superapostles preached "another Jesus," "a different spirit," and "a different gospel" (11:4) from what he preached. He accused these opponents of being "false apostles, deceitful workers, who masquerade as apostles of Christ" (11:13) who actually charged others for their preaching of the gospel (11:7). Paul held up his own visions (12:1–6), his personal sufferings for the gospel (11:23–29), and his mighty deeds (12:11–12) as proof of his authentic apostleship. Cleary, this is not a friendly conversation aimed at achieving reconciliation between Paul and the superapostles. Rather, Paul seeks reconciliation with the Corinthians and hopes that they will cast out the other anti-Pauline apostolic claimants.

## Is 2 Corinthians a Single Letter?

Scholars continue to debate the literary integrity of 2 Corinthians.[7] Those who argue that 2 Corinthians is a composite of two or more letters typically cite the following observations:[8]

---

7. In addition to Schnelle, *Apostle Paul*, and Lambrecht, see also Schnelle, *The History and Theology of the New Testament Writings*. Trans. M. Eugene Boring (London: SCM, 1998), 79–87, for a brief survey of the various partition hypotheses associated with 2 Corinthians.

8. Most scholars no longer support one of the traditionally cited criteria for asserting that 2 Corinthians is a composite letter: the language and content of 2 Corinthians 6:14–7:1 differs from the rest of letter because it is an anti-Pauline fragment.

- The narrative break in subject matter and shift in tone between 2 Corinthians 1–9 and 2 Corinthians 10–13, which suggests two separate letters.
- 2 Corinthians 8 and 2 Corinthians 9, two chapters dealing with the collection of money for the poor in Jerusalem, appear to be independent and unnecessarily redundant discussions of the collection.
- 2 Corinthians 2:14–7:4, a lengthy theological reflection by Paul on his ministry, is sandwiched between Paul's discussion of the crisis with the Corinthians (2 Corinthians 1:1–2:13) and its eventual resolution (2 Corinthians 7:5–16).

These clues leave some scholars convinced that 2 Corinthians may contain as many as six letters or letter fragments: 2 Corinthians 1:1–2:13, 2:14–6:13, 7:2–4, 7:5–16, and chapters 8, 9, and 10–13. Other scholars argue that 2 Corinthians, although a composite letter, consists of only two main parts: 2 Corinthians 1–9 and 2 Corinthians 10–13.

A principal difficulty with the various partition theories is that they require numerous hypothetical scenarios that cannot be verified. Furthermore, the manuscript evidence of this letter gives no indication of a lack of integrity. In other words, 2 Corinthians has been preserved in manuscripts only as a single letter.

Scholars who hold that 2 Corinthians is a single letter often explain that the composition of this letter likely took place over an extended period, even more so than the usual two to three weeks it took for an author to dictate and a scribe to write a letter in its final form. This may account for the various breaks in tone and subject matter. The most significant seam in the letter—between chapters 9 and 10—can be attributed to Paul's receiving news of the opponents in Corinth, who challenged his authority and status as an apostle, during the writing of 2 Corinthians. If correct, this would mean that Paul was once again naively optimistic about the situation in Corinth. When he wrote 1 Corinthians, he assumed that he had the authority to give numerous instructions to this community, which he clearly did not. And again, when he wrote 2 Corinthians 1–7, he senses that a previous crisis has been reconciled when, as of 2 Corinthians 10–13, the drama continued. Given these arguments, the position taken in this book is that 2 Corinthians is a single letter composed over an extended period, because it allows for a simpler explanation than most partition theories. Nevertheless, other scholars maintain that 2 Corinthians 10–13 reflects a crisis situation prior to the reconciliation reflected in 2 Corinthians 1–7. Scholarly debates on this point will likely continue for some time.

## Summary: Historical Context of 2 Corinthians

### CORE CONCEPTS

- Second Corinthians is Paul's most personal and apologetic letter.
- Paul defends himself against his opponents and defines his ministry in 2 Corinthians.
- Serious debate exists about the literary integrity of 2 Corinthians because of the variety of topics it addresses and the possibly different situations reflected in its different parts.

### SUPPLEMENTAL INFORMATION

- Second Corinthians was co-sent with Timothy but authored only by Paul.
- Between the writing of 1 and 2 Corinthians, Paul sent a now-lost "letter of tears" to the church in Corinth after he had a humiliating visit to Corinth and realized that 1 Corinthians was not at all adequate for solving that congregation's problems.
- Opponents in Corinth challenged Paul's authority and status.
- Second Corinthians reveals the important role Titus played as one of Paul's co-workers.
- The idea that 2 Corinthians was written over an extended period best accounts for its often sudden change in tone and subject matter.
- Some scholars think 2 Corinthians may contain as many as six letter fragments.

# THEOLOGY AND ETHICS OF 2 CORINTHIANS

The theology and ethics reflected in 2 Corinthians are closely tied to the situation in Corinth, as Paul understood it. The crisis resulting from his second brief visit and the presence of superapostles (and their considerable followers) in the Corinthian congregation prompted Paul to offer some theological reflections on his ministry and apostleship.

## Theology

### Paul's Ministry

Early in this letter, Paul offers an extended discussion of his ministry (2 Cor 2:14–7:4). The discussion likely stems from Paul's conflicts with Christian opponents in Corinth who challenged the legitimacy of his ministry, including during the last visit. In these chapters, Paul develops two points: he and Timothy are "ministers of a new covenant" (2 Cor 3:6) and called by God to deliver a "ministry of reconciliation" (2 Cor 5:18).

In his first letter to Corinth, Paul used the language of *new covenant* to refer to the tradition he received and passed on regarding Jesus' words at his final meal with the disciples (1 Cor 11:23b–26). In 2 Corinthians and in the context of defining his own ministry, Paul further develops this idea of the new covenant. He contrasts the new covenant, "written on our hearts . . . by the Spirit" (2 Cor 3:2–3), producing a ministry of life, with the covenant given to Moses, "carved in letters on stone" (2 Cor 3:7), further suggesting that Paul's opponents are Jewish Christians.

Paul also uses the image of the "veil" to further differentiate between the old covenant with Moses and the new covenant with Christ. Moses covered his face with the veil because the Israelites could not look at him directly after Moses had seen God face to face and received the law. The image of the veil allows Paul simultaneously to further define his ministry of a new covenant and to point out the shortcoming of Jews who refuse to acknowledge Jesus as the Messiah (2 Cor 3:14b–18). For Paul, Christ-believers reflect on the full glory of God—unveiled—in the person of Christ and enjoy the transformative power of the new covenant.

## The Spirit as "a First Installment"

Twice in 2 Corinthians, Paul writes about the Spirit as "a first install-ment," meaning a guarantee (1:21–22; 5:5).

Paul uses a Greek legal term (1:22 and 5:5), *arrabōn* (install-ment or guarantee), to indicate that Christians receive God's "first installment" of the Spirit in their hearts as a guarantee of the Spirit's presence at the eschaton, the end-time. Paul will develop this idea further in his next two letters, Galatians and Romans, in which he refers to the in-dwelling Spirit as a guarantee from God of Christian resurrection (Gal 6:7–8; Rom 8:11,22–23). Paul saw the role of the Spirit as integral to the life of a Christian.

Paul also uses the language of reconciliation to define the nature of his ministry to the Corinthians. Paul holds up God's reconciliation to the world through Christ as the model for his ministry of recon-ciliation (2 Cor 5:17–21). Paul sees himself and Timothy as "ambas-sadors for Christ" (5:20), calling all to reconciliation with God and with each other. The reconciliation between Paul and the believers in the Corinthian church communicates the point that Paul's reconcili-ation with this congregation is emblematic of humanity's reconcili-ation with God in Christ. The closing words of his letter urge that a process of reconciliation continue in this community: "Mend your ways, encourage one another, agree with one another, live in peace, and the God of love and peace will be with you" (2 Cor 13:11).

### The Role of Suffering

In addition to using the language of *new covenant* and *reconcili-ation* to define his ministry, Paul also speaks of the role of suffering. The language of affliction and suffering in relation to Paul's ministry appears throughout this letter (see "The Sufferings of Paul" on page 114). In discussing what he has suffered, Paul makes the point that he endures so much for the Corinthians' benefit. Reconciliation after a conflict is often a difficult process. Here Paul highlights that he is already paying a high price for the Corinthians' benefit. Hopefully, they too will see the value of continuing to invest themselves in a process of reconciliation and, more broadly, in the service of the gospel.

Paul sees the afflictions and persecutions to his body (and, by extension, the sufferings of all believers) as a living example and witness to all of "carrying about in the body the dying of Jesus" (4:10a). The suffering Paul endures within his ministry serves a greater purpose of making it possible for "the life of Jesus" to "be manifested in our body" (4:10b).

Paul also views his ministering of this new covenant and reconciliation as a "treasure" to be cherished, acknowledging the suffering it brings upon his body (4:7). However, Paul also acknowledges the transient nature of the earthly vessel, or "tent" ("our earthly dwelling"), which will be replaced by "a building from God, a dwelling not made with hands, eternal in heaven" (5:1). Paul affirms Christian suffering ("For in this tent we groan," 5:2) and places it in its proper perspective (5:4).

## Paul's Diatribes[9]

One of the remarkable features of 1 and 2 Corinthians is the prevalence of the rhetorical device known as a diatribe. This type of rhetoric was a common technique used for argumentation among ancient philosophers. In a diatribe, the author posits a rhetorical question reflecting a position (often that of one's opponents) that he wishes to refute. Paul employs the diatribe with impressive force in his explanation of a crucified Christ as well as in his defense of his ministry and himself.

Diatribes are scattered throughout both 1 and 2 Corinthians (1 Cor 1:26–31, 4:6–21, 9:1–27, 13:1–13; 2 Cor 4:7–15, 6:3–10, 11:12–15,21–29, 12:5–10, 13:3–4). Sometimes put into question-and-answer format, other times topically based (for example, divine reversal, strength in weakness), Paul's diatribes helped sway the Corinthians to take his side of the argument. See, for instance, 1 Corinthians 9:1–2; 2 Corinthians 11:13–15.

Also in the Letter to the Romans, Paul uses this rhetorical device to present his theology (responding to criticisms and correcting possible misunderstandings) to the faithful in Rome.

---

9. For a good discussion on Paul's rhetoric in 1 and 2 Corinthians, see Witherington, 35–48.

## Paul's Apostleship

Toward the end of his letter, Paul includes another extended discussion—this time in defense of his apostleship (2 Cor 10–13). This four-chapter section stands on its own within 2 Corinthians, both in structure and in content. In it, Paul launches a legal defense of his status as an apostle in direct response to Christian opponents and their followers in Corinth who challenged Paul's apostolic authority and gospel message.

Paul begins the formal defense of his apostleship by identifying up front two of his opponents' main accusations: (1) Paul boasts about his authority (2 Cor 10:8); and (2) Paul writes powerful letters, but his body is weak and his speech is poor (2 Cor 10:10). Paul responds at some length to these criticisms. Later, Paul offers a list of charges (11:1–15) against the opponents (the superapostles, 11:5) who challenge him in Corinth. Paul begins by accusing the superapostles of preaching another Jesus and spirit as well as a different gospel to the Corinthians (11:4). He then addresses the issue that he did not collect payment from Corinthian Christians for the gospel he preached (11:7; 1 Cor 9:6–18). For his opponents, this would have been an ominous sign, indicating that Paul did not possess the authority to do so. Paul responds that he robbed (11:8) other congregations in order not to be a burden to the Corinthians. Here, Paul *agrees* with his opponents that a legitimate apostle has the right to be supported by those to whom he ministers. Notably, Paul seeks reconciliation with the Corinthians—but not with these superapostles. Instead he offers insults: they are false prophets, deceitful workers, and ministers of Satan (11:13–15a), and "their end will correspond to their deeds" (11:15b).[10]

In 2 Corinthians 11:16–12:10, Paul offers two additional arguments to defend his authority and status as an apostle: his unparalleled suffering for the gospel and his unique mystical experiences. Paul begins by speaking of his Jewish identity (11:22), highlighting that he, like the superapostles, has a background on which he could base his authority. However, Paul refuses to do so. Next, he discusses in some detail the suffering he has experienced in his apostolic missionary work (11:23–29).[11] Listing his many persecutions and the

---

10. See "Paul's Opponents in Corinth," on pages 116–117 of this book.

11. See "The Sufferings of Paul," on page 114.

physical torture that he endured for the gospel highlights Paul's profound dedication—a dedication that, Paul alleges, the superapostles do not possess.

The letter also mentions mystical experiences, "visions and revelations of the Lord" (12:1).[12] Paul does not reveal what he has heard or seen, stating only that he "was caught up into Paradise and heard ineffable things, which no one may utter" (12:4). Paul also says he avoids sharing his mystical experiences so that others do not think too much of him (12:6b–7). The elation Paul receives from his visions and revelations is tempered by "a thorn in the flesh" and "an angel of Satan" (12:7), which offers another indication of his close relationship to Christ amid hardships. Another interpretation of this text is that Paul is speaking ironically here, offering a parody of what his opponents would boast about. In either interpretation, the central point is that Paul takes a strength of his rivals—presumably an asset they found lacking in Paul. He concludes his central defense by summarily stating that his strength lies in his weakness (12:10).

## Paul's Thorn in the Flesh

Paul writes of "a thorn in the flesh" that was given to him and, also, an "angel of Satan" that beat him so that he would not be "too elated" from the "abundance of revelations" he receives (12:6–9a). Scholars have not reached a consensus on what exactly Paul refers to by the thorn that afflicted him and the satanic angel that beat him. Theories range from a physical disability—for example, a speech impediment (2 Cor 10:10, 11:6) or an eye disease (Gal 4:13–15) to more mental or psychological problems such as Paul's "daily pressures" and "anxiety" for his churches (2 Cor 11:28) or his "despair" from his afflictions (2 Cor 1:8). Paul turns this negative point against his apostolic authority into a positive one: through this thorn, Paul has enjoyed closer fellowship with Christ, whose "grace is sufficient" in all the apostle's afflictions.

---

12. See Paula Gooder, *Only the Third Heaven? 2 Corinthians 12.1–10 and Heavenly Ascent* (London: T & T Clark, 2006), especially chapter 3, "Caught Up into Heaven: Ascending into Heaven," 68–78.

In 2 Corinthians 12:11–18, Paul then reinforces his central point that he is not inferior to the superapostles, reminding the Corinthians: "The signs of an apostle were performed among you with all endurance, signs and wonders, and mighty deeds" (12:12). Paul hopes that he has sufficiently defended himself and that another visit will be possible (12:14). Paul's hope is that the visit will be more collegial than his earlier humiliating visit. This serves well as the backdrop for the final warnings and appeals that conclude this section of the letter (12:19–13:10).

# Ethics

Second Corinthians highlights two ethical matters of particular significance. The first, the collection as a moral duty, expands upon Paul's comments at the end of 1 Corinthians 16:1–4. The second, a call to live a holy life, arises in several parts of this letter.

## The Collection as Moral Duty

Second Corinthians includes Paul's most extensive discussions about the collection of money for the poor in Jerusalem (2 Cor 8–9). Already in 1 Corinthians, Paul mentions his project of the collection of money for the poor Christians in Judea (1 Cor 16:1–4).

Underlying the moral imperative for the collection are numerous Pauline theological principles. First, participation in the collection models the Christological example: Christ became poor so that others might become rich (2 Cor 8:9). Second, by giving generously, Gentile Christ-believers will share "fellowship" (*koinōnia*) with needy Judean Christ-believers. This is a fellowship with those whom one has never met through helping those in need; it is a partaking in the work of the whole church. Third, sharing in the collection has an eschatological element: the Gentiles themselves (rich or poor) owe a debt because, in Christ, they share in the inheritance of the fulfillment of ancient Israel. For Paul, there is one church—comprising Jews and Gentiles, and Christ is the fulfillment of the Israelite covenant. By receiving this fulfillment in Christ the Gentiles are already in debt to their Jewish brethren and recognize their indebtedness by helping their Judean Christ-believing sisters and brothers in need. At the heart of Paul's theological justification for this offering is a concept of *reciprocity*, or payback. The Gentiles benefit from the spiritual legacy of ancient Israel and, thus, are obliged to pay back their poor Judean brethren in need.

## Titus and the Collection

Second Corinthians 8:16–24 details how Titus coordinated the collection of money for the poor in Jerusalem. Described by Paul as his "traveling companion," "partner," and "co-worker," Titus took on the collection as a project within the churches established by Paul. In letters written subsequent to 1 and 2 Corinthians (see Gal 2:10; Rom 15:25–28), it is evident that the collection for the poor Christbelievers in Jerusalem remained a central concern in Paul's missionary work among the Gentiles.

### The Call to Live a Holy Life

Paul presents two aspects as central to the call to holiness. The first has to do with external relations—how the Corinthian Christians should live within the larger world of Roman Corinth. The second has to do with internal relations, resolving the troubles within the congregation.

Paul clearly worries about how believers interact with the wider society of Roman Corinth. He urges the Corinthian believers to separate themselves from nonbelievers (2 Cor 6:14). Paul called the Corinthians to radically break from their former way of life as nonbelievers as one of the means to living a holy life, a charge that surely posed a whole host of challenges, not the least of which would have been handling interactions with nonbelieving family members. As noted in 1 Corinthians, written less than a year before 2 Corinthians, this was a reality for at least some of the Corinthian families (see 1 Cor 7:12–16).

In addition to separating from the larger society, Paul called upon the Corinthians to heal and resolve their internal troubles. This was a grave concern for Paul in writing 1 Corinthians. Dealing appropriately with internal division and strife was essential to living as a holy community (2 Cor 12:20–22). Paul challenges the Corinthians to live a life of holiness in the closing remarks of his letter. He promotes an ethical standard to separate the Corinthians from the larger society and heal the strife within the community: "Finally, brothers, rejoice. Mend your ways, encourage one another, agree with one another, live in peace, and the God of love and peace will be with you. Greet one another with a holy kiss" (13:11–12a). Paul, of course, hopes this action will include his relationship with the Corinthian congregation.

## Summary: Theology and Ethics in 2 Corinthians

### CORE CONCEPTS

- Paul defines himself and Timothy as ministers of a new covenant and ministers of reconciliation.
- Paul defends his apostolic role and authority based on his sufferings for the gospel and his mystical visions and revelations.
- Paul viewed the collection for the poor in Jerusalem as an act of Christian charity and as a moral duty.

### SUPPLEMENTAL INFORMATION

- Paul uses the historic image of Moses and the veil to help define his ministry as well as attack his Jewish opponents.
- Paul makes the point that he suffers for the Corinthians' benefit, modeling the suffering of Christ.
- Paul's Corinthian opponents accuse him of abusing his authority and being weak in physical presence and rhetorical speech.
- Paul accuses the superapostles of preaching a different Jesus and spirit to the Corinthian Christians.
- Paul calls for a radical separation from the larger society in Corinth as a means to holiness for the Corinthian Christians.
- Second Corinthians preserves Paul's most extended discussions on the collection for the poor of Jerusalem.

## Questions for Review

1. What information in 2 Corinthians can help establish its historical setting?
2. What circumstances prompted the writing of 2 Corinthians?
3. On what grounds do some scholars argue that 2 Corinthians was originally more than one Pauline letter?
4. In what ways does Paul define his ministry?
5. In what context does Paul speak of "earthen vessels" and heavenly buildings?
6. What words does Paul use to describe his opponents in the church at Corinth?
7. On what grounds do Paul's opponents criticize him? What are the different accusations against Paul?
8. Does Paul agree that any of his opponents' perceptions are correct?
9. According to Paul, why did the Lord place "a thorn in [his] flesh"?
10. What role did Titus play in collecting money for the poor?

## Questions for Reflection

1. What do you imagine Paul wrote in the now-lost "letter of tears" that he sent to the church in Corinth between the writing of 1 and 2 Corinthians? How might this letter have differed from 1 and 2 Corinthians?
2. Paul endured much suffering and affliction in his ministry. What do you think this says about Paul's character and personality?
3. Paul states that by giving generously, Gentile Christ-believers will share "fellowship" (*koinōnia*) with needy Judean Christ-believers. Our world has so many needy people. Is it possible to share *koinōnia* with the poor through service and generosity to them?
4. After reading 2 Corinthians 1–7, 8, 9, 10–13, consider whether 2 Corinthians is best viewed as a single letter of Paul or as parts of letters written to the Corinthians before Paul's reconciliation with them (2 Cor 10–13) and after his reconciliation with them (2 Cor 1–7).

# Recommendations for Further Reading

Cameron, Ron, and Merrill P. Miller, eds. *Redescribing Paul and the Corinthians.* Atlanta, GA: Society of Biblical Literature, 2011.

The volume contains nine essays, many of which challenge the conventional approaches and presuppositions in modern Pauline studies. Typical discussions associated with the Corinthian correspondences, such as Paul and his relationship with the Christians in Corinth and the nature of Pauline opposition in Corinth, are approached in new ways, resulting in some rather unconventional conclusions.

Gooder, Paula. *Only the Third Heaven? 2 Corinthians 12.1–10 and Heavenly Ascent.* London: T & T Clark, 2006.

Gooder offers an extensive literature survey on heaven from relevant primary sources (biblical and ancient texts, including Jewish and Christian apocalyptic literature) and secondary sources from modern authors covering topics such as God, heaven, mystical visions, and angels. Gooder argues that heaven is best understood within the larger biblical and ancient view as God's dwelling place, an experience of God more so in the here and now and less in the distant future.

Kelhoffer, James A. *Persecution, Persuasion and Power: Readiness to Withstand Hardship as a Corroboration of Legitimacy in the New Testament.* WUNT 270. Tübingen: Mohr Siebeck, 2010.

In the chapter on "The Pauline Letters: Faithfulness in Withstanding Persecution as Corroboration of Believers' Standing in Christ and of Paul's Apostleship," Kelhoffer examines how a readiness to endure persecution offers a confirmation to both Paul (as a legitimate apostle) and to believers in general (as those who belong to Christ, the suffering Messiah). In particular, Kelhoffer discusses 2 Cor 11:23–33, in which Paul's many sufferings on behalf of the gentile mission answer criticisms of the superapostles' objections to Paul's authority (see pp. 53–61).

Lim, Kar Yong. *"The Sufferings of Christ Are Abundant in Us" (2 Corinthians 1:5): A Narrative Dynamics of Paul's Sufferings in Second Corinthians.* New York and London: T & T Clark, 2009.

After a brief literature review and explanation of his methodological approach, Lim focuses on four passages from 2 Corinthians that speak to Paul's sufferings: 1:3–11 (the thanksgiving); 2:14–16 (Paul's apostolic ministry); 4:7–12 (Paul's ministry of suffering as treasure in an earthen vessel); 6:1–10 (Paul's self-commendation through suffering in the ministry of reconciliation). For all four passages, Lim begins with an explanation of the structure and line of thought behind the text and then examines each passage in light of the story of Jesus.

Longenecker, Bruce W. *Remembering the Poor: Paul, Poverty and the Greco-Roman World.* Grand Rapids, MI: Eerdmans, 2010.

Longenecker approaches the topic of Paul and the poor in the ancient world with a twofold division of his book: "The poor in their ancient places" and "The poor in Pauline places." He begins with an analysis of wealth and poverty in the Greco-Roman cities of the ancient world. He then argues the case for Paul's strong conviction for the Christian moral obligation to care for the poor as central to the gospel and the message he conveyed to the communities he founded.

# CHAPTER 5

# Galatians

## INTRODUCTION

Shortly after (or perhaps during) the writing of 2 Corinthians, Paul composed a letter to the believers in Galatia. This is the only letter addressed to multiple churches in a larger geographic region than a city. The first section of this chapter focuses on the historical context of the letter: the setting, the crisis that prompted the writing to the Galatians, and Paul's apologetics. The second section examines both the theology of this letter—justification by faith, the Jewish law, and freedom in Christ—as well as the ethical teachings that stem from this freedom on life in the Spirit and guidelines for community relations.

## No Thanksgiving

In his earlier letters, immediately following the greeting, Paul inserted a thanksgiving as part of the introduction, following the pattern typical of a Hellenistic Greek letter. For example, in 1 Thessalonians, Paul expressed his gratitude for the faith of the Thessalonians, seeing this community as a "model for all the believers in Macedonia and in Achaia" (1 Thess 1:7). Likewise, in 1 Corinthians, Paul thanked God for the abundance of discourse, knowledge, and spiritual gifts that were bestowed upon the believers of the Corinthian congregation (1 Cor 1:4–7). In addition, in 2 Corinthians, Paul thanked God for the encouragement in the afflictions that he and the Corinthians suffered (2 Cor 1:3–11).

In his letter to the Galatians, however, Paul offers no opening words of thanks. Replacing the standard thanksgiving indicates Paul's shock and disappointment with the Galatian Christians for following a different gospel than the one he delivered to them (1:6–9). Twice, in the space normally reserved for words of thanks, Paul says of the person(s) preaching this different gospel: "let that one be accursed!" (1:8,9). The contrast with earlier letters is striking. As the letter unfolds, Paul reveals his objections to this different gospel and his reasons for omitting a thanksgiving become clear.

## Emerging Ideas

The letters Paul wrote before Galatians show how some of his ideas emerged over time. For instance, in 1 Thessalonians 1:3 and 5:8, Paul connects the virtues of faith, hope, and love. Then, in 1 Corinthians, he orders these virtues, with love (*agapē*) as the supreme theological virtue (13:13). The language of *new covenant* in 1 Corinthians 11:23–26—a "received" tradition on the Lord's supper that Paul inserts into his letter—offers another example. In 2 Corinthians 2:14–3:18, Paul further develops the idea of new covenant as a way of defining his own ministry.

Scholars have long recognized that some of the major ideas and themes (even the "train of thought") present in the Letter to the Romans begin to emerge in a preliminary way in Galatians.[1] Paul's discussion of justification of faith and the role of Abraham provide a good example. In Galatians 2:15–21, Paul introduces the idea that faith (and not works of the law) justifies one before God. Then, he goes on to cite Abraham's belief in God as the exemplar of justification (3:6–18). In Romans, Paul significantly elaborates on the idea of justification by faith apart from the law (3:19–31) and further develops the connection between Abraham's faith in God and the Gentiles' (the uncircumcised) faith in Christ (4:1–25).

## HISTORICAL CONTEXT OF GALATIANS

As was the case with Paul's previous letters, Galatians includes information that can help answer the historical questions of authorship,

---

1. See Udo Schnelle, *The History and Theology of the New Testament Writings*, trans. M. Eugene Boring (London: SCM Press, 1998), 94–95.

date and place of composition, and intended audience. Information from two of Paul's other letters (1 Corinthians and Romans), as well as the Acts of the Apostles, assists in determining the date and place of composition for Galatians.

## Outline of Galatians

| | |
|---|---|
| 1:1–10 | **Greeting and Concern Prompting the Letter**<br>The letter opens with a greeting from Paul and "all the brothers who are with me" (1:2) to the churches in Galatia. Of the seven undisputed letters, this is the only one clearly sent to multiple congregations. Omitting any thanksgiving, Paul moves directly to his concern: the churches of Galatia are exposed to a different gospel from the one that Paul preached to them. He then twice curses those who pervert the gospel message and who lead the Galatians astray. He also says "as we have said before"(1:9), which is likely a reference to a previous time when Paul had similar problems in Galatia. |
| 1:11–2:14 | **Paul's Apologetic and Relationship with Peter**<br>Paul begins the defense of his status as an apostle by highlighting the source of his gospel message: a "revelation" from Jesus Christ (1:12b). Paul next mentions parts of his life, including his initial persecution of the church, which ended when he received a revelation from God of his resurrected Son and led to Paul's evangelization of the Gentiles. Paul then narrates some encounters with Peter (Cephas) over the years in Jerusalem to Antioch. |
| 2:15–4:13 | **Justification by Faith and Freedom in Christ**<br>These precedents from Paul's life set the stage for Paul's authoritative theological teachings on justification, the law, and freedom. This backdrop allows Paul to define clearly the tenets of his gospel message: all people (Jews and Gentiles |

*Continued*

| | |
|---|---|
| | **Outline of Galatians** *Continued* |
| | alike) are justified by their faith in Christ. The crucifixion and Resurrection of Jesus fulfilled the Jewish law, because through Christ, God's fidelity to the covenantal promises to Israel was realized. No longer bound to the law, Christians experience a new freedom in the Spirit to live as children of God. |
| 5:1–6:10 | **The Christian Moral Life** Paul begins the final section of this letter with a prohibition against male circumcision because it forfeits Christians' freedom in the Spirit. For a Gentile follower of Christ to become circumcised would result in being "separated from Christ" (5:4). Paul lists both vices (works of the flesh) and virtues (fruits of the Spirit), emphasizing that believers should act of out of love for one another. Paul then presents a list of moral exhortations for community life. |
| 6:11–18 | **Final Appeal and Blessing** Paul concludes by signing his letter and castigating once again those who have compelled the Galatians to circumcision. The letter ends with a warning from Paul and a brief blessing. |

## Author and Audience

The letters from Paul to the churches of Thessalonica and Corinth all had clearly identified co-senders: 1 Thessalonians (Paul, Silvanus, and Timothy); 1 Corinthians (Paul and Sosthenes); and 2 Corinthians (Paul and Timothy). In Galatians, Paul identifies himself as the sender as well as "all the brothers who are with me" (1:2). Nowhere in the letter, though, does Paul identify who "all the brothers" are. Furthermore, Paul's consistent use of the first personal singular *I* throughout the letter implies that he is the sole author of Galatians. The reference to "all the brothers" may have been Paul's attempt to claim a widespread support for the strong tone and the theological assertions of the letter.

In the greeting, Paul directs his letter "to the churches of Galatia" (1:2). Two clues in the letter suggest that the members of these congregations were predominantly Gentile. The first occurs in Galatians 4:8 in which Paul speaks of Christian freedom: "At a time when you did not know God, you became slaves to things that by nature are not gods." Paul refers here to the Galatian Christians' past practice of worshipping idols. The second clue occurs in references in which Paul warns against male circumcision of the Gentile Christ-believers (5:2–3,12; 6:12–13). Given Torah-observant Jews' strict practice of circumcision and the opposite prevailing trend in Gentile circles, this prohibition was clearly directed to non-Jewish (that is, Gentile) Christians.

## Paul's Aggressive Defense Strategy

The opening words of the Letter to the Galatians signal Paul's intent to forcefully defend his apostolic call and authority: "Paul, an apostle not from human beings nor through a human being but through Jesus Christ and God the Father who raised him from the dead" (1:1).

The spread of a different gospel being adopted by some Galatian Christians, as well as questions about Paul's theology and authority as an apostle of Christ, prompted Paul to begin his letter by reminding the various congregations of Galatia of his unique call and authority.

The internal evidence suggests that the Christian congregations of Galatia were primarily Gentile. Additionally, the letter gives some clues about the geographic location of these congregations. Scholars have debated this issue, which has led to two competing theories: the North Galatian (region) hypothesis and the South Galatian (province) hypothesis.[2] The location debate has direct implications for the dating of Galatians, especially when cross-referenced with details found in the Acts of the Apostles.

---

2. For an extended discussion on these two hypotheses, see Frank J. Matera, *Galatians* (SP 9; Collegeville, MN; Liturgical Press, 1992), 19–24. See also Udo Schnelle, *Apostle Paul: His Life and Theology*, trans. M. Eugene Boring (Grand Rapids, MI: Baker Academic, 2005), 266–271.

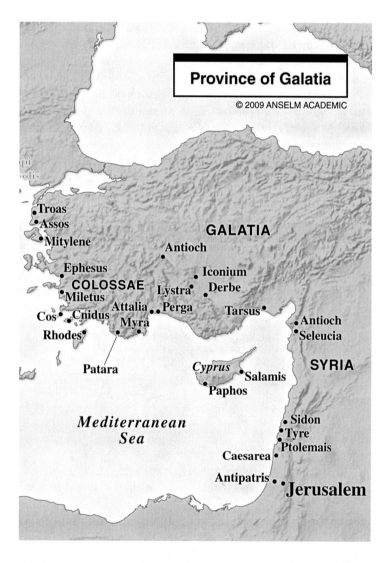

## Province of Galatia

© 2009 ANSELM ACADEMIC

Troas
Assos
Mitylene
GALATIA
Antioch
Ephesus
Iconium
COLOSSAE
Lystra
Derbe
Miletus
Attalia
Perga
Cos
Cnidus
Myra
Tarsus
Antioch
Seleucia
Rhodes
Patara
Cyprus
Salamis
SYRIA
Paphos
Mediterranean
Sea
Sidon
Tyre
Ptolemais
Caesarea
Antipatris
Jerusalem

Debate remains among scholars as to whether "the churches of Galatia" to which Paul wrote refer to the Christian congregations in the northern or southern region of Galatia.

Some scholars, who date Galatians before 1 Corinthians, tend to favor the South Galatian hypothesis. They argue that Paul wrote to the churches in the southern area of the Roman province of Galatia, in the districts such as Pisidia, Lystra, Iconium, and Derbe, during his first missionary trip (Acts 13–14). Thus, scholars associating Paul's Letter to the Galatians with his first missionary journey, as reported in Acts, tend to date Galatians in the late 40s or early 50s CE. Most scholars today, however, support the North Galatian hypothesis and hold that *internal* evidence from the letter indicates that Paul addressed his letter to those in the northern region of Galatia. They argue Paul's reference to the ethnic name *Galatians* in 1:2 and 3:1, for example, more aptly fits the inhabitants in the north. This theory holds that Paul established the churches of northern Galatia on his second missionary journey, narrated in Acts 15:36–18:22, and wrote his letter during his trip through Macedonia (Acts 20:1–3), on his third missionary journey, in the mid 50s CE.[3]

## Date and Place of Composition

In determining the date and place of composition for Galatians, scholars have focused on two other undisputed Pauline letters, 1 Corinthians and Romans. The point of contact between Galatians and 1 Corinthians has to do with the collection for the poor in Jerusalem, one of Paul's projects. At the end of 1 Corinthians, Paul writes: "Now in regard to the collection for the holy ones, you also should do as I ordered the churches of Galatia" (16:1).

Paul's comments here do not indicate any tension between himself and the Galatian congregations. In fact, quite the opposite could be inferred—the Galatians are still following Paul's authoritative directives at the writing of 1 Corinthians. Paul's mention of the collection for the poor in Galatians 2:10 demonstrates that this project was his initiative and not a command from the Jerusalem church. Paul writes about the collection as though already accomplished, which suggests that Galatians was written sometime after 1 Corinthians.

---

3. See Brigitte Kahl, *Galatians Re-Imagined: Reading with the Eyes of the Vanquished* (Minneapolis, MN: Fortress Press, 2010), 31–39, who offers an alternative read of the location of Galatians beyond the north-south debate.

As mentioned earlier, the structure and even train of thought that first appears in Galatians is later expanded upon in Romans (compare, for example, discussions of justification by faith, Abraham, baptism, slavery and freedom, law, and promise in Galatians 2–4 with those in Romans 3–9).[4] This has led many scholars to date the writing of Galatians before Romans.

The date for the composition of Galatians, then, falls somewhere between the writing of 1 Corinthians and the writing of Romans. Indeed, Paul probably composed it during or immediately after 2 Corinthians, in late 55 CE. Chapter 4 of this book indicated that Paul was in Macedonia for the writing of 2 Corinthians, which may have taken an extended period (more than even the typical two to three weeks). Therefore, it is most likely that Paul wrote Galatians in Macedonia. Galatia, the inland region of modern Turkey, was a long way from the region of Macedonia, more than five hundred miles. Nonetheless, Paul needed to send a letter to the Galatians, probably with one of his co-workers accompanying the letter, to mediate the crisis occurring in the churches of Galatia.

## Summary: Historical Setting for Galatians

| | |
|---|---|
| Author | Paul |
| Audience | The congregations of north Galatia (an inland region of modern Turkey) |
| Date of Composition | Late 55 CE |
| Place of Composition | Region of Macedonia |

## The Crisis That Prompted the Writing of Galatians

Immediately following the brief greeting, Paul launches into the heart of the crisis affecting the churches of Galatia: "some"

---

4. See Schnelle, *Apostle Paul*, 270–271, for a useful comparative chart.

people are inducing the believers in Galatia to follow "a different gospel" (1:6–7).

Two basic questions emerge concerning this crisis: (1) What is this "different gospel"? (2) Who are the agitators (the "some" people) who have brought this other gospel to the Galatian congregations? Regarding the first question, scholars generally agree that the different gospel involves requiring male circumcision of the Gentile Christians (5:3; 6:12–13) and following the Jewish cultic calendar as outlined in the Torah (4:8–11), as well as keeping oneself pure in food and other regulations. In other words, this different gospel seems to have involved believers in Galatia who were convinced that Jesus was the Messiah and that he brought the law to fruition, but who did not believe that this meant people should stop observing the law.[5] Much of Paul's theology and ethics in Galatians attempts to dismantle the core of this different gospel. The second section of this chapter addresses these matters in more detail.

As for the identity of the "some" who brought this different gospel to Galatia, there is general scholarly consensus that these were ethnically Jewish Christians, likely from Judea.[6] However, in Galatians, Paul does not offer much background on these Jewish Christians beyond their push for Gentile circumcision and cultic calendaring. Thus, scholars have many unanswered questions, such as, Did these Jewish Christians oppose Paul's gospel, or were they trying to complement it? Were they supported by the Jerusalem leadership of James, Cephas (Peter), and John (Gal 2:9), or were they acting on their own? The uncertainty surrounding these questions has led scholars to suggest various titles for these Jewish Christian missionaries, ranging from "Judaizers" (a traditional, problematic, and potentially anti-Jewish title indicating that these people stood in opposition to Paul) to "rival teachers" (a more recent title that downplays such opposition).

---

5. Schnelle, *Apostle Paul*, 276, summarizes this different gospel: "a movement in which strict Jewish Christians in a variety of ways attempted to make faith in Jesus Christ *and* Torah observance, baptism *and* circumcision obligatory not only for Jewish Christians but Gentile Christians as well."

6. Matera, *Galatians*, 2–6, presents a brief history on the research of the identity of the agitators and the content of their gospel message.

### The Apologetic of Paul

Paul offers selective parts of his autobiography only twice in his surviving letters, in Galatians 1:11–24 and Philippians 3:4–11. In both instances, Paul addresses a particular issue. In Philippians, Paul differentiates between faith in Christ and works of the law. In Galatians, it is part of a larger strategy to remind the Galatians of his own credentials while also discrediting the rival Jewish Christian missionaries and the legitimacy of their "different gospel," which was apparently being accepted by some in the congregations of Galatia.

## James, the Brother of the Lord

One of the many interesting details Paul offers in Galatians 1:11–24 is that Jesus had a brother. He writes that during his fifteen days in Jerusalem with Peter, "I did not see any other of the apostles, only James the brother of the Lord" (1:19).

This is the New Testament's earliest attestation of Jesus having a brother (in Greek, *adelphos*). James, the brother of the Lord, is mentioned in later New Testament writings: Mark 6:3; Matthew 13:55; Acts 12:17, 15:13, 21:18. In both Paul's Letter to the Galatians (2:1–11) and in Acts, James is presented as a leader in the Jerusalem church. In the gospel accounts, James is mentioned only as one of Jesus' siblings. For the early church, the matter became a point of theological dispute.

Paul uses parts of his autobiography to stress (at least) three important points: First, his gospel is "not of human origin . . . it came through a revelation of Jesus Christ" (1:11–12; see also 1:1). Therefore, challenging or altering Paul's gospel message is tantamount to blasphemy. Second, God "reveal[ed] his Son to me, so that I might proclaim him to the Gentiles" (1:16a). Paul's call for missionary outreach specifically to the Gentiles emanates directly from God, confirming Paul's apostolic authority. Third, Paul worked through the meaning of the revelation on his own, conferring with Cephas (Peter) only three years later in Jerusalem (1:16b–18). Paul's delay in seeking consultation about the revelation affirms the grounding of his apostolic authority in the divine, which does not require information from the Jerusalem Church, on whose authority the rival missionaries rely.

## Ancient Rhetoric and Galatians

In the predominantly oral culture of Paul's day, rhetoric (the learned art of persuasion) was a popular form of expression and even entertainment.[7] Galatians offers a good example of a surviving Pauline letter structured according to the rules of rhetoric. Most of the letter is in the form of a rhetorical speech, lacking the typical Pauline thanksgiving, greetings to individuals, and travel plans. Scholars have debated whether Galatians is better categorized rhetorically as juridical (attempts to persuade an audience primarily from past events) or deliberative (attempts to persuade an audience to take some future action). In Galatians, it can be argued that the letter is deliberative because of its attempts to convince the Gentile Christians not to submit to male circumcision and the Mosaic Law.

Galatians 1:11–2:14—select aspects of Paul's autobiography (1:11–24); the apostolic council in Jerusalem (2:1–10), and the incident in Antioch (2:11–14)—can be viewed as a single rhetorical unit that lays out the precedence for Paul's authority and gospel message that all are saved by faith in Christ and not by works of the law.

## Summary: Historical Context of Galatians

### CORE CONCEPTS

- The occasion for writing Galatians is the successful spreading of a "different gospel" among the churches of Galatia.

*Continued*

---

7. See Ben Witherington III, *Grace in Galatia: A Commentary on Paul's Letter to the Galatians* (Grand Rapids, MI: T & T Clark, 1998), 25–36, for a discussion on ancient rhetoric and the rhetoric of Galatians.

Summary: Historical Context of Galatians *Continued*

- Scholars generally agree that the opponents were Jewish Christians from Judea who were trying to convince Gentile Christians to submit to male circumcision.
- Paul inserts selective parts of his autobiography as a way of defending his gospel message and his apostolic authority and independence.

**SUPPLEMENTAL INFORMATION**

- Paul is the sole author of Galatians.
- Paul offers no thanksgiving in this letter, instead launching into a tirade against rival Christian missionaries and their message.
- Scholars debate about the location of the churches of Galatia.
- Paul composed the Letter to the Galatians from Macedonia, a region more than five hundred miles away from Galatia.
- The long distance between Macedonia and Galatia required a letter and possibly the sending of one of Paul's co-workers to mediate the dispute.
- The outsiders who infiltrated the Galatian Gentile congregations demanded consistency between the Mosaic Law and the message about Jesus.

# THEOLOGY AND ETHICS OF GALATIANS

When he wrote to the Galatians, Paul was facing an unanticipated and difficult situation. Gentile Christians in Galatia were in danger of embracing a different gospel. This circumstance required Paul to affirm his authority and debunk the theology and authority of his rivals. Thus, new figures and ideas emerge in Galatians (for example, Abraham and justification by faith) in a way not seen in the previous letters of 1 Thessalonians and 1 and 2 Corinthians.

Paul stakes out three theological areas to define the heart of his gospel message: justification by faith, the Jewish law, and freedom in Christ. The ethical implications of his gospel message are evident in Paul's argument for life in the freedom of the Spirit and for proper Christian conduct in community life.

## Theology

### Justification by Faith

When speaking about justification, Paul often uses the verb form *dikaioō*, meaning to put in a right relationship with God. Paul viewed justification as a divine initiative that facilitates the right relationship between God and humanity.[8] For Paul, God restored sinful humanity through the death and Resurrection of Jesus Christ. This restoration was a gift, a "grace" from God. *Faith* in God's saving work is required of believers in order to be acquitted of sin and restored to a right human-divine relationship. For Paul, justification is tied to reconciliation. It is in this context that Paul speaks about "justification by faith," and it is for this reason he writes: "I do not nullify the grace (gift) of God; for if justification comes through the law, then Christ died for nothing" (2:21).

In Galatians 2:15–21, Paul introduces his theology of justification by faith for which he will argue in Galatians 3–4. Galatians 2:15–16 succinctly presents Paul's position on justification by faith and works of the law. Paul's insistence on justification by faith versus the works of the Mosaic Law is rooted (at least in part) in his desire to dismantle the "new" gospel message—requiring the circumcision of male Gentile Christians—that was circulating among the congregations of Galatia. Paul sees the practical problem of continuing to rely on the works of the law, especially in male circumcision: it divides believers in Christ into the circumcised and the uncircumcised, separating them into social situations like table fellowship in which the celebration of the Eucharist occurred. If the congregation was not eating together, then neither was it worshipping together. Paul agreed for the church to have separate missions but not to have a divided community (see Gal 2:11–14). For Paul, this divided body of Christ violated "the truth of the gospel" that he originally brought to the Gentile Christians of Galatia (2:14).

---

8. For a good discussion of the Pauline term *justification*, see A. E. McGrath, 517–523 in Gerald F. Hawthorne, Ralph P. Martin, and Daniel G. Reid (eds.), *Dictionary of Paul and His Letters* (Downers Grove, IL: InterVarsity Press, 1993).

Paul then turns to what the believers of Galatia knew to be true from their experience: they were baptized and received the Spirit because of their faith in Paul's original preaching of the gospel and not from works of the law (3:1–5). From this perspective, Paul sarcastically writes: "Are you so stupid? After beginning with the Spirit, are you now ending with the flesh [circumcision]?" (3:3).

To further solidify his opposition to compelling Gentile Christians to become circumcised and his promotion of justification by faith, Paul turns to Abraham, using him to establish the scriptural basis for his position (3:6–14). Paul begins by quoting Genesis 15:6: "Thus Abraham 'believed God, and it was credited to him as righteousness'" (3:6). He then describes that Abraham is the vehicle through which God has orchestrated salvation for the Gentiles (3:7–11). Because of their faith in the gospel message that Paul preached to them, the Gentile Christians of Galatia are "children of Abraham," recipients of the same promise that God made to Abraham. Further and equally significant, the uncircumcised Gentiles are not subject to the curse of the law. For Paul, once marked in the flesh (circumcised), the Gentiles then become subject to "doing all the things written in the book of the law" (3:10).

## The Covenants of Genesis 12, 15, and 17

In Genesis 12 and 15, Abraham receives promises and blessings before the covenant of circumcision in Genesis 17. For Paul, the argument "between the lines" is that the chronological priority of Genesis 12 and 15 points to the temporal nature of the covenant of circumcision, given in Genesis 17. But Paul had to deal with the problem of the perpetual nature of circumcision (Genesis 17:12–13). If Paul begins his argument that his gospel was not "of human origin" with Genesis 17, then his line of reasoning is lost before it even begins. Therefore, Paul begins with the uncircumcised Abraham as the essential precedent to his argument.[9]

---

9. In fact, it may have been the case that the rival teachers in Galatia appealed to the circumcised Abraham in promoting the circumcision of male Gentile Christians.

Continuing with his scriptural argument, Paul speaks of the cross of Christ as the event that "ransomed us from the curse of the law by becoming a curse for us" (3:13a). He then goes on to quote Deuteronomy 21:23: "Cursed be everyone who hangs on a tree" (Gal 3:13b). Jesus' death on the cross connects the Gentiles to the promise made to Abraham: "that the blessing of Abraham might be extended to the Gentiles through Christ Jesus, so that we might receive the promise of the Spirit through faith" (3:14).

## Paul's Reliance on the Torah for Justification by Faith

In his initial attempts to explain his doctrine of justification by faith, Paul relies on three of the five books of the Torah: Genesis, Leviticus, and Deuteronomy.

| Galatians | Torah |
|---|---|
| Galatians 3:6 | cf. Genesis 15:6 |
| Galatians 3:8 | cf. Genesis 12:3, 18:17–19 |
| Galatians 3:10 | cf. Deuteronomy 27:26 |
| Galatians 3:12 | cf. Leviticus 18:5 |
| Galatians 3:13 | cf. Deuteronomy 21:23 |

Paul's training as a Pharisee (Phil 3:5; Gal 1:13–14) equipped him with a breadth and depth of knowledge of the Jewish written and oral traditions. Furthermore, the citation of these texts helps Paul's point of the absurdity of trying to keep the whole law.

### The Jewish Law

Paul discusses the Jewish law in the next section of his letter, 3:15–29. Central to his gospel message on justification by faith is knowledge of the proper place and function of the Mosaic Law within God's plan of salvation. Paul begins by juxtaposing two

Early Christian fresco depicting a scene from Genesis 22, which tells of God's promises to Abraham after he believed God and prepared to sacrifice his son, Isaac

concepts: promise and law. He applies a chronological approach to prioritizing promise over law. God's covenant and promise—of land, descendants, and divine blessings to all the nations of Earth—were made repeatedly to Abraham and his descendants (see Gen 12:2–3,7, 13:15, 17:7–8, 22:16–18, 24:7). These promises take precedence over the law given to Moses because the Law "came four hundred and thirty years" (3:17) after the promise. The law, therefore, does not alter or annul the original promise.

To reinforce how the promise takes priority over the law, which reinforces the temporal argument that the law came after the promise was made, Paul connects Abraham directly to Christ through the promise by pointing out that, in addition to Abraham, the promises were made to one descendent, Christ (3:16). With the tie between Abraham and Christ established, Paul can now connect the Gentiles directly to the inheritance of the divine promises. God's covenant and promise were based upon Abraham's *faith* in God, "who attributed it to him as an act of righteousness" (Gen 15:6). Therefore, it is the Gentiles' *faith* in the gospel message proclaimed by Paul that justifies them before God, allowing them to share in the Abrahamic covenant and promises.

Given the opponents' emphasis on observance of the Torah (such as male circumcision, calendar regulations, and purity regarding food and other regulations), Paul then asks two central rhetorical questions about the function of the law. First, "Why, then, the law?" (3:19a). His answer offers something positive about the law, commenting that "it was added for transgressions," and that it was secondary in nature to the promise, as it was "promulgated by angels at the hand of a mediator [Moses]," (3:19b). The answer to the second question—"Is the law then opposed to the promises of God? Of course not!" (3:21)—may, at first glance, appear more positive. However, Paul's explanation makes it clear that while the law does not oppose God's design (3:22), it serves only the (limited) purpose of raising awareness of sin (transgressions).

## "Neither Jew nor Greek . . ."

In three of Paul's letters, a radical and countercultural equality quickly emerges for those justified by God because of their faith in Christ.

| 1 Corinthians 12:13 | Galatians 3:28 | Romans 10:12 |
|---|---|---|
| For in one Spirit we were all baptized into one body, whether Jews or Greeks, slaves or free persons, and we were all given to drink of one Spirit. | There is neither Jew nor Greek, there is neither slave nor free person, there is not male and female: for you are all one in Christ Jesus. | For there is no distinction between Jew and Greek; the same Lord is Lord for all, enriching all who call upon him. |

Both Jewish and Gentile Christians enjoyed a freedom in Christ that was prohibited under the Mosaic Law.

Paul then speaks of the law metaphorically, as a "disciplinarian" (in Greek, *paidagōgos*) (3:24). The literal translation of *paidagōgos* is "leader of a child." The term referred to the older household slave who had the responsibility of acting as the moral guide and limit-setter for a boy from his youth (age seven) through late adolescence.[10] The task was time limited: the *paidagōgos* functioned specifically to protect and constrain the youth in preparation for adulthood. This slave was not the instructor but, rather, the "disciplinarian" who accompanied the child to the lessons. For Paul, this parallels how the Jewish law functioned in anticipation of the revelation of Jesus Christ: "The law was our disciplinarian for Christ, that we might be justified by faith. But now that faith has come, we are no longer under a disciplinarian" (3:24–25). In other words, the law was like a chaperone, keeping people in line until the coming of Christ.

Paul concludes his discussion on the law by reaffirming the primacy of faith for the Gentile Galatians and their new identity as "children of God," heirs to the promise made to Abraham (3:26–27,29). For Paul, Abraham was the key Old Testament figure for understanding the Gentiles' place in God's plan of salvation.

### Freedom in Christ

After establishing the link between the Gentile Christians and the promise made to Abraham, Paul addresses a certain "freedom" that the Gentile Christians enjoy because of their faith in Christ and their newfound status as "heirs." Paul uses the analogy of a free child (heir) and a slave, some shared history, and a final appeal to Scriptures.

Paul begins by speaking of both Jews and Gentiles as being at one time enslaved: the Jew, a slave to the law, and the Gentile, a slave to the "elemental powers of the world" (4:1–3). However, "when the fullness of time had come," God sent his Son into the world "so that we might receive adoption" (4:4–5). The presence of the Spirit in the life of the Christian is "proof" that the believer, whether Jew or Greek, has been liberated from slavery to the law and the elemental powers and has been elevated to the status of heir (4:6–7). Paul fears

---

10. Matera, *Galatians*, 139–40. See also N. H. Young, "*PAIDAGŌGOS:* The Social Setting of a Pauline Metaphor," *NovT* 39 (1987): 150–176.

that if the Gentile Christians should submit to circumcision, they will relinquish their freedom from the "elemental powers" and, thus, their status as heirs. Adhering to the regulations of the law—now required because of circumcision—would once again enslave the Gentiles not only to the elemental powers, but also to the "curse" of the law. The consequences of the Gentiles accepting and practicing this "different gospel" exasperate Paul: "I am afraid on your account that perhaps I have labored for you in vain" (4:11).

## Born of a Woman

Galatians 4:4 contains Paul's only reference to the mother of Jesus, noting that Jesus was born of a woman. Paul mentions her in relation to defining Jesus as the Son of God and the Gentiles' status as adopted children of God. A theology of Mary (Mariology) does not fully develop until centuries later.

Paul then recalls the history he and the Galatians share, starting with when he first proclaimed his gospel message to them (4:12–14; also 3:1–5). Paul acknowledges the presence of this different gospel within the Galatian congregations and that it has challenged Paul's authority. In response, Paul asks, "So now have I become your enemy by telling you the truth"? (4:16). Employing maternal imagery of himself laboring "until Christ be formed in you" (4:19), Paul concludes, "I would like to be with you now and to change my tone, for I am perplexed because of you" (4:20).

Paul makes a final appeal to Scriptures in support of his gospel message by drawing an allegory between the two mothers (Sarah and Hagar) and the two covenants (one from Mount Sinai and one from "the Jerusalem above," 4:24–26). Hagar, the slave woman, bearing Ishmael, represents the law given at Mount Sinai, which enslaves those bound to it. Sarah, the freeborn woman, bearing Isaac "through a promise," represents the freedom coming from "the Jerusalem above" that is granted to those who have faith. Paul makes the connection for the uncircumcised Gentile Christians:

"Now you, brothers, like Isaac, are children of the promise" (4:28). Paul then appeals to the Gentiles of Galatia to expel from their congregation those who promote the different gospel advocating male circumcision (4:30). Paul's interpretation here is allegorical and his Christian opponents would have likely not accepted such an interpretation.

## Ethics

Paul devotes the final section of his letter to discussing the ethical implications for the Galatian congregations who are justified by faith in Christ and "called for freedom" (5:13) to live in the power of the Spirit. He sets the stage for these moral standards by reminding the Galatians of the grave consequences of following a gospel message different from his: "Christ will be of no benefit to you" (5:2). Paul's strong language here underscored the depth of his conviction that faith, and not works of the law, justifies one before God.

### Life in the Freedom of the Spirit

Being justified by faith brings with it a newfound freedom, which a Christian can enjoy after being liberated from the curse of the law and the influence of the elemental powers. Per Paul, this freedom must be first and foremost grounded in loving service to others (5:13). This freedom must also be rooted in the life of the Spirit. Paul is careful here to emphasize that the Spirit leads people to live properly in order to keep complaints from surfacing about his not requiring the law as a guide to human behavior.

In this regard, Paul presents a list of virtues and vices that represent the tension between Spirit and flesh (Gal 5:19–23), elaborating on the idea of Spirit versus flesh presented earlier in Galatians 3:3. There is nothing particularly Pauline in this list of virtues and vices. They reflected the Hellenistic cultural norms of the day. Paul sees no need for the law for those who live according to the fruit of the Spirit: "love, joy, peace, patience, kindness, generosity, faithfulness, gentleness, self-control" (5:22–23). There is no need for circumcision either, as "those who belong to Christ Jesus have crucified their flesh with its passions and desires" (5:24).

## Guidelines for Community Relations

Paul draws his letter to a close by offering some guidelines for proper relations within the Galatian congregations. Unlike in previous letters, in which he addresses behavioral norms for community life in some detail (for example, 1 Corinthians 5–6), in this one, Paul simply lists a set of recommendations for the congregations of Galatia. Paul's advice includes being gentle in fraternal corrections, bearing one another's burdens, examining one's conscience, being open with one's instructor in the faith, and doing good to everyone (6:1–10). He takes a less detailed approach to the Galatian congregations than to the Corinthians on this topic since he has other more pressing matters.

### Bearing "the Marks of Jesus"

Paul concludes his Letter to the Galatians with a rather startling declaration: "From now on, let no one make troubles for me; for I bear the marks of Jesus on my body" (Gal 6:17).

In 2 Corinthians, Paul chronicles the marks on his body, injuries sustained from floggings and stonings and from being beaten by rods (see 2 Cor 11:24–28). Paul is likely commenting here on the legitimacy of his "marks," which connect him to the sufferings of Christ, versus the "marks" of circumcision, which separated one from Christ.

### The Pauline Signature "Sign-Off"

In three of the seven undisputed letters, Paul concludes his letter by writing a brief, final message saying he has written in his own hand (1 Cor 16:21–22; Phlm 19; Gal 6:11–12). In each instance, this Pauline "sign-off" connects in some measure with the occasion for writing the letter. These handwritten insertions by Paul suggest that he likely employed a secretary or scribe (known as an amanuensis) for his letter writing, as was commonly done in the writing of

*Continued*

**The Pauline Signature "Sign-Off"** *Continued*

Hellenistic Greek letters. In Paul's Letter to the Romans, the actual writer of the letter identifies himself: "I, Tertius, the writer of this letter, greet you in the Lord" (Rom 16:22).

## Summary: Theology and Ethics in Galatians

### CORE CONCEPTS

- Paul asserts that God justifies all Jews and Gentiles because of their faith in Christ, not because they perform "the works of the law."
- For Paul, the promises made to Abraham in Genesis 12 and 15 take priority over the Mosaic Law (including circumcision) later given to Israel.
- The letter to the Galatians is not just a dialogue between Paul and the believers in Galatia. It is a kind of "trialogue": Paul must defend his authority and theology in the face of accusations from rival Christian missionaries.

### SUPPLEMENTAL INFORMATION

- The presence of a "different gospel" in Galatia required Paul to explain more fully the theology and ethics of his gospel message.
- Through baptism and the Holy Spirit, believers in Christ experience freedom from the curse of the law and the elemental powers.
- According to Galatians, the Mosaic Law served the time-limited function of preparing Israel for the arrival of Christ.
- Jewish and Gentile Christians alike are "heirs" to the promise made to Abraham because of their faith in Christ.
- Those who live in the life of the Spirit have no need for the Mosaic Law as a guide for human behavior.
- Paul draws a sharp contrast between the works of the Sprit and works of the flesh.

## Questions for Review

1. How do 1 Corinthians and Romans help establish the historical setting for Galatians?
2. Why does Paul omit a thanksgiving in his letter to the Galatians? What rhetorical "punch" does he deliver by this omission?
3. What are the competing hypotheses regarding the location of the Galatian congregations?
4. What lies at the core of the "different gospel" influencing the Galatians? How did these other Christians interpret the Mosaic covenant in relation to faith in Christ?
5. In what ways does Paul attempt to influence the churches of Galatia with select portions of his autobiography?
6. How does Paul use Abraham to argue for justification by faith?
7. Why does Paul speak of the law as a *paidagōgos* (chaperone)?
8. How does Paul's allegory between the two mothers (Sarah and Hagar) and the two covenants (from Mount Sinai and "the Jerusalem above") contribute to his self-defense and argumentation in Galatians?
9. What does Paul expect from those who live in the freedom of the Spirit?
10. What ethical standards does Paul hold for the community life in the congregations of Galatia?

## Questions for Reflection

1. What do you find most revealing about Paul from his autobiography in Galatians 1:11–24?
2. How do you think the rival Christian missionaries in Galatia reacted to Paul's argument in Galatians?
3. What tensions do you imagine occurred between the circumcised and uncircumcised Gentile Christians as a result of Paul's letter?
4. How might the later church have looked if Paul's opponents had won and circumcision had been required for all male followers of Jesus?

## Recommendations for Further Reading

Cummins, Stephen Anthony. *Paul and the Crucified Christ in Antioch: Maccabean Martyrdom and Galatians 1 and 2*. Cambridge, UK: Cambridge University Press, 2001.

> Cummins offers interesting insights into the well-known "Antioch incident" (Gal 2:11–21), in which Paul confronts Peter over his "hypocrisy" toward Gentiles and table fellowship (2:11–14) as well as some theological reflections on 2:15–21. Cummins argues that a Maccabean martyr model can provide another perspective on Paul's reaction to Peter. Cummins provides the historical context for Maccabean martyrdom and its impact on first-century Judaism and Paul as well as its connections to the crucified Christ.

Koperski, Veronica. *What Are They Saying about Paul and the Law?* Mahwah, NJ: Paulist Press, 2001.

> By asking the question, "What is wrong with the law?" Koperski divides past and current scholarly understandings about Paul and the law into various categories. Chapter 1 deals with the category "Human Effort vs. Gift of God." Chapter 2 looks at the category "Through Christ vs. Not Through Christ." Chapter 3 examines the category "Particular vs. Universal." Chapter 4 explores the "Lutheran" position. Chapter 5 looks at scholars who attempt to find coherence and consistency regarding Paul's view of the law within all his undisputed letters. Chapter 6 explores some possible "new centers" of Pauline theology.

Martyn, James Louis. *Galatians*. The Anchor Yale Bible Commentaries. Yale University Press, 2004.

> Widely regarded as one of the best commentaries available on Galatians, Martyn presents relevant cultural, historical, political, and theological aspects to his interpretation of Galatians. The aim of the commentary is to allow modern readers to hear this letter as one of the original Gentile congregations to which it was originally written.

Matera, Frank J. *Galatians*. Sacra Pagina 9. Collegeville, MN: The Liturgical Press, 1992.

> Matera presents a very readable commentary on Paul's Letter to the Galatians. His introduction includes an analysis of the crisis at Galatia and Paul's response to it as well as a discussion on the much-debated analysis of the identity of the Galatians. He concludes the introduction with a discussion titled "Galatians Today," bringing the reader up to date on both traditional and new understandings of Galatians. Matera's notes and interpretations for each section of Galatians offer many interesting insights.

Nanos, Mark D. *The Irony of Galatians: Paul's Letter in First-Century Context.* Minneapolis: Fortress Press, 2002.

Paying attention to the dynamics of irony as it applies to the letter's frame, structure, and body, Nanos argues that the Letter to the Galatians is best interpreted as a letter of ironic rebuke. He draws many interesting conclusions, such as the identity of the "influencers" in the Galatian churches as Jewish nonbelievers in Christ whose primary concern was to properly initiate (circumcise) these Gentiles into the Galatian Jewish communities. Paul responds to this news with a letter of rebuke to the Gentile Christian congregations of Galatia.

# CHAPTER 6

# Romans

## INTRODUCTION

Not long after the completion of Galatians, Paul wrote Romans, which is his most detailed letter in terms of theology and ethics. Following the pattern of chapters 2–5 in this book, the first section examines the historical context of the letter: the setting; the founding of the Christian community in Rome, and Paul's mission strategy. The second section of chapter 6 explores the theology of Romans—the righteousness of God; justification for all who have faith in Christ; life in Christ; and the status of Israel within God's overarching plan of salvation. It also gives attention to Paul's ethical admonitions in this letter, including obligations to fellow Christians and to state authorities, avoiding judgment of others, and respecting others' consciences.

## An Interesting Occasion

One characteristic that ties together Paul's letters is their occasional nature. All of Paul's undisputed letters address specific circumstances. For example, Paul composed 1 Corinthians, in large measure, to heal the factions that developed in the congregation; Paul's hope was that the Corinthians would find their unity in Christ alone. Paul wrote Galatians out of his significant concern that the Gentile Christians in the churches of Galatia had adopted another gospel message, different from Paul's, that required male circumcision of the Gentiles. In other words, Paul sent his letters to congregations he founded in order to address particular problems that had arisen after his departure.

In Romans, Paul does not address a specific problem in the church at Rome, a community he did not found and had not visited. Rather, it was a change in location of Paul's mission that occasioned this letter. Paul writes to the Christians in Rome in order to clarify his ministry to the Gentiles, and his theology, anticipating certain objections to his theology in the wake of the Galatian crisis. He wants to secure financial support as he seeks to evangelize the western part of the Roman Empire, beginning in Spain.

## A Changing Situation

Among the seven undisputed letters of Paul in the New Testament, Romans is widely regarded by scholars as containing his most mature theological thinking. Earlier correspondence shows that Paul adapts his thinking on certain theological ideas from letter to letter as he addresses different contingent situations in churches he established. For example, Paul presents the three theological virtues of faith, hope, and love, using varying formats and metaphors (compare 1 Thessalonians 1:3; 5:8; 1 Corinthians 13:13; Galatians 5:5–6). Romans, too, reflects a changing situation, as can be seen, for instance, in Paul's position on the Jewish law. In Galatians, Paul adopts a polemical tone to offset the inroads made by the rival teachers, whereas in Romans, he explains his understanding of the Jewish law to a church he did not establish, a church that appears to have its origins within Jewish Christianity. In many ways, the Letter to the Romans can be viewed as Paul's attempt to anticipate objections before his visit. As this chapter details, Romans allows Paul to give voice to a coherent theological vision on topics such as the universal need for salvation, justification by faith apart from the works of the law, Jewish-Christian relations, and the obligations associated with Christian freedom. Unlike the other undisputed letters, Romans does not address the practical problems faced by the letter's audience.

## HISTORICAL CONTEXT OF ROMANS

Romans provides some internal evidence about the letter's authorship and intended audience. Moreover, the letter offers interesting historical details on matters such as Paul's evolving mission and the personal contacts he had in the Christian congregations in Rome. Additional sources that help establish the date and place of composition for Romans include Galatians, 1 Corinthians, and the Acts of the Apostles.

## Outline of Romans

| 1:1–17 | **Greeting, Thanksgiving, and Theological Focus of the Letter** |
|---|---|
| | The letter opens with a greeting from Paul (no co-senders) "to all the beloved of God in Rome." (1:7). Unlike previous letters, he does not direct his letter to an identifiable congregation or congregations. Paul offers thanks to God for the faith of the Christians in Rome and twice mentions his past attempts to visit them. At the end of his thanksgiving, Paul identifies one reason for his visit: "I am eager to preach the gospel also to you in Rome" (1:15). Verses 16–17 offer the overarching theological argument of the letter—that God offers salvation to all through faith in Christ. |
| 1:18–3:20 | **All People in Need of Salvation, Jew and Gentile Alike** |
| | Paul begins the body of his letter by stating his conviction that everyone (Jew and Gentile) deserves the "wrath of God" (1:18) because everyone is under the dominion of sin. All of humanity sins either against the law written on their hearts (as is the case for all Gentiles) or against the Mosaic Law (as is the case for all Jews). As a result, no one escapes the judgment of God. All who do evil experience God's wrath and fury. In this judgment, God shows no partiality. |
| 3:21–4:25 | **All Are Justified by Faith apart from the Law, Jew and Gentile Alike** |
| | Paul begins this section with the transition "But now" (3:21), indicating a shift in fortune for all |

*Continued*

| | |
|---|---|
| | sinful humanity. The righteousness of God is now available to all who have faith in Jesus Christ. First revealed to Abraham, later affirmed by David, and now testified by Paul, all who have faith are justified. |
| 5:1–8:39 | **The Christian Life Resulting from Justification by Faith** |
| | The sin and death that Adam brought into the world is now countered by the peace and reconciliation with God and the gift of eternal life brought into the world through Christ. Freed from sin, the Christian enjoys a newfound life, one rooted in baptism and marked by having died to sin and being alive in Christ. No longer under the law or enslaved by sin, those with faith in Christ "have become slaves of righteousness" (6:18). The Christian is called to live in the Spirit and to abandon the works of the flesh that lead to sin and death. As adopted children of God, the faithful cannot be separated from the love of God. |
| 9:1–11:36 | **God's Plan for Israel** |
| | Paul begins this section by confessing his anguish over many Jews' rejection of Christ. Relying heavily on the Old Testament prophetic tradition, Paul surmises that the rejection of Jesus as the Messiah serves God's larger goal in salvation history: "A hardening has come upon Israel in part, until the full number of Gentiles comes in" (11:25b). Nevertheless, Paul is sure that a remnant of Israel will survive, chosen by God's grace. |
| 12:1–13:14 | **Christians' Duty to Each Other and to the Authority of the State** |
| | Paul offers his advice on proper moral and ethical behavior for those who share the faith. Relying on his "many parts in one body" metaphor |

*Continued*

| | |
|---|---|
| | **Outline of Romans** *Continued* |

| | |
|---|---|
| | (see 1 Corinthians 12:12–26), Paul urges a sharing of the Spirit's gifts with each other. He places a heavy stress on mutual love and self-sacrifice for neighbor. He also emphasizes obedience to state authority, because all authority ultimately derives from God. Paul concludes with a reminder of the approaching and imminent eschaton (end-time) when Christ will return. |
| 14:1– 15:13 | **Refraining from Judgment and Respecting Other Believers' Consciences** <br><br> Paul discusses at length the prohibition against the strong in the faith casting judgment on the weak in the faith, especially around matters of food and drink. Paul ends this section with references from the Law and Prophets foretelling the Gentile inclusion in salvation history. |
| 15:14– 16:27 | **Travel Plans and Personal Greetings** <br><br> As his letter draws to close, Paul reiterates his call from God "to be a minister of Christ Jesus to the Gentiles" (15:16). At this very late point in the letter, he discloses a central reason for writing to them, explaining his decision to begin evangelizing the western part of the Roman Empire, stopping in Rome for a long-awaited visit before heading to his ultimate destination, Spain. Paul concludes his letter with personal greetings to twenty-six people and households who serve as a connection between Paul and the recipients of his letter. |

## Author and Audience

Previous letters sent from Paul have clearly identified co-senders (1 Thessalonians, 1 Corinthians, and 2 Corinthians). In Romans, Paul is the sole sender of the letter. It is particularly interesting that no co-sender is identified with Romans, as Timothy, a co-sender for 1 Thessalonians and 2 Corinthians, is evidently present with Paul for the writing of Romans (16:21). This could be because Timothy, like Paul, had not had any contact with the church in Rome.

Whereas in earlier letters, Paul addressed his letter to a specific *ekklēsia /ekklēsiai* (to the "church" in Thessalonica; the "church" in Corinth; the "churches" in Galatia), in Romans, Paul addresses his letter not to a specific church but, rather, to the "beloved of God." Evidence from Romans 16 also indicates that this letter's intended audience is neither a single church nor a single individual. This likely reflects the existence of multiple congregations (house churches) and groups of Christians in Rome. The city of Rome was home to numerous house churches (for example, the house churches that met in the homes of Prisca and Aquila, Aristobulus, and Narcissus) and a number of influential individuals such as Phoebe, the deaconess and patron of Paul, and others. The multiple congregations is not too surprising, as Rome was a very large city, much larger, in fact, than Corinth.

## The City of Rome

During Paul's lifetime, Rome was universally recognized as the imperial capital city of the known civilized world. With a population of nearly one million people, Rome exerted tremendous influence in the first century CE.

The city was home to diverse groups of people, religious traditions, and practices. It hosted a flourishing polytheistic religious culture as well as thousands of Jews and numerous synagogues. The Roman state and its citizenry publicly honored and worshipped many different gods and goddesses. Among the most important were Jupiter, protector of the state, and Mars, the god of war. Other popular deities included Juno, the protector of women, and Minerva, the goddess of craft and wisdom. Roman citizens also believed in familial and household spirits who protected the home and family. Often a family would erect a shrine, called a *larium* (*lar* in Latin meaning "protective spirit"), in their home. The head of the household, typically the father or eldest male, would offer regular sacrifices to the household sprit, ensuring an ever-watchful protective eye.

Internal evidence from the letter indicates that Paul was writing to a largely Gentile Christian population in Rome. The letter includes numerous direct references to the Gentile Christ-believers in Rome (see, for example, 1:5–6,13–15; 11:13, 28) as well as some extended discussions of Israel's rejection of the Messiah, which Paul understood as part of God's plan of universal salvation for Jew and Gentile alike (see 11:11–32, 10:1–3). However, the fact that Paul also quotes from the Hebrew Scriptures, especially the Prophets and the Psalms (most extensively in Romans 9–11, Israel's role in God's plan), suggests that some believers in Rome were still Torah-observant Jews and likely had their roots in Jewish Christianity. In addition, some of the Gentle Christ-believers may have been "God-fearers" (Gentiles worshipping the God of Israel) before embracing Christianity.

## "Paul, a Slave of Christ Jesus"

In all his letters written earlier than Romans, except 1 Thessalonians, Paul identifies himself in the opening line of the letter as "an apostle" of Christ Jesus (see 1 Corinthians 1:1; 2 Corinthians 1:1; Galatians 1:1). But in Romans, Paul replaces the designation of *apostle* with that of *slave*. It is probably the case that Paul presents himself more humbly to congregations that may not know of or respect his authority. Phrases in the greeting and thanksgiving such as "we have received the grace of apostleship" (1:5) and "that you and I [we] may be mutually encouraged by one another's faith" (1:12), reflect such humility.

## Date and Place of Composition

Galatians, 1 Corinthians, the Acts of the Apostles, and Romans provide only indirect evidence for establishing the date of the letter. In Romans 15, Paul speaks of a sense of closure to his mission to the Gentiles in the eastern part of the Roman Empire, explaining that he "finished preaching the gospel of Christ" from Jerusalem to Illyricum (15:19). The crises prompting the Second

Letter to the Corinthians and the Letter to the Galatians, which had threatened Paul's authority and gospel message, may very well have encouraged him to consider evangelizing the western part of the Roman Empire, beginning in Spain (15:23–24). Further, several parts of Romans elaborate on ideas presented earlier in Galatians (compare, for example, Galatians 2–4 with Romans 3–9 on justification by faith and the role and function of the law). These factors support the dating of Romans sometime after the writing of Galatians.

## Tertius, the Scribe for Romans

Paul may have dictated his letters to a scribe, which was a common practice in the ancient world, but the evidence that he did so is limited. Some indirect evidence, such as concluding remarks in which Paul "signs off" the letter in his own hand (see Gal 6:11–12; 1 Cor 16:21–22; Phlm 19), suggests that Paul used a scribe. The most direct evidence of Paul employing a scribe to write his letter is found in Romans 16:22, "I, Tertius, the writer of this letter, greet you in the Lord." This is the New Testament's only mention of Tertius; thus, information about him is very limited. Obviously, he was a scribe and, therefore, literate. Paul trusted him. His greeting to the recipients of the letter suggests that Tertius knew some of the Christians in Rome, and his phrase "in the Lord" suggests that he, too, was a Christian.

One important clue indicating the place of composition for Romans appears toward the end of the letter and can be compared with 1 Corinthians. Tertius, the scribe writing this letter to the Romans, sends a greeting to the Christians in Rome from "Gaius, who is host to me and to the whole church" (Rom 16:23). Paul writes in 1 Corinthians 1:14: "I give thanks to God that I baptized none of you except Crispus [the synagogue official in Corinth, Acts 18:8] and Gaius." It is plausible, then, that Paul composed his letter to the Romans in the house of Gaius in the city of Corinth. The dictation of this letter to Tertius could have taken up to three entire weeks.

This would have been quite an undertaking. After spending the winter months reflecting on his next steps for the evangelization of the Gentiles, Paul sent off his Letter to the Romans from Corinth, possibly in the spring of 56 CE.[1]

## Summary: Historical Setting for Romans

| | |
|---|---|
| Author | Paul |
| Audience | Christian congregations in Rome (mostly Gentiles) |
| Date of Composition | Probably spring 56 CE |
| Place of Composition | Probably Corinth |

## The Founding of the Christian Community in Rome

Scholars are uncertain about who founded the Christian congregations in the city of Rome. Many theorize that Christianity was originally brought to Rome by a combination of Jewish travelers from Jerusalem and by trade merchants who had accepted faith in Christ and were seeking opportunities for evangelization.[2] What is clear is that by the time Paul wrote his Letter to the Romans in the mid-50s CE, a significant contingent of Christians were living in Rome and practicing the faith. They met in house churches to celebrate Eucharist and gathered together on other occasions to share the faith.

---

1. Most scholars identify the city of Corinth as the place of composition for Romans, see Brendan Byrne, SJ, *Romans*. SP 6 (Collegeville, MN; Liturgical, 1996), 8–10; Ben Witherington III, *Paul's Letter to the Romans* (Grand Rapids, MI: Eerdmans, 2004), 7. There is less scholarly consensus on the exact date of composition. See Byrne who notes that "the winter of any year between late 54 CE and early 59 CE is possible," 9. Witherington, 7, dates Romans to the spring of 57 CE. Udo Schnelle, *The History and Theology of the New Testament Writings*, trans. M. Eugene Boring (London: SCM, 1998), 109, dates the writing of Romans to the spring of 56 CE.

2. See Byrne, 10–13, for a discussion on the origins and problems of Christians in Rome. See also Schnelle, 112–114.

Evidence suggests that within the first two decades after the death of Jesus, established groups of Jewish Christians were already living in Rome. Sources outside of the New Testament seem to verify the presence of Christ-believing Jews living in Rome. The Roman historian Suetonius writes of the expulsion of the Jews from Rome by Emperor Claudius in the year 49 CE because of riots started by a man named Chrestus: "As the Jews were making constant disturbances at the instigation of Chrestus, he expelled them from Rome" (*Life of Claudius* 25.4). Some scholars suspect that Suetonius may be referring to Christus (Christ), mistakenly referred to as Chrestus. As discussed in chapter 3, this reference is consistent with what Luke reports in Acts 18:2. The expulsion of the Jews and Christians from Rome in 49 CE may account for the fact that the Christian congregations Paul writes to in the mid-50s CE are predominantly Gentile.

## Paul's Ongoing Mission

In Romans, Paul spends a considerable amount of time sharing his travel plans, which in turn reveals something about his ongoing mission to a new location. Paul begins by acknowledging that he cannot take credit for planting the seeds of Christianity in Rome. He makes it clear that he has no desire to claim ownership of a congregation he did not personally establish and that he favors evangelizing people and territories that are hearing the gospel message for the first time (15:20–21).

Paul's attitude here reflects his desire not to "boast" in the success of others' evangelization efforts. In one of his earlier letters to the Corinthians, Paul speaks directly to this issue about not accepting credit "in other people's labors" or "of work already done in another's sphere" (2 Cor 10:15–16). Paul probably also found it preferable to evangelize those Gentiles who had few or no preconceived notions of Christianity and who had not heard another's gospel message. Paul saw firsthand in Corinth and in the churches of Galatia the dangers of mixing another gospel with his own.

Paul's quote from Isaiah 52:15 in Romans 15:21 also sheds some light on his changing mission location. The Isaiah citation belongs to one of the "Servant of the Lord" oracles found in Isaiah 40–55. The servant was called to bring the good news of Yahweh's salvation to all the nations. Paul's use of Isaiah indicates that he may have viewed his mission as a continuation of sorts of Israel's call to bring salvation to all the nations.

## The Answer to a Diatribe: Of Course Not!

Throughout his Letter to the Romans, Paul employs the literary device of a diatribe. The context is one in which an author (here, Paul) poses a hypothetical (or actual) objection, in order to refute that objection. Paul often responds, *mē genoito* (Of course not!), to these objections. The list of objections reveals either real or anticipated challenges to Paul's gospel message to the Christians in Rome and elsewhere.

- What if some [Jews] were unfaithful? Will their infidelity nullify the fidelity of God? (3:3)
- Is God unjust, humanly speaking, to inflict his wrath? (3:5)
- Shall we persist in sin that grace may abound? (6:1)
- Shall we sin because we are not under the law but under grace? (6:15)
- What then can we say? That the law is sin? (7:7)
- Did the good, then, become death for me? (7:13)
- Is there injustice on the part of God? (9:14)
- I ask, then, has God rejected his people? (11:1)
- Hence I ask, did they [the Jews] stumble so as to fall? (11:11)

With the diatribe, Paul writes not simply to present his theology but also to defend it.

## Paul's Missionary Field: From Jerusalem to Illyricum

Romans is the only letter in which Paul makes specific geographic references to his larger Gentile mission to the eastern half of the

*Continued*

**Paul's Missionary Field** *Continued*

Roman Empire in the 1st Century CE

© 2009 ANSELM ACADEMIC

Paul's missionary outreach to the Gentiles covered a wide range of territory in the eastern half of the Roman Empire.

Roman Empire. In the context of explaining his desire to travel to Spain, Paul informs the Christians in Rome that he "finished preaching the gospel of Christ" from "Jerusalem all the way around to Illyricum" (Rom 15:19).

The city of Jerusalem near the far eastern border of the Roman Empire and Illyricum was a Roman province northwest of Macedonia and Achaia on the eastern shore of the Adriatic Sea. The straight-line distance between Jerusalem and Illyricum (whose modern-day city is north of Greece in the former Yugoslavia) was about 1,200 miles. Scholars estimate that Paul traveled approximately 18,000 miles over his thirty-year career evangelizing the Gentiles with his gospel message.

## Summary: Historical Context of Romans

### CORE CONCEPTS

- The occasion for writing Romans was Paul's desire to clarify his ministry and theology for the Christians in Rome, at several points defending his theology and mission against objections.
- Paul introduces himself to believers in Rome in order to gain support for his anticipated new missionary work farther to the west, in Spain.
- Christianity in Rome in the mid-50s CE consisted of numerous house churches comprised of mostly Gentile Christ-believers.

### SUPPLEMENTAL INFORMATION

- Scholars do not know who established Christianity in the city of Rome.
- Paul's authorship of Romans, a letter addressed to a community Paul did not establish, is undisputed.
- Paul may have dictated his Letter to the Romans from the home of Gaius in the city of Corinth in the spring of 56 CE.
- Romans 16:22 indicates that Tertius was a Christian scribe who, working for Paul, recorded the Letter to the Romans. The process of dictation by Paul and writing by Tertius likely took up to three weeks.
- Emperor Claudius expelled Jews and Christians from Rome in 49 CE.
- Rather than collaborate (as in Corinth) or compete (as in Galatia), Paul preferred to evangelize people who are hearing the gospel message for the first time.

# THEOLOGY AND ETHICS OF ROMANS

As is the case with each of his letters, the theology and ethics of Romans are best understood within the context of the letter's composition and the specific circumstances of Paul's ministry. In presenting himself to the Christians in Rome, Paul needed to explain his mission to the Gentiles and his gospel message. Among the undisputed

Pauline letters, Romans provides Paul's most coherent theological vision. In Romans, he addresses the righteousness of God, justification for everyone (Jew and Gentile alike) who has faith in Christ, life in Christ, and the status of Israel within God's overarching plan for salvation.

This more detailed presentation of his gospel message allowed Paul to expand upon ideas he had begun to develop in his Letter to the Galatians. It also gave Paul the opportunity to apply his theology to the particular ethical circumstances that may have been faced by the Christians in Rome, such as the proper relations to state authorities in the imperial city and the shifting demographics of the community members.

The beginning of the letter to the Romans (1:16–17) presents the overarching theological argument of the letter, which also serves as the focus of the first main part of Romans, 1:18–11:36.[3] With this opening statement, Paul presents himself and the core his gospel message to the Christians in Rome.[4] The heart of Paul's gospel message—the righteousness of God revealed through Jesus Christ—provides a key to understanding the structure and theology of 1:18–11:36.

# Theology
## The Righteousness of God

The opening section of the letter establishes one of the important building blocks of Paul's gospel message: All people (Jews and Gentiles) are "under the domination of sin" (3:9). An awareness of sin's universal hold and the law's inability to prevent sin is key to grasping how humanity can be justified and avoid the impending wrath of God. For Paul, the reality of sin and the limits of the law are linked to the righteousness of God.

Paul begins his explanation of God's righteousness with the assertion that *all people* (both Gentiles *and* Jews) are under the

---

3. Romans has two main parts on theology (1:16–11:36) and ethics (12:1–15:13). This structure is similar to that in Galatians and Philippians.

4. See A. Katherine Grieb, *The Story of Romans: A Narrative Defense of God's Righteousness* (Louisville, KY: Westminster John Knox Press, 2002), who argues that Romans is a sustained narrative defense of God's righteousness.

domination of sin and thus deserve "the wrath of God" (1:18). He first presents the case against the Gentiles, a case that to a Jewish (or a Christian) audience would have been easy to make, if not obvious (see 1:18–32). Although the Gentiles do not have the Jewish law as a guide, "what can be known about God is evident to them" (1:19) because "the demands of the law are written in their hearts" (2:15). Therefore, their sin against God—a fundamental sin of idolatry—as outlined in 1:22–32, cannot be attributed to ignorance of God. Paul concludes, "As a result, they have no excuse" (1:20b).

## "For Jew First, and Then Greek"

Twice in Romans (1:16 and 2:9–10) Paul speaks of an ordering in salvation history: "Jew first, then Greek." The ordering of the Jews first, then Gentiles, has two different connotations in these passages. In 1:16, Paul refers to the past and present revelation of the righteousness of God, first made manifest historically to the Jews and later realized by the Gentiles. Here, Paul shows his respect for the priority of Judaism in salvation history. The ordering also places the expectation on the Jews to be the first to respond in faith to the good news of Jesus Christ. In 2:9–10, Paul refers to the future revelation of how both affliction and distress (for those who do evil) as well as glory, honor, and peace (for those who have faith) will be visited upon the Jews first and then the Gentiles.

Despite the evidence of a clear ordering, Paul continues by making the point that God's judgment is just and impartial: "There is no partiality with God" (2:11). God's impartiality is found in the *ordering* of both the judgment and the reward of humanity: Jews are the first to be judged and also the first to be rewarded.

Paul next turns to the sins of the Jews, beginning with the caution against judging the sins of the Gentiles (see 2:1). God alone will judge the sins of all people, and no one will escape the wrath and "just judgment of God" (2:5). Although the Jews have the benefit of the law, which provides instruction, knowledge, and truth, the law itself does not prevent the Jewish fundamental sin of disobedience.

Paul rhetorically points out: "You who boast of the law, do you dishonor God by breaking the law?" (2:23). Paul even highlights the Jewish practice of male circumcision—the ethnic mark in the flesh separating Jews from the other nations—as insufficient for the purpose of preventing sin (2:25–26).

Paul argues that circumcision does not release the Jew from the bondage to sin. Neither does the law, good and holy as it is, prevent sin (3:20a). For Paul, neither being circumcised nor keeping the Mosaic Law establishes a person's religious identity. Instead, both lead to sin. This is central in Paul's thought. Paul acknowledges, however, that the law does serve an essential function with regard to sin: the law raises the awareness of sin (3:20b). However, knowledge of the problem and a solution to the problem are not the same thing. Christ, the solution for sin, comes after the law and takes precedence over the law.

## God's Divine "Wrath"

Paul refers to God's "wrath" throughout Romans. See, for example, the following verses: 1:18; 2:5,8; 4:15; 5:9; 9:22.

Israel's prophets spoke of the "wrath of God" in terms of God's anger at human sinfulness (see, for example, Isaiah 9:7–20) as well as in an eschatological sense on "the day of the Lord" (see, for example, Zephaniah 1:15). Paul appears to use the idea of God's divine wrath both ways (for example, Romans 1:18; 2:5,8).

First Thessalonians is the only other letter in which Paul speaks about the "wrath of God" (1 Thess 1:10; 2:16b; 5:9). In 1 Thessalonians, Paul connects it to the Second Coming of Christ, giving it an apocalyptic tone closely associated with the impending judgment of God. Paul reveals a new element to divine "wrath" in Romans in light of God's righteousness: those who have faith in Christ will be justified and spared from the wrath of God through the blood of Christ (Rom 5:9).

### Justification for All Who Place Their Trust in Christ

Paul moves into the next section of his letter with the simple turn of the phrase, *Nuni de* (But now) at 3:21. Although Paul has laid a solid foundation for God's just judgment and coming wrath on all of sinful humanity (both Greeks *and* Jews), the phrase "But now" indicates an important transition in Paul's argument about sinful humanity in relation to God: the righteousness of God is now shown by the faith of those who believe in Christ (3:21-23).

In a sense, Romans 3:21–23 develops further the theological focus of the letter found in 1:16–17. However, in these later verses Paul asserts that God's righteousness is now manifested in the *faith* of the sinner (Jew and Gentile alike): "For we consider that a person is justified by faith apart from the works of the law" (3:28). For Paul, faith in Christ Jesus saves the sinner from God's coming judgment and wrath, and herein lies the righteousness of God offered to everyone who places their trust in Christ.

Expanding upon his earlier discussion of justification by faith in the Letter to the Galatians (3:6–18), Paul turns once again to the story of Abraham as a key precedent from the Hebrew Scriptures of one rendered righteous by faith alone. Abraham's belief in God's promise that he (at nearly one hundred years old) and his wife Sarah (whose "womb was dead") would bear a son "was credited to him as righteousness" (4:22). Critical to Paul's argument is that Abraham's belief in God's promise and status as "righteous" occurred *before* Abraham was circumcised and *before* the law was given to Moses. In fact, for Abraham, the "sign of circumcision" became "a seal on the righteousness received through faith while he was uncircumcised" (4:11a). Paul also notes that the promise made to Abraham came not from the law but through his faith (4:13). Because Abraham was "father of all the uncircumcised who believe . . . as well as the father of the circumcised" (4:11b–12a), those who likewise have faith will be credited as righteous (4:24–25). In Romans 1–4, Paul notes that all of humanity, both Gentiles and Jews, share equally in the problem of sin, for which the Mosaic Law offered no solution. Uncircumcised Gentiles who place their trust in Christ find a "precedent" in the uncircumcised Abraham, who placed his trust in God.

## Adam and Abraham in Romans

In both Galatians and Romans, Paul speaks in great detail about the uncircumcised Abraham as a precedent for uncircumcised Gentiles who come to faith. As compared with Galatians, a novelty in Romans is the mention of the first human, Adam. For Paul, the sin of Adam (and Eve) represents the beginning of the problem of sin, that affects all humanity, including the later patriarch Abraham and his Israelite descendants. The problem began already with Adam (and Eve). Only Christ—and not the Law—offers a solution to the problem of sin and death.

### Life in Christ

Having established faith as the fruit of God's righteousness, Paul can now speak about the Christian life of those who placed their trust in Christ. For both Jew and Gentile, life in Christ is first and foremost a life grounded in peace and reconciliation with God (5:1,11), saved from God's coming wrath (5:9). Furthermore, it is a life of enjoying the gifts of grace and justification from Christ who destroyed the power of sin and death brought into the world by Adam's trespass (5:12–21). Through baptism, the life justified by faith is now "dead to sin and living for God in Christ Jesus" (6:11).

The one freed from sin now stands under the power of grace and righteousness, which leads to sanctification, and ultimately eternal life (6:22). A key point Paul wishes to make in defense of his theology is that, for the uncircumcised Gentile Christians, life without the Mosaic Law *does not* entail living like lawless "pagans." Rather, the metaphor of dying with Christ in baptism (6:4–5) entails a death to one's previous way of life.

Equally important, the life of one justified by faith is now freed from the law, which brought an awareness of sin and death that dominated one's life (7:5–12). Using the first person singular *I*, Paul gives voice to the old self dominated by sin and death (Rom 7:17–18). Paul employs the *I* as a literary device to show the reality of sin and the insufficiency of the law to overcome sin. In doing so, Paul is able to contrast this old self with new self, now living under the power of the Spirit as adopted children of God, "joint heirs with Christ" (8:17).

### The Status of Israel within God's Overarching Plan of Salvation

In Romans 9–11, Paul discussed his views on the status of Israel within God's plan for salvation history. Paul struggles with the reality of God's righteousness in relation to Israel's rejection of Jesus as the Messiah. Israel's unfaithfulness clearly caused great personal unrest for him: "I have great sorrow and constant anguish in my heart" (9:2). Paul could not fathom how God's fidelity to the covenantal promises could result in the judgment against Israel.

Paul begins by dividing Israel between "children of the flesh" and "children of the promise." For Paul, only the latter belong to the true "children of God" to be counted among the "descendants" of Abraham (9:6–8). To support this doubtless controversial point, Paul offers some examples from the Old Testament in which Israelites and others received God's judgment and, as a result, became cut off from the covenant people. Drawing heavily upon Israel's prophetic tradition, Paul cites the historic pattern of Israel's failure as God's covenantal people, countered by God's assurance that a remnant of Israel will be saved (9:25–29). Paul sees Israel's pursuit of righteousness based on the law as their "stumbling block" (9:30–10:21).

Speaking directly to the Gentile Christians in Rome, Paul challenges them to see Israel's current rejection of Jesus as the Messiah as a vehicle for Gentiles' salvation, a further manifestation of God's righteousness (11:11–12). Paul ultimately concludes that despite Israel's infidelity, God remains faithful: "all Israel will be saved" (11:26), for God remains true to his "gifts" and his "call" (11:29). Using the metaphor of grafting (11:17–24), Paul presents a theology of the one people of God, with roots in ancient Israel. Here a warning is given to Gentile Christians, lest they become proud.

## Ethics

Paul reserves most of his ethical and moral exhortations for the latter part of his letter. Just as the discussion in 1:16–17 served as the theological focus for first part of the letter (1:18–11:36), Paul's moral instruction for the Roman congregations in Romans 12:1–2 functions as the ethical thesis for the second part (12:3–15:13). Paul draws upon the ironic metaphor of a "living sacrifice." By definition, a sacrifice is dead. However, with analogy to the death one experiences through baptism (6:3–4), the Christian lives, yet without unlimited freedom. Further, a sacrifice is offered to God. Thus, the life of the believer is to be seen as a gift offered in service to God.

### Obligations to Fellow Christians and State Authorities

Paul offers a specific set of ethical duties to the Christians who comprised the congregations of Rome. He expected compliance from all believers who live now in the Spirit, dead to sin and graced with the righteousness of God. No longer under the legal obligations of the law, the Christians in Rome were expected to exercise good judgment and to recognize the many and varied gifts (parts and functions) of fellow believers. Paul urged them to live as "one body in Christ" with "many parts" (12:4–5). As members of the body of Christ, they were called to mutual love and affection. In the daily living of community life, members of the various Roman congregations were expected to share the gifts that each received (such as, prophecy, ministry, teaching, 12:6–8), maintain their zeal for the faith, show compassion for each other, give generously to the poor, and offer love to enemies, (12:9–21).

Paul also expects that Christians will submit themselves to the state authority (13:1–7), an ethical obligation not seen in previous Pauline letters. Paul appears to be very sensitive to the reality that the city of Rome is the imperial city of the Roman Empire—the headquarters of the state authority. While Paul sees God as the ultimate authority (13:1b), he strongly encourages obedience to the state (13:3b–4). In Paul's view, both the coming wrath of God and individual conscience guide one's behavior in relation to the state. He sees compliance with civil authorities as a constituent element to life in Christian community, including paying taxes and tolls as well as showing respect and honor to those in authority (13:7).

The Letter to the Romans was written in Emperor Nero's "good," or early, years. Paul never envisioned that, just a few years after Romans was written, the Roman state would persecute Christians after the fire that consumed a third of Rome. In Romans,

Paul envisions Gentile Christianity flourishing within the Roman Empire. The apostle's theology was in need of updating once Nero punitively started executing Christians—likely, some of those very same believers who heard Paul's advice in Romans 13.

### Avoiding Judgment and Respecting Conscience

Paul also offers some ethical advice to those "strong" in the faith on treating those who may be "weak in faith" (14:1–15:13). Paul's discussion centers on purity laws associated with eating or abstaining from certain food and drink. The issue may refer to ongoing debate between the Gentile and Jewish Christians in Rome about the observance of some Jewish purity laws associated with eating (14:3). Paul clearly shows his bias in this debate, favoring the "strong" in faith who do not allow food and drink to become a divisive issue with the community (14:14,17).

Paul encourages the "strong" not to pass judgment on the "weak," allowing all believers in Christ to exercise their own conscience in this regard. The stakes are too high for Paul to allow the "strong" to dictate to the weak, "For the sake of food, do not destroy the work of God" (14:20). Above all, Paul wants for the one church to be united in Christ and not to be divided over cultural matters, such as food and drink.

## A Profile of Paul's Twenty-six Co-workers of Romans 16[5]

As his letter draws to a close, Paul sends personal greetings to an astonishing twenty-six people who count themselves among "the beloved of God in Rome" (1:7) and whom Paul considers as co-workers.

*Continued*

---

5. Scholars often note the text-critical problem of whether Romans 16 was (1) originally a part of this letter, (2) Pauline but not originally part of this letter, (3) not written by Paul. Notably, most of the names are Greek, not Latin.

| A Profile of Paul's Twenty-six Co-workers *Continued* | |
|---|---|
| Nine women | Prisca (or Priscilla [Acts 18:2]), Junia (an "apostle" who had been imprisoned with Paul), Mary, Tryphaena and Tryphosa (sisters, possibly twins), Persis, the mother of Rufus, the sister of Nereus, and Julia (five of the nine bear epithets that denote service and labor on behalf of the community and the gospel) |
| Fourteen men | Aquila, Andronicus, Ampliatus, Urbanus, Stachys, Apelles, Rufus, Asyncritus, Phlegon, Hermes, Patrobas, Hermas, Philologus, and Nereus |
| Jewish husband/wife | Aquila and Prisca, Andronicus and Junia |
| Families | Philologus and Julia (parents), Nereus and his sister (children) |
| Entire households | Of Aristobulus and of Narcissus |
| Paul's "relatives" | Herodion, Lucius, Jason, and Sosipater |

Notably, Romans 16 begins with Paul's commendation of Phoebe: "our sister" and "a minister of the church at Cenchreae" (the eastern seaport of Corinth), a "benefactor of many and of me" (16:1–2). Phoebe was the probable letter carrier to the city of Rome. By sending such an unusually large number of greetings, Paul claims a certain rapport with the church in Rome, hoping that they will welcome him and support his anticipated missionary work farther west, in Spain.

## Summary: Theology and Ethics in Romans

### CORE CONCEPTS

- The theology and structure of Romans are grounded in the idea of the righteousness of God.
- Paul warned the Gentile believers not to be proud of Israel's role in salvation history.
- Mutual love, sharing of gifts, and obedience to civil authorities constitute ethical obligations for Christians living in Rome.

### SUPPLEMENTAL INFORMATION

- Romans 1:16–17 contains the theological focus for part one of the letter, 1:18–11:36.
- Paul believed that all people (Jew and Gentile alike) were under the domination of sin, in need of salvation, and deserving of "God's wrath."
- Paul relies on the figure of Abraham as one rendered righteous by God because of his faith.
- The fruits of God's righteousness include peace and reconciliation with God, sanctification, a "new self" in the Spirit, and eternal life.
- Israel's rejection of Jesus as the messiah is part of God's plan to save all people, including Israel.
- Romans 12:1–2 functions as the ethical thesis for part two of the letter, 12:3–15:13.
- Paul strongly encouraged that one's conscience be the guide in matters of food and drink.

## Questions for Review

1. What occasion prompted Paul to write the Letter to the Romans?
2. Why does Paul address his letter to the "beloved of God" in Rome rather than to an individual church?
3. When and where do scholars think Paul may have written Romans?

4. Who is Tertius?
5. How might the gospel message have been brought to Rome?
6. According to Romans, what was the function of the Jewish law?
7. What does Paul mean by saying in Romans 2:11 that God shows "no partiality"?
8. According to Paul, why has God "hardened" the heart of Israel?
9. What is Paul's attitude toward the civil authorities in the city of Rome?
10. What are the "strong" and the "weak" debating about in the congregations in Rome?

## Questions for Reflection

1. What do you imagine the relationship was like between Paul and Tertius?
2. Explain which you think is more likely: Christians in Rome embracing Paul's correspondence with them or Christians in Rome finding Paul's letter objectionable.
3. How do you think Romans 9–11 can help facilitate interfaith dialogue between Jews and Christians today?
4. In Romans, Paul advocates for Christians to submit to the authority of the state. Must Christians today always submit to the governing authorities?

## Recommendations for Further Reading

Grenholm, Cristina, and Daniel Patte, eds. *Gender, Tradition and Romans: Shared Ground, Uncertain Borders.* New York: T & T Clark, 2005.

Presented from the perspective of feminist criticism, this book addresses Paul's view of gender in the Letter to the Romans. Leading feminist scholars contribute essays to this book, which is divided into three parts: (1) Mapping traditions in Romans; (2) challenging gendered traditions in Romans; and (3) gender and the authority of Romans. The essays are grounded in the conviction that the various traditions found in Romans either promote or challenge gender injustice.

Grieb, A. Katherine. *The Story of Romans: A Narrative Defense of God's Righteousness*. Louisville, KY: Westminster John Knox Press, 2002.

Grieb argues that the Letter to the Romans is best understood from the perspective of story. Grieb maintains that Paul presents a sustained narrative argument of God's righteousness made evident through a series of Old Testament stories (for example, Adam and Abraham) embedded within the larger story of the death and Resurrection of Jesus Christ. Grieb also makes the case for how Paul's narrative defense of God's righteousness speaks to Christians today.

Jewett, Robert. *Romans: A Commentary* (Hermeneia: A Critical & Historical Commentary on the Bible). Minneapolis, MN: Fortress Press, 2006.

Jewett provides a variety of critical approaches to his analysis of Romans: historical criticism, rhetorical criticism, sociological analysis, and cultural-anthropological analysis. Jewett pays close attention to the cultural, social, political, and ideological contexts of this letter, arguing that Romans was written, at least in part, to encourage reconciliation between the churches in Rome and to support his mission to Spain.

Reasoner, Mark. *Romans in Full Circle: A History of Interpretation*. Louisville, KY: Westminster John Knox Press, 2005.

Reasoner focuses on key texts in the Letter to the Romans (for example, 1:16–17, the thesis of the letter; 3:21–28, humanity made righteous by Christ; 11:25–27, Israel's salvation), that have been subject to various interpretations throughout history, going back to the year 240 CE. Reasoner presents the interpretations of these texts from key figures in the early Church (such as Origen and Augustine), Middles Ages (for example, Aquinas and Luther), modern period (Karl Barth), and the so-called "new perspective" on Paul (Dunn, Sanders, and Wright).

Westerholm, Stephen. *Understanding Paul: The Early Christian Worldview of the Letter to the Romans*. 2d ed. Grand Rapids, MI: Baker Academic, 2004.

Westerholm presents the Letter to the Romans from the perspective of Paul's thought world. Rather than focus on standard historical questions such as the date and place of composition, Westerholm engages the reader by making sense of Paul's vision of life as he articulates it in Romans. His aim is to make Paul's presuppositions clear to the modern reader, and in turn, assist the modern reader in seeing his/her presuppositions brought to Romans.

# CHAPTER 7

# Philippians

## INTRODUCTION

Paul wrote his Letter to the Philippians while in prison, but during *which* imprisonment (Rome, Caesarea, Ephesus, or Corinth), remains the subject of scholarly debate and also affects the dating of the letter.[1] Many scholars date Philippians to Paul's imprisonment in Rome, which means that he wrote it after the Letter to the Romans. The first section of this chapter considers the historical context of the letter: its setting; that Philippi was likely Paul's first congregation; and the literary unity of Philippians. The second section examines the theology of Philippians, especially in regard to the Parousia, Church unity, and God's righteousness and as has been done in the other chapters, it considers the letter's ethical themes, including being "blameless" for the day of Christ and serving each other in humility.

## A Letter of Joy

Philippians is commonly referred to as Paul's "letter of joy." Indeed, the terms *joy/rejoice* (in Greek, *chara/chairō*) appear throughout the letter. See, for example, the following verses: 1:4,5,18,25; 2:2,17,28,29; 3:1; 4:1,4,10. Because the Philippian congregation was one of the earliest communities he founded (4:15; Acts 16:11–15), Paul has much to rejoice about. He considers them true "partners" in

---

1. The theories associated with each possible imprisonment are discussed in the section "Date and Place of Composition." The traditional location for Paul's imprisonment is Rome, but there is also considerable scholarly support for Ephesus.

the proclamation of the gospel (1:5,7) and is grateful for their consistent support from the very beginning of his ministry (4:15).

Given that Paul wrote the letter while in prison, its joyful tone may seem a little unusual. Paul, however, was well aware of the Philippians' concern for him and his present situation (4:10). The letter's joyful tenor (for example, 1:3–4) likely reflects Paul's desire to ease their worries about his imprisonment as well as to show them that faith in Christ relativized earthly troubles. Unlike the previous letters discussed, this is a letter of genuine friendship between Paul and the Christians at Philippi. Aside from an attack on false teachers and opponents (1:15–18,28; 3:2–4,18–19), Philippians maintains a positive focus with an emphasis on past successes with the congregation, present opportunities in prison, and future rewards when Christ returns from heaven.

## A Letter from Prison

Philippians and Philemon are the only two of Paul's surviving letters written from prison. (The other two Pauline imprisonment letters, Ephesians and Colossians, are considered deutero-Pauline.) During his nearly three decades of preaching his gospel message, Paul appears to have been imprisoned numerous times and in different cities. In the Acts of the Apostles, Luke speaks of Paul's imprisonment in Philippi (Acts 16:16–40), Caesarea (Acts 23–26), and Rome (Acts 28:30). Furthermore, Paul himself testifies to being in prison (2 Cor 11:23—in fact, "far more imprisonments" than others preaching the gospel) and even writing from prison (Phil 1:7,13,14,17; Phlm 1,9,10,13,23).

During his imprisonments, Paul remained in contact with his congregations. In Philippians, Paul speaks of having visitors (2:25–30). These visitors include Timothy, who may have delivered Paul's letter to Philippi (2:19–23), and Epaphroditus, who had brought Paul a monetary gift from the Philippians (4:18). In the Letter to Philemon, Paul writes to Philemon from prison fully expecting the letter to reach its destination (Phlm 21). Luke also mentions Paul having visitors, even friends, call upon him during his imprisonments in Caesarea (Acts 24:23) and in Rome (Acts 28:23). Imprisonment apparently did not deter Paul from continuing his apostolic ministry.

# HISTORICAL CONTEXT OF PHILIPPIANS

Philippians offers some good information about its intended audience. The Acts of the Apostles also discusses Paul's ministry at Philippi, which offers some context about the intended audience.[2] The date and place of composition, on the other hand, remains a subject of debate among scholars, since the primary sources offer few clues.

## Outline of Philippians

| | |
|---|---|
| 1:1–11 | **Greeting and Thanksgiving** <br> The letter is co-sent by Paul and Timothy and is written from Paul's imprisonment to the community in Philippi.[3] As in Romans, Paul does not address a specific church. Paul begins by giving thanks to God for the true "partnership" (1:5) experienced between himself and the Philippians, and he prays that the Philippians will be found "pure and blameless for the day of Christ" (1:10). |
| 1:12–26 | **Reflections from Prison** <br> Paul reflects on his imprisonment, seeing his time in prison as an opportunity to "advance the gospel" (1:12). Faced with the possibility of being put to death, Paul speaks about the resulting personal dilemma: He is torn between welcoming death to "be with Christ" (1:23) and desiring life so as to continue his "fruitful labor" (1:22) among the Philippians and others. Paul bemoans, "I am caught between the two" (1:23) alternatives. |

*Continued*

---

2. However, Paul's silence about Lydia, according to Acts 16, his first convert, suggests the secondary nature of Acts as a source.

3. On the translation and role of these terms, see information under heading "Author and Audience" on page 185.

**Outline of Philippians** *Continued*

| | |
|---|---|
| 1:27–2:18 | **Instructions to the Philippian Congregation**<br><br>Paul's initial instructions center on standing firm in the faith together. He speaks of not being "intimidated in any way by your opponents" (1:28). Paul urges the Philippians to learn from the opponents' negative example, and act instead out of humility and love, united in mind and spirit. Paul includes some elative prose (the so-called Christ hymn of 2:5–11), which speaks of Jesus as the model of humility, and encourages the Philippians to have "the same attitude" (2:5). He concludes by speaking of the Philippians as "children of God" (2:15), obedient to the gospel message and ready for "the day of Christ" (2:16). |
| 2:19–3:1 | **The Travel Plans of Paul, Timothy, and Epaphroditus**<br><br>Paul next speaks of his desire to send both Timothy and Epaphroditus back to the Philippians. Paul considers both of these co-workers as models of the faith and true allies in spreading the gospel. Paul anticipates that Epaphroditus will recover from a grave illness and that Epaphroditus' arrival in Philippi will be a relief to all. |
| 3:2–4:9 | **Further Instructions to the Philippian Congregation**<br><br>Paul's second set of instructions advises the Philippians against opponents of the gospel message who wrongly encourage circumcision as a means of attaining righteousness. After inserting a brief autobiography, Paul testifies that faith in Christ rather than works of the law provides the only means for justification. Rather than conduct themselves as "enemies of the cross of Christ" (3:18) as the opponents do, Paul urges the Philippians to follow his example. Paul also mentions the disagreement between two female co-workers. |

*Continued*

| | |
|---|---|
| **Outline of Philippians** *Continued* | |
| 4:10–20 | **A Note of Personal Gratitude** <br> Paul offers a final note of thanks to the Philippians for their consistent support from the very "beginning of the gospel" (4:15). |
| 4:21–23 | **Personal Greetings and Farewell** <br> Paul concludes with greetings from those with him in prison and "especially those of Caesar's household" (4:22). He ends with a brief blessing. |

## Author and Audience

Philippians is not the first letter co-sent by Paul and Timothy. Paul sent 2 Corinthians with Timothy and 1 Thessalonians with both Timothy and Silvanus. However, the pervasive use of the first person singular (*I*) throughout the letter, along with the absence of the first person plural (*we*), leaves little question that Paul is the sole author.

For the first and only time in his surviving letters, Paul refers to "the overseers and ministers" in his greeting. This implies some level of organization among the Christians in the city of Philippi. The Greek terms used here, *episkopos* (overseer) and *diakonos* (minister), are translated elsewhere in the NAB as *bishop* and *deacon* (see the Pauline Pastoral Letters of 1 Timothy 3:1–7 and Titus 1:5–9). This translation is more appropriate for the Pastorals, which date to the late-first or early-second century CE, by which time more formalized and structured offices existed within Christian communities.[4] The translation of *overseer* and *minister* in the Letter to the Philippians more accurately connotes the presence of some organizational elements but indicates that they may have not yet developed to the level of an official office. However, the Philippian congregation was likely more structured than what is evidenced in the congregation in Corinth (see 1 Cor 12).

---

4. See second-century documents that refer to bishops and presbyters in Church offices: *Didache* 15; *1 Clement* 42:5; Ignatius's *Letter to the Magnesians* 6:1; 13:1.

"All the holy ones" (Phil 1:1) in Philippi appear to have been largely, perhaps exclusively, Gentile.[5] The individuals Paul mentions in the letter have Gentile (that is, non-Jewish) names: Epaphroditus (2:25), Euodia and Syntyche (4:2), and Clement (4:3). Paul's attack on opponents in Philippi who promoted male circumcision of the Gentiles ("Beware of the mutilation!" 3:2) further supports a Gentile Christian profile of the community. In Acts of the Apostles, Luke refers to another individual in Philippi by the name of Lydia, a woman whom he describes as a "worshiper of God" or God-fearer (in Greek, *sebomenē*, 16:14). The term refers to Gentiles who are attracted to the Jewish religion and who worship the God of the Jews but are not full converts to Judaism and don't follow Jewish laws about such matters as circumcision and food.[6]

## The Ancient City of Philippi

The city of Philippi was named after Philip II of Macedon who in 365 BCE defeated the Thracian tribes in that region. About two hundred years later, in 167 BCE, Romans occupied the city and made the whole region of Macedonia into a Roman province. Philippi benefited from the area's rich soil and natural-water springs, achieving economic prosperity through grain harvesting and wine production. Philippi's location on the Via Egnatia, a pathway connecting Macedonia with regions to east (Asia Minor) and north (Illyricum: cf. Rom 15), contributed to the city's trade and wealth. Over time, the city grew in popularity and influence, eventually being named a senatorial province by Claudius in 44 CE.

In Paul's day, Philippi had a population of about 10,000. The city was a Roman military colony and had become the home to many Roman veterans. Luke refers to Philippi as "a leading city

*Continued*

---

5. Scholars, however, are uncertain about any Jewish presence there. See Bonnie B. Thurston and Judith M. Ryan, *Philippians and Philemon*. SP 10. Collegeville, MN; Liturgical Press, 2005, 9.

6. According to Luke's account, Lydia and her entire household were among Paul's first converts in Philippi (16:15). For other examples of God-fearing Gentiles, see the centurion in Luke 7 and Cornelius in Acts 10.

> ### The Ancient City of Philippi  *Continued*
>
> in that district of Macedonia and a Roman colony" (Acts 16:12). Archeological evidence reveals that Philippi had many religious cults. Its inhabitants worshipped various Roman, Greek, and Egyptian gods/goddesses as well as the older Thracian deities such as Apollos and Artemis. To date, there is little archeological evidence to suggest a Jewish presence in the city of Philippi during Paul's lifetime.

# Date and Place of Composition

Scholars disagree on when and where Paul wrote the Letter to the Philippians. Two factors contribute to the debate. First, the main sources—the letter itself and the Acts of the Apostles—offer little direct evidence. Although Paul makes numerous references to his imprisonment (Phil 1:7,13,14,17), these provide no clues about date and place of composition. This lack of evidence leads to the second complicating factor: Which imprisonment is Paul referring to? At least three possibilities exist: Rome, Ephesus, and Caesarea.[7] The Philippians knew where Paul was imprisoned, thus, Paul's silence about this.

Traditionally scholars date Philippians to Paul's final imprisonment in Rome in the very early 60s CE. Scholars often point to Paul's reference to the "whole praetorium" (Phil 1:13) and the final greeting from "those of Caesar's household" (Phil 4:22) which supports this theory, as a *praetorium* (a military headquarters) and members of Caesar's household, would be located in Rome. However, a *praetorium* was not restricted to Rome. Acts mentions Paul's imprisonment in Rome "for two full years in his lodging" (Acts 28:30), noting that he was allowed visitors (Acts 28:17). According to Paul's own testimony, Timothy and Epaphroditus visit him

---

7. See Udo Schnelle, *Apostle Paul: His Life and Theology*, trans. M. Eugene Boring (Grand Rapids, MI: Baker Academic, 2005), 2, 366–69, who favors the traditional location of Rome. Compare with Thurston, 28–30, who favors Ephesus. Thurston also cites a Corinthian imprisonment as a possible location for the writing of Philippians. Both Schnelle and Thurston lay out the arguments for each possible location.

during his incarceration, and he hopes to send them back to the Philippians (Phil 2:19–24,25–30). The long distance from Rome to Philippi (about seven hundred miles) and the time Timothy and/or Epaphroditus would need to travel back and forth, also suggest a long imprisonment.[8]

A second theory proposing Ephesus as the site of Paul's imprisonment during the composition of this letter also garners considerable scholarly support. The distance between Ephesus and Philippi (about four hundred miles) makes the back-and-forth travel of Timothy and Epaphroditus more realistic. Paul's references to the *praetorium* and members of Caesar's household would certainly have been possible in the provincial residences of Ephesus. Although Luke speaks about Paul and Timothy being together in Ephesus (Acts 19), Acts does not mention a lengthy imprisonment there.

## Women in the Church at Philippi

Both the Letter to the Philippians and the Acts of the Apostles provide some insights into the leadership roles of women in the Christian congregation in Philippi.

Paul speaks of two women, Euodia and Syntyche, as his co-workers who "struggled at my side in promoting the gospel" (Phil 4:2–3) among the Philippians. In the context of the letter, Paul expresses concern about a misunderstanding that has developed between the women. That disagreement between two church leaders could have had implications for the congregation as a whole. Because the unity of the congregation in the body of Christ comprised an important part of Paul's gospel message (see, for example, 1 Cor 6:15–17; 10:16–17; 12:12–27; Rom 12:45), he was eager to resolve the conflict among two of its more prominent leaders. Notably, Paul does not mention these co-workers' gender. For Paul, the problem was that two co-workers, who happened to be women, had a significant and unresolved disagreement.

*Continued*

---

8. Schnelle, 369, estimates that a sea trip from Philippi to Rome would take about two weeks and a land trip covering about seven hundred miles (23 miles per day) would take about four weeks.

In Acts, Luke refers to the wealthy businesswoman, Lydia, "a dealer in purple cloth" (16:14), as one of Paul's initial Gentile converts in Philippi. Lydia's conversion led to the baptism of her entire household (16:15). Luke also states that Paul and Silas later visited her (16:40).

Modern Greek Orthodox Church that commemorates the conversion and baptism of Lydia, located in Philippi a few yards from the stream where Paul is thought to have baptized her

Acts 23–26 discusses Paul's imprisonment in Caesarea that appears to have extended for two years or more (24:27). He was held in custody in "Herod's praetorium" (23:35) and was allowed to have visitors (24:23), during that time. These details from Acts do support the scant information about his imprisonment that Paul includes in his Letter to the Philippians. However, the distance between Caesarea and Philippi is nearly one thousand miles, making numerous trips back and forth by Timothy or Epaphroditus unrealistic.

Each of the imprisonments merits consideration, but the available evidence gives no compelling reason to support the Ephesian or Cesarean hypotheses over the traditional view of Rome as the place of composition for Philippians. With Paul's imprisonment in Rome commonly dated to the early 60s CE, this book assumes the date and place of composition for Philippians is Rome in 60 CE. Dating Philippians so late in Paul's apostolic mission has implications for understanding the letter's theology and ethics.

## Summary: Historical Setting for Philippians

| | |
|---|---|
| Author | Paul |
| Audience | Gentile converts |
| Date of Composition | 60 CE (early-mid-50s CE, if Ephesus; late 50s CE, if Caesarea) |
| Place of Composition | In prison, possibly Rome (or possibly imprisoned in Ephesus or Caesarea) |

## Philippi as Paul's Macedonian Congregation

Philippi had personal significance for Paul because this was probably one of his first congregations established in Macedonia, likely around 49 or 50 CE. According to Luke's account, Paul established a community of Gentile Christ-believers in Philippi (Acts 16:11–12) during his second missionary journey (15:36–18:22). Paul converted and baptized two people (Lydia and the jailer) and their entire households in Philippi (16:15,32–34). If these dates are accurate, then, by the time Paul wrote his letter to the Philippians in 60 CE, the church there would have been about ten years old. Paul alludes to a long-term relationship with the Philippians in his opening prayer of thanksgiving (1:3-5). Paul's reference in the greeting to the "overseers and ministers" in Philippi may also be better understood in the context of this ten-year history.

Paul visited the Philippians (perhaps more than once), and the letter to the Philippians indicates a good relationship. Paul seems to sincerely appreciate the Philippians' sustained "partnership" with him—a likely reference to the Philippians' financial support of Paul's ministry. Previous correspondence, for example, with the Corinthians and the churches of Galatia, indicate that such consistent support for and advancement of Paul's gospel message was not the norm. The Corinthian congregation was characterized by factions and various allegiances, troubled by numerous crises, and influenced by opponents such as the "superapostles" who challenged the authority of Paul and his gospel. The situation in the churches of Galatia was even worse, with Gentiles actually embracing a different gospel from Paul's after his departure, going so far as to support male circumcision of Christ-believing Gentiles.

In contrast to his relationship with some other congregations, Paul and the Philippians shared a bond of trust. Whatever opponents the Philippians faced (Phil 1:15–20,28–30, 3:2–3,18–19), there is no indication that, insofar as Paul understands the situation there, they

## Who Was Epaphroditus?

As is the case with Sosthenes in 1 Corinthians 1:1, or Phoebe in Romans 16:2, Epaphroditus is mentioned nowhere else in the New Testament except in Philippians 2:25 and 4:18. Both Paul and the Philippians must have thought highly of Epaphroditus, because Paul uses numerous descriptors to explain his value: *brother*, *co-worker*, *fellow soldier*, *messenger*, and *minister*; and the Philippians entrusted Epaphroditus as their representative to bear their gift to Paul.

The terms Paul uses to describe Epaphroditus provide some clues about his identity. Epaphroditus was a messenger between Paul and the Philippians (2:25b,28–30; 4:18). Because many Roman prisons provided little more than a cell for those under arrest, Paul's reference to Epaphroditus as "minister in my need" indicates that he may have supplied Paul with necessities such as additional food and water. He may also have treated any injuries Paul may have sustained. Paul often uses the language of *brother* and *co-worker* to refer to those who worked directly with him in spreading the gospel message (see for example, 1 Thes 3:2; Rom 16:1; Phil 4:3), but he rarely used the term *fellow soldier* to describe a co-worker. (As will be seen in chapter 8, the only other place Paul uses the term *fellow soldier* is Philemon 2 in reference to Archippus.) There may be a connection between this military language and that Paul wrote both Philippians and Philemon from prison.

did not fully defend Paul's gospel message. Furthermore, Paul seems confident that internal communal conflicts can be resolved (Phil 4:2–3). Even after ten years, Paul could refer to his original founding community as "partners with me . . . in the defense and conformation of the gospel" (Phil 1:7).

## The Literary Unity of Philippians

Scholars have strenuously debated the issue of the literary integrity of Philippians. By *literary integrity*, scholars mean the question of whether this was just *one* letter Paul wrote to *one* congregation at *one* point in time. Current scholarship has not reached a consensus on this point. Whereas some scholars see Philippians as originally consisting of parts of two or three different letters, others view the letter as a single composition from Paul. Scholars who champion the former view point to apparent sudden transitions and differences between different parts of the letter. Champions of the fragmentary hypothesis have offered several proposals for where these purportedly fragmentary letters begin and end.[9] Regardless of the number of fragments in Philippians, or where the seams occur, scholars supporting the fragmentary hypothesis agree that a clear change in mood appears between 3:1 and 3:2, and that 4:10–20 seems to be a singular, separate letter of thanksgiving.

Scholars who argue for the unity of Philippians remain unconvinced by the fragmentary proposals, in part, because of the disagreements among the fragmentary theorists and the lack of any manuscript evidence. They also call attention to recurring vocabulary and thematic patterns throughout the letter, as well as formal, literary structures that point to a single letter. Equally important is the application of rhetorical analysis to Philippians in recent decades. Scholars doing this work argue that the rhetorical patterns and forms of Greco-Roman letters in Paul's day suggest that Philippians is a single, unified letter that basically "uses deliberative rhetoric for a

---

9. For example, the following are common two-fragment divisions of Philippians: Letter A: 1:1–3:1a and 4:10–23; Letter B: 3:1b–4:9. Or, Letter A: 1:1–3:1 and 4:20–23; Letter B: 3:2–4:20. Scholars arguing for a tripartite division of Philippians offer competing divisions as well: Letter A: 4:10–20; Letter B: 1:1–3:1; 4:4–7, 21–23; Letter C: 3:1b–4:3, 8–9. Or, Letter A: 4:10–20; Letter B: 1:1–3:1; 4:2–9; Letter C: 3:2–4:1.

hortatory purpose."[10] In other words, Philippians is best understood as a letter structured to persuade the "holy ones" of Philippi to accept Paul's support, advice, and instructions to them.

The similar vocabulary in the supposed fragments (for example, *form* in 2:6,7 with *conform* in 3:21) bolsters the argument for the literary and theological unity of Philippians. Further, certain themes that emerge throughout the letter—such as the focus on Paul's opponents and enemies (1:15–20,28–30; 3:2–3,18–19), the motif of unity (1:27–28; 2:2) and the overarching tone of joy/rejoice—undermine the idea of numerous fragments.[11] Thus, Philippians is treated here as a single, unified letter.

## Paul's Opposition in Philippi

Although Paul maintains a good and open relationship over the years with the Christians of Philippi, he acknowledges various opponents (1:28) and enemies (3:18) who wish to affect the Philippian community. At three points in the letter, Paul discusses the influence of these outsiders: 1:15–18; 1:28–30; 3:2–3,18–19. The limited information Paul provides allows for only a sketchy profile of these opponents.

| | |
|---|---|
| 1:15–18 | Some preach the gospel out of rivalry and envy or out of selfish ambition. These people do not appear to be much of a threat. |

*Continued*

---

10. Thurston, 35. Thurston, 34–37, provides a good summary of the work of rhetorical critics of the past few decades. Scholars applying rhetorical criticism to Philippians recognize that ancients could have viewed the letter as "a letter of friendship, a letter of consolation, and as a family letter," 34.

11. Some recent scholars suggest the debate has been won by those favoring the theory that Philippians is a single, unified letter. See John Paul Heil, *Philippians: Let Us Rejoice in Being Conformed to Christ* (Atlanta, GA: Society of Biblical Literature), 6, who states, "In the past the Letter to the Philippians has been plagued by various theories that it is a composite of different letters, so that it lacks literary unity and integrity. Recent research, however, seems to have largely discredited such theories, so that one could speak of a current consensus against such an idea."

**Paul's Opposition in Philippi** *Continued*

| 1:28–30 | Paul identifies a second, separate group of opponents whom the Philippians may be "intimidated" by. Paul implies these opponents may be the civil authorities who have the power to arrest them, as they did Paul. |
|---|---|
| 3:2–3; 3:18–19 | This group appears to be the biggest concern to Paul and the Philippians. Paul reserves his strongest language for them, calling them: dogs, evil-workers, enemies of the cross. This section of the letter presents Paul's most extensive argument to counter their message. Their emphasis on circumcision and legal issues associated with dietary laws and their deemphasis of the cross suggest a group of Jewish Christians whose message Paul has battled elsewhere. |

## Summary: Historical Context of Philippians

### CORE CONCEPTS

- Paul wrote Philippians during one of his imprisonments, possibly in Rome.
- Paul praised the Philippian community for their steadfast support of him and his gospel, including their sending Epaphroditus with a gift to support Paul in prison.
- Scholars continue to debate whether Philippians is composed of already existing letter fragments or is an original, unified letter. This chapter favors the latter hypothesis.

### SUPPLEMENTAL INFORMATION

- The Philippian congregation was largely, perhaps exclusively, Gentile.

*Continued*

> ### Summary: Historical Context of Philippians *Continued*
>
> - Philippians is often characterized as "a letter of joy."
> - Scholars remain uncertain about the date and place of composition for Philippians.
> - According to Acts, Paul founded the Christian community in Philippi. Scholars date this around 49 or 50 CE.
> - By *literary integrity*, scholars mean the question of whether this was just *one* letter written by Paul to *one* congregation at *one* point in time.
> - Scholars supporting the theory that Philippians is a fragmented letter disagree on the number of fragments or the divisions between them.

# THEOLOGY AND ETHICS OF PHILIPPIANS

The theology and ethics reflected in Paul's letters are best understood in context. In the case of Philippians, Paul writes from prison, uncertain whether he will be released or martyred (1:20). It is late in Paul's apostolic ministry, and circumstances in his beloved community in Philippi require that he revisit some of the major tenets of his gospel message: church unity, the return of Christ, and God's righteousness. Within this theological framework, Paul offers instructions to help the Philippians respond to both internal and external tensions in their community.

## Theology

### Church Unity

Throughout the letter, Paul makes appeals for unity in the church. In some cases, these requests for unity reflect the desire to defend the community from certain opponents (1:28) and "enemies of the cross of Christ" (3:18). At other times, the call for unity stems from the need to resolve internal conflict (4:2–3). In both situations, Paul sees the unity of the church best exemplified when the congregation can stand firm together in the faith (1:27; 4:1). The Philippians' unity of heart and mind offer the best defense against outsiders who seek to destroy the church (1:27–28) as well as the most effective means to overcome internal misunderstandings and strife (4:1–3).

In a personal appeal, Paul uses his suffering in prison to inspire unity in the Philippian congregation. Paul shares his internal struggle as he faces an uncertain future: release from prison or death (1:20). Both life and death bear fruit for him (1:21–22,23b–24), and he confesses: "I am caught between the two" (1:23a). Paul urges the Philippians to "rejoice" in his suffering because "I know that this will result in deliverance for me through your prayers and support from the Spirit of Jesus Christ" (1:19). Paul's suffering in prison as well as the suffering of the Philippians at the hands of their opponents and from internal conflicts (1:29–30) paradoxically reveals God's grace and offer opportunities for unity.

Paul connects his suffering and the suffering of the Philippian congregation to the cross of Christ by inserting the text into Philippians 2:5–11. For Paul, Christ is the ultimate source of unity, and he urges the Philippians to imitate Christ in their interactions with each other and in their willingness to suffer: "He humbled himself, becoming obedient to death, even death on a cross" (2:8). In imitating Christ and in imitating Paul, community members will find that humility and suffering can unify the church and strengthen the faith. Furthermore, the Philippians should submit to one another out of reverence to Christ. With such mutual submission, following Christ's (and Paul's) example, they will have a better chance of staying together and standing firm against internal and external threats.

### A Less Imminent Parousia

One indicator that Paul wrote Philippians late in his apostolic career is his evolving view of the Parousia, the return of Christ. Paul spoke of Christ's return in previous letters, 1 Thessalonians and 1 Corinthians, with his most extensive discussion coming in the earliest of his letters, 1 Thessalonians. There, Paul associates Jesus coming "from heaven" with God's coming "wrath" (1 Thess 1:10; 5:9. See also, 2:19; 3:13; 5:23), but acknowledges that he does not know when "the day of the Lord will come" (5:2). Paul addresses the reality that some have already died, and others will die, before the return of Christ (1 Thess 4:15–18).

## Who Wrote the Text of Philippians 2:5–11?[12]

Scholars debate whether Paul wrote Philippians 2:5–11 or whether he inherited a preexisting text and incorporated it into his letter.[13] Some scholars see this text (often called a Christ hymn) as central to the theology of the letter.

Those in favor of Paul's authorship point out that this text, an elative prose, contains theology present in other Pauline letters (for example, see Rom 8:35–39) and parallels ideas found elsewhere in Philippians (for instance, see Phil 3:20–21). Others claim that Paul inserted it as a preexisting text into the letter. They argue that these types of texts and text fragments in the New Testament (such as, Phil 2:5–11; Col 1:15–20; John 1:1–4; 1 Tim 3:16) are among the earliest attempts by the first generation of Christians to articulate their beliefs about Jesus. These texts date to the oral period of the New Testament, 30–70 CE. Paul and other New Testament writers strategically placed these texts into their larger writing to support their theology. Paul may have done this with 2:5–11. The pre-Pauline text flows well within the context of his appeal to the Philippians for unity and humility.

In antiquity, letter writers used leaves from papyrus plants to write on. The "ink" was typically made from carbon soot deposits that resulted from burning wood and other materials.

© bpk, Berlin Art Resource, NY

---

12. Some scholars refer to Philippians 2:6–11 as a Christological hymn, but there is no evidence of this text being used in a liturgical setting. For a good discussion on this misnomer, see A. Y. Collins, "Psalms, Philippians 2:6–11, and the Origins of Christology," *Biblical Interpretation* 11 (2003): 361–72.

13. Lincoln D. Hurst, "Christ, Adam, and Preexistence Revisited," in *Where Christology Began: Essays on Philippians 2*. Eds. Ralph P. Martin and Brian J. Dodd (Louisville, KY: Westminster John Knox Press, 1998), 84–95: "Philippians 2:6–11 continues to be one of the most disputed passages in the history of New Testament interpretation," 84.

Paul not only speaks of Christ's imminent return, but also states his belief that he will still be alive at the Parousia: "Then *we* who are alive, who are left, will be caught up together with them in the clouds to meet the Lord in the air" (1 Thess 4:17) (emphasis added).

Paul's discussion of the Parousia in 1 Corinthians also communicates a sense of urgency regarding the Second Coming, as he implores the Christians in Corinth to be "irreproachable on the day of our Lord Jesus Christ" (1 Cor 1:8). Later in this letter, Paul offers further specifics about the actual Parousia-event (1 Cor 15:22–25).

Philippians marks a shift in Paul's view of the Parousia. Paul no longer envisions the Parousia from an earthly perspective. He now foresees the Second Coming from a heavenly perspective and the sense of its imminence seems to fade (Phil 3:20–21). Furthermore, Paul does not speak of being "in Christ" (*en Christō*, 1 Thess 4:16; 1 Cor 15:22), when Christ comes from heaven. Rather, Paul speaks of being "with Christ" (*sun Christō*, Phil 1:23) as he reflects upon the possibility of his own death.

The three letters in which Paul discusses the Parousia span a period of ten years: 1 Thessalonians (50 CE), 1 Corinthians (55 CE), and Philippians (60 CE). Paul's belief in the *imminent* return of Christ and his witness to the associated events here on Earth during his lifetime do not figure into his theological reflection on this topic in Philippians. What remains, however, is the belief that the return of Christ will initiate the end-time, when Christ will reign and Christians will be transformed.

### Righteousness from God

In his fight against the evil-workers promoting male circumcision of the Gentile believers in Christ (3:2), Paul returns to one of the major themes from his Letter to the Romans: the righteousness of God. As he did in his Letter to the Galatians (1:11–24), Paul uses details from his own life (Phil 3:4b–6) to address the insufficiency of works of the law. In the case of the Philippians, Paul draws on his own experiences to discredit the validity of circumcision, "confidence in the flesh" (3:4), as means of attaining righteousness before God.

Paul presents a convincing case for his "confidence in the flesh." His aim here is not to show that he has such confidence but, rather, the absurdity of others who boast in the mark left in their flesh by circumcision. Paul is, by the standards of the law, exemplary in his Jewish pedigree: lawfully circumcised, descended from the tribe of Benjamin, and a trained Pharisee. Paul even mentions his earlier persecution of the church and concludes: "in righteousness based on the law I was blameless" (3:6). Once Paul experienced faith in Christ, however, he came to see aspects of his former life and its gains based on the works of the law as rubbish (in Greek, *skubalon*: "shit, dung, garbage") (3:8). Paul's insight was that righteousness comes from God, not from the works of the law, such as male circumcision. In fact, Paul considered himself and his fellow believers in Christ as the true circumcision (3:3). Paul offers a substitute for the credential of male circumcision touted by others: possession of God's Spirit and worship through that Spirit trump whatever status could (however wrongly) be claimed by the circumcision faction.

## Select Details from Paul's Life

What new personal information does Paul reveal to the Philippians that he did not communicate to the Galatians?

- Circumcised on the eighth day (as the law required, see Leviticus 12:3)
- An Israelite of the tribe of Benjamin (one of Israel's most celebrated families)
- Of Hebrew parentage (pure bloodlines)
- A Pharisee (learned and observant in the oral and written law)

These details about Paul's life were essential to his response to those "enemies of the cross of Christ" demanding male circumcision of the Gentiles. These additional details about Paul's life complement what was learned about Paul in Galatians 1–2.

## Ethics

Paul includes two main ethical exhortations in Philippians: serve each other in humility and be blameless for the day of Christ. Paul's plea for humility appears within the framework of both positive and negative models. Paul's conviction in the inevitability of the Parousia gives weight to his challenge to be blameless.

### Serve in Humility

Paul places a high value on service and sees it as a central component to community life. Authentic and effectual service must be grounded in an attitude of humility, and Paul sets a high standard in this regard (2:3b). He suggests adopting a practical perspective in meeting this ethical norm, advising each community member to care for others as much as themselves (2:4).

Paul saw Christ as modeling humble service to the world, and he urged the Philippians to adopt "the same attitude" (2:5). Jesus, who is both Christ and Lord (2:11), embodied humility, especially in his death on the cross (2:8). Precisely because of Christ's humble service, "God greatly exalted him" (2:9a).

Throughout the letter, Paul offers both positive and negative models of humble service. Paul sees himself and his attitude in prison as modeling how Christ lived his life in humility and service. This situation gives Paul a reason to rejoice (1:18b). Paul also holds up Timothy and Epaphroditus to the Philippians as examples of humble

### The Philippians' Gift to Paul in Prison

In closing the letter, Paul expresses his gratitude to the Philippians for the gifts he received from them both during his current stay in prison and earlier when he was in Thessalonica (4:16–18). Paul describes the gift he received from Epaphroditus while in prison as "a fragrant aroma, an acceptable sacrifice, pleasing to God" (4:18b). Paul draws a parallel here between the gift he receives from the Philippians and the thanksgiving offerings Israel made to God in the Temple (see, for example, Ezekiel 20:41).

In his second letter to the Corinthians, Paul refers to the financial gifts the churches in Macedonia (presumably including Philippi) gave him during his time in Thessalonica (2 Cor 11:8–9). Paul's gratitude for the gifts that he has received over time from the Philippians and the Corinthians is rooted in his belief that these gifts help advance the gospel message.

service to the gospel message (2:19–30). On the other hand, he considers his opponents and enemies negative models, for they do not act in service of others or with humble hearts (1:28–30; 3:2–4,18–21).

## Blameless for the Day of Christ

Paul uses the shared belief in the Parousia among the Gentile Christians of Philippi to frame his discussion of being blameless (in Greek, *aproskopos*, meaning "not giving offense") upon Christ's return from heaven. Paul wants the Philippians to have a clear conscience at the eschaton. He groups the characteristics of being blameless into conduct and attitude.

First, Paul urges the believers to behave in a way "worthy of the gospel" (1:27). Second, Paul advises them to exercise the proper attitude by standing as "one" in spirit and mind (1:27), united in heart and mind (2:2). Paul considered aligning one's behavior to the gospel message and standing in solidarity with fellow Christians the sure way to maintaining a clear conscience in preparation for the Second Coming of Christ.

Paul insists that the Philippians take these ethical norms of conduct and attitude seriously (2:12). They can achieve success in this regard because God instills in the believer both the will and the desire to do so (2:13). God's grace, which brings salvation to the believer, offers an alternative way of being and serves as a source of pride for Paul at the eschaton (2:14–16).

Once again, Paul urges the Philippians to act out of humility in terms of interactions with each other and preparation for the return of Christ.

## Perfect Maturity

Paul used the Greek term *teteleiōmai* (to attain perfect maturity) only once in his writings, in Philippians 3:12. (Pauline scholars refer to a term that appears only once in Paul's writings as a *hapax legomenon*.)

Clearly, Paul does not believe he has achieved perfect maturity (3:13–14). In these verses, Paul may be referring to some (perhaps his opponents) who claim to have attained full spiritual maturity.

## Summary: Theology and Ethics in Philippians

### CORE CONCEPTS

- Paul remains firm in his belief in the Parousia (the coming of Christ).
- Paul sees his own suffering and that of the Philippians as a source of unity for the church.
- Paul urges that the Philippians strive to attain the high standard of being blameless in conduct and attitude.

### SUPPLEMENTAL INFORMATION

- Paul writes of his uncertain future while in prison, especially the possibility of being put to death.
- Scholars debate whether Paul wrote the text of Philippians 2:5–11 or incorporated earlier Christian material because it fit the situation in Philippi.
- Paul urges the Philippians to "stand firm" in the faith as means of combating their opponents.
- Paul uses select details from his life as evidence of God's righteousness made manifest by faith in Christ and not works of the law.
- Paul uses himself and his opponents as models to reinforce his theology and ethics.
- For Paul, humble service to others shows one's moral and ethical behavior.

## Questions for Review

1. For what occasion does Paul write his Letter to the Philippians?
2. How do scholars use Acts to surmise that Philippians was an early Christian community Paul founded?
3. What are the most likely dates and places of composition for Philippians?
4. Who were Timothy and Epaphroditus in relation to Paul and the Philippians?

5. Why do scholars debate about the literary unity of Philippians?

6. How has Paul's view on the Parousia in Philippians shifted from in previous letters?

7. What are some characteristics of church unity for Paul?

8. How do select details from Paul's life help Paul answer his opponents?

9. According to Paul, why is being blameless essential when Christ returns?

10. For Paul, how is humility connected to service?

## Questions for Reflection

1. Why do you think Paul writes a letter filled with joy as he faces possible death in prison?

2. Do you think the Letter to the Philippians reads more like a fragmented letter or a single, unified one?

3. How do you think the Philippians might have reacted to Paul's dilemma between life and death while in prison?

4. What do you think the two female church leaders in Philippi disagreed about?

## Recommendations for Further Reading

Heil, John Paul. *Philippians: Let Us Rejoice in Being Conformed to Christ.* Atlanta, GA: Society of Biblical Literature, 2010.

Heil argues for the literary unity of Philippians. Employing the literary-critical approach of reader response, Heil views Paul as the implied author and the Philippian congregation as implied reader as a method for understanding more clearly the letter's message and intent.

Holloway, Paul A. *Consolation in Philippians: Philosophical Sources and Rhetorical Strategies.* Cambridge, UK: Cambridge University Press, 2001.

Holloway examines ancient rhetorical means of exhortation to argue that Philippians is best understood within its original social and cultural context as a "letter of consolation." Holloway sees Philippians as a single, unified letter in which Paul attempts to console the Christians in Philippi who have concerns about Paul's imprisonment as well as the current internal and external struggles of the congregation.

Martin, Ralph P., and Brian J. Dodd, eds. *Where Christology Began: Essays on Philippians 2*. Louisville, KY: Westminster John Knox Press, 1998.

This book consists of ten essays from a group of international scholars who take various approaches to interpreting the material of Philippians 2:5–11. These scholars explore the literary, theological, and lexical dimensions of this text, which has commanded the attention of New Testament interpreters for the past century.

Peterman, Gerald W. *Paul's Gift from Philippi: Conventions of Gift Exchange and Christian Giving*. Cambridge, UK: Cambridge University Press, 2001.

Peterman offers interesting insights in the language of social reciprocity found in Philippians, especially in 4:10–20. He explores the phenomenon of social reciprocity in both Jewish literature and in the Greco-Roman world, arguing that Paul viewed the act of "giving and receiving" not so much in terms of financial support between himself and his congregations but more in terms of the advancement of the gospel.

Thurston, Bonnie B., and Judith M. Ryan. *Philippians and Philemon*. Sacra Pagina 10. Collegeville, MN: The Liturgical Press, 2005.

In this commentary, Thurston presents the historical and literary background to Philippians, focusing on such areas as the place of women in the Philippian church and the form and structure of the letter in light of its purpose. Thurston sees Philippians as a hortatory letter of friendship with Paul structuring the letter by using contrasting models on how friends and enemies behave.

# CHAPTER 8

# Philemon

## INTRODUCTION

Like Philippians, Paul wrote the Letter to Philemon, a church leader, from prison. Therefore, the same question of which imprisonment arises: Rome, Caesarea, or Ephesus? This book maintains that Paul wrote the Letter to Philemon a short time after Philippians. Section 1 of chapter 8 considers the historical context of Philemon, in particular, the setting of the letter and slavery in the ancient world. Section 2 examines the letter's underlying theology, including Christian fellowship and love, and its implicit ethical themes, such as Christian freedom and social relations as well as the call for service on behalf of the gospel.

## A Narrative Theology

In his Letter to Philemon, Paul presents theological and ethical principles primarily through narrative rather than by explicitly discussing such principles, as he did in other letters. There is no discussion of the Parousia as seen in 1 Thessalonians and Philippians. Absent is any reference to justification by faith as articulated in Galatians and Romans. Paul does not mention the Resurrection of Christ or the gifts of the Holy Spirit as he does in 1 Corinthians. Missing as well are the ethical teachings found in some of Paul's previous letters, such as the call to live a holy life (1 Thessalonians and 2 Corinthians) and proper conduct at worship services (1 Corinthians).

Rather, the theology in this letter is embedded in Paul's discourse with Philemon. Throughout the letter, Paul discusses theology and ethics specifically as they pertain to Philemon's relationship to his slave, Onesimus. Paul encourages Philemon to treat Onesimus, who has converted to the faith, as "a brother . . . in the Lord" (v. 16). He urges Philemon to act out of their shared "partnership in the faith" (v. 6). In his Letter to Philemon, in fact, Paul applies his theology and ethics to a specific and focused issue: Philemon's relationship with Onesimus, making the bold assertion that Onesimus is no longer Philemon's slave but a beloved brother in Christ.

## A Letter to a Household and an Individual

The six previous letters of Paul were sent either to a single church in a city (Thessalonica and Corinth), to a cluster of churches in a province (Galatia), or to a group of Christians in a city (Romans and Philippians). The address and greeting of this letter refers to three individuals as well as the household of Philemon, "Paul, a prisoner for Christ Jesus, and Timothy our brother, to Philemon, our beloved and our co-worker, to Apphia our sister, to Archippus our fellow soldier, and to the church at your house. Grace to you and peace from God our Father and the Lord Jesus Christ" (Phlm 1–3).

With the exception of the multiple individuals addressed, the entire letter is addressed to *you*, singular, not *you*, plural. This suggests that the letter is written primarily to Philemon, though Paul also wants the congregation there to know what he is asking of Philemon. Addressing the letter to Philemon and his household is appropriate given that the nature of Paul's request would have repercussions. Asking Philemon to treat one of his slaves as a "brother" was extraordinary, it may well have had an effect on other household slaves (if he had others) who would view expressing faith in Christ as a means of manumission (that is, being freed from slavery). Paul's request also had the potential to affect other slave-owners in Philemon's community who may well have wondered about the dangers this new Christian religious movement presents, especially if it involves freeing slaves.

## HISTORICAL CONTEXT OF PHILEMON

Aside from it being written from prison, the letter offers few historical details about its date and place of composition. Close parallels to the disputed Pauline Letter to the Colossians offers some possibilities for the historical setting.

## Outline of Philemon

| 1–3 | **Address and Greeting** |
|---|---|
| | The letter is co-sent by Paul and Timothy during Paul's imprisonment (in an undisclosed location) to Philemon, Apphia, and Archippus, and to the church that met in Philemon's house. |
| 4–7 | **Thanksgiving** |
| | Paul offers thanksgiving to God for Philemon's love and faith in the Lord Jesus and for "all the holy ones" (5), and prays for success in their partnership. Paul speaks of the "joy and encouragement" (7) he and the holy ones have experienced from Philemon's love. |
| 8–20 | **Paul's Intercession for Onesimus** |
| | In the body of the letter, Paul appeals to Philemon on behalf of his slave, Onesimus, whom he had met and converted while in prison. Paul sends Onesimus back to Philemon, asking him to treat Onesimus now as a "brother . . . in the Lord" (16). Paul remarks that although he would like to retain Onesimus to serve him while in prison, he nonetheless plans to send Onesimus back to Philemon and requests that Philemon "welcome him [Onesimus] as you would me" (17). Paul offers to pay Philemon for any costs Onesimus incurred while away from home and make restitution for any loss to Philemon because of his absence. |
| 21–22 | **Closing Remarks** |
| | As the letter draws to close, Paul expresses his hope to visit Philemon soon, expressing trust in Philemon's compliance with Paul's request on behalf of Onesimus. |
| 23–25 | **Final Greetings and Blessing** |
| | Paul offers greetings to the recipients of his letter from a fellow prisoner (Epaphras), and four co-workers (Mark, Aristarchus, Demas, and Luke). He then concludes with a short blessing. |

## Author and Audience

The Letter to Philemon is co-sent by Paul and Timothy. Of Paul's seven undisputed letters, four are co-sent with Timothy: Philemon, Philippians, 2 Corinthians and 1 Thessalonians. Paul uses the first-person singular (*I*) seventeen times in this short letter, indicating that he alone wrote it. He addresses the letter to three individuals (Philemon, Apphia, and Archippus) and "to the church at your house" (1:2). Tradition has often identified Philemon and Apphia as husband and wife, but no evidence from the letter itself verifies such a claim. Philemon is head of the household in which the community gathers ("the church at your house") and Paul's trusted co-worker. The use of *sister* in reference to Apphia is likely intended to parallel the description of Timothy as *brother*. Paul uses these familial terms to designate fellow believers in Christ and co-workers. In referring

© Erich Lessing / Art Resource, NY

The city of Colossae, located in the region of the Lycus Valley in western Asia Minor (pictured here), is often identified as the location of Philemon's household.

to Archippus, Paul uses the term *fellow soldier* (*sustratiōtēs*), which appears only one other time in Paul's letters, as a descriptor for Epaphroditus (Phil 2:25). Paul considers Archippus (like Epaphroditus) a co-worker in his battle to preach the gospel message.

The intended destination of the letter—Philemon's household—is often identified as the region of the Lycus Valley (western Asia Minor), in or near the city of Colossae.[1] The names appearing in the letters of Philemon and Colossians show considerable overlap, as can be seen in the address (Timothy: Phlm 1; Col 1:10), the body of the letter (Onesimus: Phlm 10; Col 4:9), and the final greeting (Epaphras, Mark, Aristarchus, Demas, and Luke: Phlm 23–24; Col 4:10–14). These commonalities have drawn the attention of scholars, with many concluding that Philemon lived the city of Colossae.

With little solid evidence in hand, scholars can only infer basic facts about Philemon from the letter. First, he was a homeowner with a house large enough to host gatherings for the congregation. Second, he owned at least one slave, Onesimus. Third, given his status as a private homeowner with slave(s), and a home large enough for a church gathering, he probably had considerable wealth.

## A Twenty-five Verse Letter?

The Letter to Philemon contains 335 words. It is by far the shortest of Paul's surviving letters; Romans, the longest, contains 7,111 words. Although brief in comparison with the other undisputed letters, Philemon actually more closely aligns with the length of an average letter in Paul's day. Despite its brevity, it contains all the standard elements of a Pauline letter: address and greeting, thanksgiving, body, final greetings, and blessing.

---

1. See Bonnie B. Thurston and Judith M. Ryan, *Philippians and Philemon*. SP 10 (Collegeville, MN; Liturgical, 2005), 178–179; Udo Schnelle, *The History and Theology of the New Testament Writings*, trans. M. Eugene Boring (London: SCM Press, 1998), 145–146; Douglas J. Moo, *The Letter to the Colossians and to Philemon* (Grand Rapids, MI: Eerdmans, 2008), 361–363.

## Date and Place of Composition

The same questions about the date and place of composition of Philippians also apply to Philemon. Paul wrote both letters from prison (Phlm 9,10,13; Phil 1:7,13,14,17), but neither have internal evidence that would definitively identify which imprisonment: Rome, Ephesus, or Caesarea.[2]

Most scholars lean toward either the imprisonment in Rome or Ephesus as the place of composition for Philemon. The traditional view maintains that Paul wrote the letter from Rome, sometime after Philippians. However, the distance between Rome and western Asia Minor—following the theory that Philemon's home was in the Lycus Valley, possibly Colossae—is nearly one thousand miles. That would make traveling problematic for Timothy or any other letter carrier. At five hundred miles between them, Colossae and Caesarea were only about half as far apart; and less than one hundred and fifty miles separated Ephesus from Colossae, which makes the trek

### Paul: "Old Man" or "Ambassador"?

In Philemon 9, Paul refers to himself using the term *presbutēs*, which can be translated as either *old man* or *ambassador*: "I rather urge you out of love, being as I am, Paul, an old man [ambassador], and now also a prisoner for Christ Jesus." If Paul used the term *presbutēs* in the sense of *old man*, then it offers a clue to his age during his imprisonment. If *presbutēs* is more accurately translated as *ambassador*, then Paul may be playing on a paradoxical image of himself as both "prisoner" (*desmios*, Phlm 1, 9) and "ambassador" for Jesus Christ. In proclaiming his gospel message to the Gentiles, he suffers as a prisoner for Christ. As a prisoner, he also preaches the gospel, thus, serving as an ambassador for Christ.

---

2. Udo Schnelle, *Apostle Paul: His Life and Theology*, trans. M. Eugene Boring (Grand Rapids, MI: Baker Academic, 2005), 377–378, maintains that Paul wrote Philemon from his imprisonment in Rome, shortly after the writing of Philippians. Ryan, 179–181, argues that Philemon was written during Paul's imprisonment in Ephesus, in the mid-50s CE. Both Schnelle and Ryan believe that Paul wrote both Philippians and Philemon during the same imprisonment.

between those two cities much more manageable. Thus, some scholars favor Ephesus.

In terms of the date and place of composition, all three imprisonments are plausible; however, Rome and Ephesus offer better possibilities than Caesarea. Just as with Philippians, though, the available evidence does not support the Ephesian hypothesis or the Cesarean hypothesis over the traditional view of Rome as the place of composition for Philemon. Paul's imprisonment in Rome is commonly dated to the early 60s CE, affirming Rome as the place of composition and dating the writing of Philemon to sometime after Philippians, in late 60 CE, from Rome.

## Summary: Historical Setting for Philemon

| | |
|---|---|
| Author | Paul |
| Audience | Philemon, Apphia, Archippus, and Philemon's house church |
| Date of Composition | Late 60 CE (early mid-50s CE, if Ephesus; late 50s CE, if Caesarea) |
| Place of Composition | Imprisonment in Rome (possibly imprisonment in Ephesus or Caesarea) |

## Slavery in the Ancient World

Paul's Letter to Philemon has garnered much attention, in large measure, because it offers a glimpse of the first-century CE world of slavery in the Roman Empire and how the earliest Christians responded to this social and cultural reality.[3] During Paul's day,

---

3. See Keith R. Bradley, *Slaves and Masters in the Roman Empire: A Study in Social Context* (Cambridge, UK: Cambridge University Press, 1984) for a good introductory study on slavery in the ancient world; see also Ryan, 169–176, who offers background information on slavery in the Greco-Roman world, slavery in Israel, and freedom and slavery in Paul's letters. Ryan provides many additional sources for review and study on slavery in the ancient world.

Slavery was embedded in the social, political, and economic fabric of the Roman Empire. This engraving depicts a young slave serving patricians in ancient Rome.

many inhabitants of the Roman Empire were enslaved. Estimates range from 25 to 50 percent of the total population and higher for urban areas.[4] Slaves primarily came from the ranks of foreigners captured as prisoners of war, and many, born to slave parents, became slaves by birth. They provided a cheap workforce vital to the economic growth and stability of the Roman Empire. Slaves captured in war brought with them many useful skills and abilities, and slaves by birth often received education and training in specific skilled and semiskilled professions. Consequently, virtually all areas of Roman life depended upon slave labor. Slaves worked in a range of capacities, from skilled positions (for example, as lawyers, architects, physicians, philosophers, and grammarians) to manual labor (such as working on farms, in mines and refineries, and in ships' galleys). Wealthy homeowners with slaves put them to work in and around the house, which involved all levels of domestic chores from tutoring children to tending to household duties such as cooking and cleaning.

Slaves had some rights under Roman law, but these were limited. They could, for example, marry and have children, but their children became property of the master of the household. Some

---

4. Ryan, 170; Schnelle, 147.

slaves were allowed to accumulate their own money, which under certain circumstances could be used to buy the slave's freedom. A master could also grant freedom to a slave, a practice known as manumission. Typically, a slave was freed only if it worked to the advantage of the master. By and large, the treatment a slave experienced depended almost entirely upon the will and the disposition of the master. In this regard, the experience of slavery on a day-to-day basis could vary significantly.

Details from Paul's surviving letters offer some insights into the state of slaves and slavery. For example, the list of twenty-six names identified in Romans 16 contained the names of slaves—Andronicus and Urbanus (Rom 16:7,9)—as well as heads of households, for instance, Aristobulus and Narcissus. Paul's greeting to those "who belong to the family" of Aristobulus and Narcissus (Rom 16:10–11) almost certainly included the slaves within their households.

In 1 Corinthians 7:21–24, Paul offered his most extensive discussion on slavery, giving advice to slaves. This counsel to the slaves in Corinth provides a remarkable commentary on his position on the practice.[5] Paul honors the status of slave and free equally, placing greater value on "being called" than on one's current station in life. Paul dismisses the traditional markers separating people into classes and instead views all Christ-believers as in the state of God's grace. In the greetings of some letters, Paul referred to himself as "a slave of Christ Jesus" (Rom 1:1; Phil 1:1), by which he meant that he would serve no one but Christ.

Although Paul apparently did not discourage slaves from seeking freedom or masters from granting freedom (1 Cor 7:21), he saw the change in status from slave to free person as relative. From Paul's perspective, the current social structures were a temporary and even fading reality: "For the world in its present form is passing away" (1 Cor 7:31b). Paul believed the imminent return of Christ would transform the world along with its accompanying social structures. Until then, slaves should enjoy a newfound freedom within their

---

5. For a discussion on slavery and the ideological construction of the human body, see Dale B. Martin, *The Corinthian Body* (New Haven, CT: Yale University Press, 1999).

congregation of faith, which made no distinctions between slave and free, male and female, Jew and Gentile (Gal 3:28). All were united in the body of Christ.

The Letter to Philemon clearly indicates that Onesimus is one of Philemon's household slaves and applies Paul's attitude toward slavery, as described in previous letters, to this specific situation. Paul calls upon Philemon to release Onesimus from slavery (Phlm 16a), and he requests that Philemon treat Onesimus as a "brother" Phlm 16a). Paul urges Philemon, as a Christ-believer, to see no distinction between Onesimus and the other believers in his household church.

## Onesimus' Encounter with Paul in Prison: Accidental or Intentional?

Scholars have debated about the conditions under which Onesimus and Paul met in prison. One theory holds that Onesimus was a runaway slave who stole money from his master Philemon and that he met Paul in prison because of his capture. Tradition has typically identified Onesimus this way, portraying him as a thief and runaway slave based on Paul's words to Philemon in verse 18: "And if he [Onesimus] has done you any injustices or owes you anything, charge it to me."

In recent years, other theories have developed regarding the circumstances that brought Paul and Onesimus together. One such hypothesis advances the idea that Onesimus purposely sought out Paul to serve as his advocate in a dispute with his master, Philemon, a practice acceptable under Roman slave laws. Another theory maintains that Philemon may have purposely sent Onesimus to assist Paul in his imprisonment, similar to how the Philippians sent Epaphroditus to support Paul during his time in prison.

Regardless of the reasons for the meeting, it resulted in Paul converting Onesimus to the faith. Paul's joy at Onesimus' conversion prompted him to write to his co-worker Philemon with the good news.

> ## Summary: Historical Context of Philemon
>
> ### CORE CONCEPTS
> - Philemon was written from prison, probably in Rome, and sometime after the letter to the Philippians.
> - In Paul's day, slavery in the Roman Empire was embedded within the fabric of society.
> - Paul's belief in the imminent return of Christ grounded his teaching that one's status (slave or free) is relative, because social structures were a temporary and fading reality.
>
> ### SUPPLEMENTAL INFORMATION
> - Paul addresses his letter to three specific individuals and to the congregation that met in Philemon's house, but the letter is intended primarily for Philemon.
> - Onesimus was a slave within the household of Philemon.
> - Philemon's house was large enough to host gatherings of the congregation.
> - The Letter to Philemon provides no definitive information about its date or place of composition.
> - Scholars estimate that slaves comprised 25–50 percent of the population of the Roman Empire in Paul's day.
> - Paul advocated that Christian communities make no distinction between slave and free.

# THEOLOGY AND ETHICS OF PHILEMON

The Letter to Philemon provides a good case study of various aspects of Paul's theological vision. This is implicit in his discussion of some familiar themes such as fellowship and love, freedom in Christ, and service on behalf of the gospel. Paul draws on these ideas throughout his letter.

## Theology

### Christian Fellowship

The relationship between Philemon and Onesimus fundamentally changed once Paul became convinced that Onesimus truly believed in

Christ. Paul expected Philemon to view Onesimus "no longer as a slave but . . . [as] a brother" (Phlm 16). He even leveraged their relationship to try to convince Philemon to accept Onesimus into the fellowship (*koinōnia*) of the faith by asking Philemon to welcome Onesimus as Philemon would welcome Paul (Phlm 17). In doing so, Paul expresses his concern for Onesimus, the Christian in the weaker relative position.

Paul's request that Philemon accept Onesimus as he would other believers in his household is consistent with the views on Christian freedom and fellowship he expressed in previous letters (1 Cor 12:12–13; Gal 3:28). Paul applies his theology of Christian fellowship to the real-life situation of Philemon and Onesimus. Scholars are uncertain how Philemon reacted to Paul's language and approach here. Some see the reference to an "Onesimus" in the Letter to the Colossians (4:9) as evidence that Philemon complied with Paul's request.

## Paul's Familial Language

In this very brief letter, Paul uses the language of family remarkably often:

- Timothy, our brother (Phlm 1)
- Apphia, our sister (Phlm 2)
- God our Father (Phlm 3)
- Philemon, brother to Paul (Phlm 7,20)
- Onesimus, whose father I have become (Phlm 10)
- Onesimus, brother to Philemon (Phlm 16)

By including Timothy, God, and now Onesimus into the familial language of the members of Philemon's house church, Paul invites Philemon to expand his vision of Christian fellowship.

### Christian Love

Paul uses the language of love (*agapē* in Greek) in various contexts throughout his letter to Philemon. He refers to Philemon as "our beloved and our co-worker" (Phlm 1) and speaks of the "joy and encouragement" he has personally received from Philemon's love (Phlm 7). It is out of this love that Paul advocates using Onesimus "on your [Philemon's] behalf in my imprisonment for the gospel" (Phlm 13).

Christian love (*agapē*) constitutes a central tenet of Paul's gospel message, and he ranks it among the highest of Christian virtues (1 Cor 13:13). Paul sees the love of God made manifest in believers in Christ (Rom 5:5). In light of this, Paul wants Philemon to act on his request out of love rather than out of a sense of duty or obligation: "Although I have the full right in Christ to order you to do what is proper . . . I did not want to do anything without your consent, so that the good you do might not be forced but voluntary" (Phlm 8, 14).

# Ethics

In Paul's view the ethical principles of Christian freedom and service stand at the heart of the request he makes of Philemon. Paul's expectation of an impending release from prison and visit to Philemon serves as an incentive for Philemon to put into practice the moral and ethical values of the Christian congregation he leads.

## Christian Freedom and Social Relations

In his letter, Paul does not advocate for the abolition of slavery altogether. Instead, Paul holds Philemon, the leader of his house church, to the same high standard he asks of all Christ-believers. He expects Philemon to treat all household Christ-believers as brothers and sisters, in anticipation of Christ's imminent return. Paul is requesting that Philemon, as master of the household, change his attitude and disposition toward his slave, Onesimus. By enforcing such a standard, the Christian community offers a social reality counter to the norms of the larger Roman society.

This expectation for Philemon and his household is consistent with the community rules and regulations Paul established elsewhere. Paul even exhorted members of the Christian congregations in Rome—a community he did not establish and, therefore, held no authority over—to adhere to his high ethical standards. He desires Christ-believers to celebrate with each other the freedom all enjoy in the Christian fellowship that developed as a result of the death and Resurrection of Christ.

## Instructions to Philemon

In this short letter, Paul lists four expectations for Philemon:

- Allow Paul to retain Onesimus in order to serve him in prison (Phlm 13)
- Welcome Onesimus back home as you would welcome Paul (Phlm 17)
- Charge to Paul anything that Onesimus owes (Phlm 18)
- Prepare a guest room for Paul (Phlm 22)

### Service on Behalf of the Gospel

Paul's request can be summed up as follows: He wants Philemon to release Onesimus to Paul so that Onesimus can serve Paul while in prison. However, Paul offers no details about what this might entail. Whatever assistance he required of Onesimus, Paul saw that assistance as helpful in spreading the gospel message.

In his Letter to the Philippians, Paul viewed his imprisonment as an opportunity to advance the gospel (Phil 1:12–14). He even praised the Philippians for their assistance to him in this effort (Phil 1:7). Paul expressed his gratitude to the Philippians for sending him Epaphroditus, whom he considered "your messenger and minister in my need" (Phil 2:25), during his imprisonment. Paul acknowledged, "I am very well supplied because of what I received from you through Epaphroditus" (Phil 4:18). It may be that Paul expects Philemon to offer similar service to him through his slave, Onesimus.

## The List of Paul's Co-workers

Paul identifies several "co-workers" in the final greeting of his Letter to Philemon: Epaphras, Mark, Aristarchus, Demas, and Luke (Phlm 23–24). Paul's co-workers have captured the attention of scholars

*Continued*

for two reasons: First, these same names, as well as the name of Onesimus, appear in the Letter to Colossians, which provides details about each of them (Col 4:7–14). Second, the names of Mark and Aristarchus appear in the Acts of the Apostles, and the name of Demas is mentioned in 2 Timothy 4:10.

Later church tradition identifies two of the co-workers Paul mentions in the Letter to Philemon—Mark and Luke—as the Gospel writers. The four New Testament Gospels, all written between 70–100 CE, were originally composed anonymously. About one hundred years after their production, church fathers attributed two of the New Testament Gospels to apostles of Jesus (Matthew and John) and two to co-workers of Paul, Mark and Luke.

## Summary: Theology and Ethics in Philemon

### CORE CONCEPTS

- Theology and ethics in the Letter to Philemon is more implicit than in Paul's other undisputed letters.
- In his request regarding Onesimus, Paul appeals to Philemon's sense of Christian love and fellowship.
- Paul expects Onesimus to experience freedom in Christ within Philemon's house church.

### SUPPLEMENTAL INFORMATION

- Paul anticipates release from prison when he writes his letter to Philemon.
- Paul expects Philemon and Onesimus to experience "fellowship" given Onesimus' status as a Christ-believer.
- Paul relies on Philemon's "love" to persuade Philemon to grant his request of Onesimus.
- According to Paul, Christian communities structure social relationships differently from the larger society.

*Continued*

> **Summary: Theology and Ethics in Philemon** *Continued*
>
> • Paul hopes to retain Onesimus to attend to his needs during imprisonment.
> • The list of Paul's co-workers in the final greeting parallels those in the Letter to the Colossians.

## Questions for Review

1. To whom does Paul address his Letter to Philemon? What aspect of the letter suggests that Philemon is the main recipient of the letter?
2. Who were Philemon and Onesimus?
3. What are the possible dates and places of composition for Philemon?
4. What is known about slavery in the ancient world?
5. Which of Paul's surviving letters offer insights into his view of slavery?
6. What does Paul request from Philemon with regard to Onesimus?
7. How does Paul expect the relationship between Philemon and Onesimus to change?
8. What are Paul's specific instructions to Philemon?
9. What evidence in the letter suggests that Paul anticipates release from prison?
10. Whom does Paul list as co-workers in his final greeting?

## Questions for Reflection

1. How do you imagine Philemon and his household reacted to Paul's letter?
2. Is slavery always wrong?
3. What challenges might Onesimus have faced upon his return?
4. Why do you think the Letter to Philemon was included among Paul's surviving letters?

# Recommendations for Further Reading

Balch, David L., and Carolyn Osiek, eds. *Early Christian Families in Context: An Interdisciplinary Dialogue.* Grand Rapids, MI: Eerdmans, 2003.

Thirteen scholars contribute essays to this book, which focuses on the role of families within the Roman, Jewish, and Christian world. The essays are grouped into six categories: Archeology of *Domus* and *Insulae* (household and islands/dwellings); Domestic Values; Women; Slaves; Children; and Implications for Theological Education. In the section on slaves, the essays include "Slave Families and Slaves in Families" and "Female Slaves, *Porneia*, and the Limits of Obedience."

Bradley, Keith R. *Slaves and Masters in the Roman Empire: A Study in Social Context.* Cambridge, UK: Cambridge University Press, 1984.

Although somewhat dated, Bradley's work is often cited in scholarly discussions on slavery and is a very good introductory book on Roman imperial society. Bradley covers a range of topics including the loyalty and obedience of slaves, the family life of slaves, the process of manumission (masters freeing slaves), and the fear, abuse, and violence endured by slaves living in a "slave society."

Fitzmyer, Joseph A. *The Letter to Philemon.* The Anchor Bible. New York: Doubleday, 2000.

Fitzmyer provides a verse-by-verse commentary on the Letter to Philemon. It includes an excellent introduction addressing the standard historical questions of authorship and date and place of composition along with a discussion on slavery in antiquity, the significance of the letter, and theological teaching of the letter.

Harrill, Albert J. *Slaves in the New Testament: Literary, Social, and Moral Dimensions.* Minneapolis: Fortress, 2006.

Harrill provides an analysis of slaves and slavery in the New Testament. He examines three letters of Paul (Philemon, 1 Corinthians, and Romans), Luke-Acts, and the household codes related to slaves. Harrill concludes with a chapter on the use of the New Testament in the history of American slavery.

Joshel, Sandra R. *Slavery in the Roman World.* Cambridge, UK: Cambridge University Press, 2010.

Joshel covers various topics in her treatment of slavery in the Roman world. She begins with an introduction to Roman slavery, including how slavery was viewed as part of the Roman social order. Joshel then explores topics such as the sale of slaves, the practice of slave owners, and the type of labor slaves engaged in. She includes a helpful annotated bibliography of ancient sources on slavery.

# PART 2

The Disputed Letters and
Post-Pauline Writings

# CHAPTER 9

# Colossians, Ephesians, and Second Thessalonians

## INTRODUCTION

Most scholars today categorize the letters of Colossians, Ephesians, and 2 Thessalonians as deutero-Pauline.[1] *Deutero-* is a Greek prefix meaning "second or secondary." Although these letters are attributed to Paul and, thereby, draw upon Paul's authority, they were, in fact, written by unknown authors, probably a generation or two after his death.[2] The authors who wrote under Paul's name applied aspects of his theology and ethics to their contemporary situation. The first section of this chapter considers the historical context of these three deutero-Pauline letters. In addition to discussing their historical settings (authors and audiences, dates and places of composition), it explores three topics that offer insight into the nature of the deutero-Pauline letters: pseudepigraphic writings; the theory of a Pauline school; and the theological, linguistic, and stylistic features peculiar to these three letters. The second section of this chapter examines the theology of each letter: the themes of Christ, the church, and the Parousia in Colossians; Christ and the church in Ephesians; and the Parousia in 2 Thessalonians. It also discusses ethical instructions

---

1. Scholars are largely unanimous in categorizing Ephesians as deutero-Pauline. There is scholarly debate on the deutero-Pauline status of Colossians and 2 Thessalonians. For this reason, these two letters are commonly labeled *disputed*. The nature of the dispute for each of these letters will be addressed later in the chapter.

2. The date of Paul's death remains uncertain, but early church tradition holds that Paul was beheaded in Rome during the reign of Emperor Nero (54–68 CE), most likely during the years between 62 and 64 CE when persecution of Christians in Rome was widespread. See chapter 1, Paul of Tarsus, for further details on his death.

associated with "household codes" of conduct, various vices to avoid and virtues to practice, and the confrontation of disorder within the community.

## The Dispute Begins

The question of who actually authored the thirteen New Testament letters bearing Paul's name first surfaced in the late eighteenth and early nineteenth century with the rise of modern historical criticism. Over time, scholars studied all the writings of the Old and New Testaments in order to answer fundamental questions: Who were the actual biblical authors? To whom did these authors originally address their writings? When were these texts written, from what location, and why? When they applied the historical and critical methods of interpretation to the thirteen letters of Paul, scholars began noticing differences among them in language, style, and theology.

An application of these differences resulted in their further categorization, with some letters classified as "undisputed" and others considered "deutero-Pauline" or written by someone other than Paul. Scholars, however, have not universally accepted this modern division into undisputed and deutero-Pauline. Indeed, it has led to a dispute about the status of the six letters that are typically classified as deutero-Pauline: Colossians, Ephesians, and 2 Thessalonians, and the three Pastoral Letters (1 Timothy, 2 Timothy, and Titus). Thus, scholars commonly speak of the undisputed and disputed Pauline letters.

## The Dispute Today

Scholars today have reached a consensus regarding the seven undisputed letters of Paul. The language, style, and theology of Romans, 1 and 2 Corinthians, Galatians, Philippians, 1 Thessalonians, and Philemon exhibit a general consistency that unifies these letters and clearly points to a single author, Paul. Discrepancies in the language, style, and theology of the six remaining letters convince many scholars of their secondary, or deutero-Pauline, status within the Pauline tradition. However, those arguing in favor of Pauline authorship of one or more of these letters have offered plausible explanations for the differences. A majority of scholars today believe that Paul's followers wrote Ephesians, 1 Timothy, 2 Timothy, and Titus after his death. However, scholarly opinion about the authorship of Colossians and 2 Thessalonians is not nearly as settled; thus, these letters are considered disputed.[3]

# HISTORICAL CONTEXT OF COLOSSIANS, EPHESIANS, AND 2 THESSALONIANS

Background information on the literary phenomenon of pseudepigraphy and the possible existence of one or more Pauline schools are helpful to understanding the letters of Colossians, Ephesians, and 2 Thessalonians. Additional information on their historical setting as well as the distinctive linguistic and stylistic features of each of these letters is also important for interpreting them and supporting the claim of their deutero-Pauline status.

## Pseudepigraphic Writings[4]

Within ancient Greek (and Latin) literature, texts ranging from philosophical treatises to personal letters were written by unknown authors in the name of notable historical figures such as Plato, Socrates, Aristotle, and Alexander the Great. In Jewish tradition, pseudepigraphy was also common.[5] For example, in the Torah, the Book of Deuteronomy is ascribed to Moses. The wisdom writings attribute numerous books to King Solomon, including for instance, sections of Proverbs and the Book of Ecclesiastes. Jewish apocalyptic literature, in particular, provides good examples of pseudepigraphy. Many texts, composed in Greek centuries after the Old Testament, were attributed to great figures of Israel's past, such as Adam and Eve (*The Life of Adam and Eve*), Enoch (*1*, *2*, and *3 Enoch*), the patriarchs

---

3. Although these letters are treated as deutero-Pauline in this book, arguments for Paul's authorship will be presented later in the chapter.

4. See Udo Schnelle, *The History and Theology of the New Testament Writings*, trans. M. Eugene Boring (London: SCM Press, 1998), 276–280, for a good discussion on pseudepigraphy as a historical and theological phenomenon.

5. For a comprehensive resource on the pseudepigrapha writings of the Old Testament, see *The Old Testament Pseudepigrapha*, vols. 1 and 2, ed. James H. Charlesworth (New York: Doubleday, 1983, 1985).

(*Testaments of the Twelve Patriarchs*), Moses (*Assumption of Moses*), and Elijah (*Apocalypse of Elijah*).

Relative to these ancient Greco-Roman and Jewish literary contexts, it is not so strange that some New Testament writings may also be pseudepigraphic. In fact, of the twenty-seven texts of the New Testament, almost half (twelve) fall into the category of pseudepigrapha. These were written in the name of a variety of figures from the apostolic period, including Paul (the letters of Colossians, Ephesians, 2 Thessalonians, 1 Timothy, 2 Timothy, and Titus), Peter (the letters of 1 and 2 Peter), James (the Letter of James), Jude (the Letter of Jude), and John (the letters of 2 and 3 John).

As part of the next generation of Christ-believers, these Christians and their congregations faced new and unprecedented challenges. Most of the original followers of Jesus, including Peter and Paul, had died; Christ had not yet returned; some Christ-believers experienced persecution; and false teachings were taking hold. Confronting these new realities required authoritative voices and some sense of a tradition, including an updated set of teachings upon which to draw. The authors of Colossians, Ephesians, and 2 Thessalonians believed that letters sent in Paul's name would invest contemporary teachings with a greater authority and a sense of tradition. These authors addressed their current circumstances and drew upon the names of the authority figures to legitimize their writings.

## Pauline Schools?

Scholars have asked what might account for the production of the deutero-Pauline letters. In addition to the precedent set by existent Jewish and Greek pseudepigraphic writings, other factors were likely at work. Some scholars have speculated that these may have included Paul's own training in a school, a developing tradition already at work about Jesus, and the dozens of co-workers associated with Paul and his missionary outreach to the Gentiles. Given these factors, some scholars have hypothesized about the existence of "Pauline schools" in order to explain the source of the deutero-Pauline letters.[6]

---

6. See Udo Schnelle, *Apostle Paul: His Life and Theology*, trans. M. Eugene Boring (Grand Rapids, MI: Baker Academic, 2005), 146–57, for an extended discussion on the Pauline school.

The idea of Pauline schools could perhaps be traced to Paul's own experience in a Pharisaic school. In Philippians 3:5–6, Paul mentions his training as a Pharisee, and in Galatians 1:14, he boasts of his success in the study of the law among his contemporaries.[7] However, because Paul never directly says where he received his Pharisaic training or from whom, scholars can only speculate about these specifics.

Coinciding with Paul's background was that, soon after the death of Jesus, "traditions" about Jesus' words and deeds had already formed and were being passed on to other believers, including Paul. In turn, Paul passed on these traditions to others (see, for example, 1 Cor 11:23–26 on Jesus' words at his final meal with this apostles; 15:3–7 on the list of Resurrection appearances). Also embedded within Paul's letters are baptismal formulas (see 2 Cor 1:21–22) and Christological texts (see Phil 2:6–11) used by the earliest Christ-believers, which offer some evidence of the formation of traditions and beliefs. A school of thought associated with Jesus appears to have been developing during Paul's missionary work with the Gentiles.

The many co-workers affiliated with Paul and the congregations he established also point to the possibility of one or more Pauline schools producing the deutero-Pauline letters.[8] Paul's seven surviving letters, written between 50 and 60 CE, attest to the apostle's collaboration with other believers in this literary endeavor. Five of the seven surviving letters were co-sent: 2 Corinthians, Philippians, and Philemon, by Paul and Timothy; 1 Thessalonians, by Paul, Timothy, and Silvanus; and 1 Corinthians, by Paul and Sosthenes. Paul also sent numerous delegates to communicate and problem-solve various theological and ethical issues within Pauline congregations; for example, he sent Timothy (1 Cor 4:17; Phil 2:19); Titus (2 Cor 8:6); Onesimus (Phlm 12); and Phoebe (Rom 16:1–2). Congregations also sent delegates to Paul to maintain lines of communication; for instance, Epaphroditus (Phil 4:18). It appears that during his nearly thirty years evangelizing the Gentiles, Paul surrounded himself with

---

7. According to Luke, Paul was trained in Jerusalem "at the feet of Gamaliel" and "was educated strictly" in Israel's ancestral law (Acts 22:3).

8. Paul's seven surviving letters mention nearly forty individuals by name.

many like-minded Christ-believers who viewed him as their leader, forming a loose network of relations that could have developed into one or more Pauline schools.

If these Pauline schools existed during Paul's lifetime, it is probable that Paul's co-workers contributed to their survival. Letters and other writings ascribed to Paul, such as Colossians, Ephesians, and 2 Thessalonians, may stem (at least in part) from the work of the Pauline schools continuing after the death of Paul. Whether the product of Pauline schools or other sources, these unknown authors used Paul's name and adapted his theology and ethics to their current circumstances after the loss of their leader.

## The Theology, Language, and Style Peculiar to These Letters

Scholars who argue for the deutero-Pauline status of these three letters often cite theological, linguistic, and stylistic characteristics that separate them from the seven undisputed letters. To be sure, each of the undisputed letters has varying features due to the different occasions for which Paul wrote; for instance, 1 Thessalonians is void of central Pauline themes such as justification by faith and Paul's anger at the Galatians for adopting a different gospel. However, in the case of Colossians, Ephesians, and 2 Thessalonians, the totality of the theological, linguistic, and stylistic aspects support the idea of non-Pauline authorship.

The theology present in each of these letters suggests development beyond Paul's lifetime. For example, even though Paul wrote on occasion of the cosmic significance of Christ (see 1 Cor 8:5–6), this idea dominates the letter to the Colossians, which offers an extensive discussion of Christ's saving work in the universe. The role and function of "the church" in Ephesians goes well beyond the assembly of the congregation that is seen in the undisputed letters. Ephesians describes the church as Christ's "body" and integral to God's plan for salvation (see Ephesians 1:22–23). The imminent return of Christ—which informs much of Paul's thinking (see Phil 1:6; Rom 13:11), and is especially prominent in 1 Thessalonians (see 1 Thess 4:13–18, 5:1–11)—receives a different treatment in 2 Thessalonians, which presents explanations for its delay.

The distinctive language in Colossians, Ephesians, and 2 Thessalonians, as compared with the vocabulary of the seven undisputed letters, likewise raises serious questions about Paul's authorship. These letters contain many words and phrases found nowhere else in the New Testament (*hapax legomena*).[9] Although the undisputed letters also contain some *hapax legomena*,[10] these appear with far greater frequency in Colossians, Ephesians, and 2 Thessalonians.[11] Furthermore, key Pauline terms such as *dikaiosunē* (righteousness), *koinōnia* (fellowship), and *nomos* (law) are altogether absent in these three letters.

The style of writing in these letters also supports their deutero-Pauline classification. Colossians and Ephesians, for example, contain much longer sentences and many more relative clauses than the undisputed letters (see Col 1:3–11; Eph 1:3–14). Rhetorical questions, frequent throughout Paul's letters (for example, 1 Thess 1:19; 1 Cor 1:13; 2 Cor 2:2; Gal 3:1; Rom 3:27; Phil 1:18) are completely absent from Colossians and Ephesians; only one rhetorical question occurs in 2 Thessalonians (2:5).

In some ways, the language and style of each of the undisputed letters is unique. Therefore, changes in language and style alone may not be enough to justify the claim of non-Pauline authorship. However, as the second section of this chapter will show, the theology and contents of Colossians, Ephesians, and 2 Thessalonians separate these letters from the undisputed seven.

## Historical Setting of Colossians (Author, Audience, Date and Place of Composition)

All three letters are examples of early Christian pseudepigrapha; therefore, the real authors of Colossians, Ephesians, and 2 Thessalonians

---

9. For example, Colossians 2:20, *dogmatidzō* (submit to regulations), Ephesians 2:14, *mesotoichon* (dividing wall), 2 Thessalonians 2:2, *eis to mē tacheōs saleuthēnai humas apo tou noos* (not to be shaken out of your minds suddenly).

10. For instance, Romans 3:25, *proginomai* (happen beforehand) or Philippians 3:12, *teteleiōmai* (perfect maturity).

11. Schnelle, *New Testament Writings,* 283, counts thirty-seven *hapax legomena* in Colossians; thirty-five *hapax legomena* in Ephesians, 300; seventeen *hapax legomena* in 2 Thessalonians, 317.

are, by literary design, unknown.[12] So, although the author of Colossians is anonymous, two clues within the letter indicate the audience was Gentile Christ-believers (Col 1:27; 2:13).

## Outline of Colossians

| | |
|---|---|
| 1:1–14 | **Greeting, Thanksgiving, and Prayer**<br>The letter, presented as co-sent by Paul and Timothy, is written from prison (Col 4:3) "to the holy ones and faithful brothers"(1:1) in Colossae. "Paul" gives thanks to God for the faith of the Colossians, acknowledging Epaphras as the founder of their church. Paul assures the Colossians of his ongoing prayer of intercession on their behalf for continued spiritual wisdom and understanding. |
| 1:15–2:3 | **The Preeminence of Christ and the Ministry of Paul**<br>A text (Col 1:15–20) presenting Christ as the mediator of creation and the mediator of redemption frames the Christology of the letter and counters the false teachings addressed later on in the letter. Paul then speaks of himself as a "minister in accordance with God's stewardship" (1:25) in proclaiming the gospel message of Christ to the Gentiles. He refers to the struggle to do so to those in Colossae and Laodicea and to all who have not seen him in person. |

*Continued*

---

12. Of these three letters, there is considerably more scholarly support for Pauline authorship of 2 Thessalonians and Colossians than for Ephesians. See, Gordon D. Fee, *The First and Second Letters to the Thessalonians* (Grand Rapids, MI: Eerdmans, 2009), 237–38, who raises points in favor of Paul as the author of 2 Thessalonians. See Douglas J. Moo, *The Letters to the Colossians and Philemon* (Grand Rapids, MI: Eerdmans, 2008), 28–41, for an extended and balanced discussion on the authorship of Colossians.

| | |
|---|---|
| **Outline of Colossians** *Continued* | |

| 2:4–23 | **Defense against False Teachings**<br>Paul encourages the congregation in Colossae to stand firm against false teachings, which he characterizes as an "empty, seductive philosophy according to human tradition" (2:8). He reminds the Colossians of Christ's saving work in the world and how his death on the cross unified Jew and Gentile, "obliterating the bond against us" (2:14). Paul urges the Colossians to resist participating in activities associated with "the elemental powers of the world"(2:20) that deny Christ's supremacy in the universe. |
| 3:1–4:6 | **Christian Moral Behavior**<br>Paul begins his moral exhortations by redirecting the Colossians' focus: "Think of what is above, not of what is on earth" (3:2). He then lists vices to avoid and virtues to emulate. Paul then instructs members of households (husbands, wives, children, slaves, and masters) on proper Christian conduct, emphasizing that they should persevere in prayer. |
| 4:7–18 | **Closing Remarks and Final Blessing**<br>Paul informs the Colossians he is sending Tychicus and Onesimus with updated news. He conveys greetings from various co-workers (Aristarchus, Mark, Justus, Epaphras, Luke, and Demas) and to various churches (Laodicea and Hierapolis), with personal messages to Nympha and Archippus. He concludes with a postscript and blessing "in my own hand"(4:18). |

The letter offers very little information about its date and place of composition. Although references within Colossians claim that it was written from prison (Col 4:3,10,18), scholars who favor its deutero-Pauline status see the prison reference as a mark of pseudepigraphy, intended to suggest that Paul wrote it. Because the Letter to the Colossians mentions three cities, all in southwest Asia Minor (Colossae, 1:2; Laodicea, 2:1; 4:13,15,16; and Hierapolis, 4:13), some scholars have suggested that this general area is the likely place of its composition. In terms of dating Colossians, that Ephesians depends heavily on Colossians indicates that Colossians was written sometime before Ephesians. Assuming the list of Paul's co-workers in Colossians 4:7–14, which closely parallels the names of the final greeting in Philemon 23–24, was known by the author of Colossians and not just an attempt to affirm Paul's authorship of Colossians, then it can be assumed that Colossians was written after Philemon. Therefore, Colossians was probably written after Philemon and before Ephesians, sometime between 70 and 100 CE.

## Possible Authors of the Deutero-Pauline Letters

Scholars convinced of the pseudepigraphy of Colossians, Ephesians, and 2 Thessalonians often suggest co-workers mentioned in the undisputed letters as possible authors. Timothy, a co-sender of four of the seven undisputed letters, is a frequent candidate for authorship. So, too, are Epaphras and Titus, who served as Paul's co-workers and sometimes as delegates to his congregations.

## Historical Setting of Ephesians (Author, Audience, Date and Place of Composition)

As a pseudepigraphic letter, the real author of Ephesians is unknown. However, one clue exists that the author may have been a Jewish Christ-believer. In Ephesians 2:11–22, the text clearly addresses Gentiles using the contrasting language of *you* and *we* (vv. 11, 13, 17, 19, 22). The author's references to the prophetic tradition in this text (Isa 28:16, 57:19; Zech 9:10), and desire to clarify the Gentile-Jewish relationship both suggest Jewish authorship. However, similar to Colossians, a few clues in Ephesians suggests that this letter was intended for Gentile Christ-believers (Eph 2:11; 3:1; 4:17).

Most scholars agree that whoever authored Ephesians relied heavily upon Colossians as a literary source.[13] Indeed, the literary dependency is striking: Ephesians uses more than one-third of Colossians; it often closely quotes phrases from Colossians (for instance, Col 2:13 and Eph 2:5; Col 1:22 and Eph 1:4). It also relies heavily upon the virtues and vices listed in the ethical section of Colossians (compare the virtues, Col 3:12–14 and Eph 4:2–3, and the vices, Col 3:8 and Eph 4:31). The author of Ephesians appears to have had access to additional Pauline letters, as evidenced by many literary parallels (compare, for example, Eph 2:9 with 1 Cor 1:29; Eph 1:13–14 with 2 Cor 1:22; Eph 5:5 with Gal 5:21; Eph 2:6 with Rom 8:10–11; Phil 3:20).

## Virtues and Vices of Colossians and Ephesians

| Virtues | Vices |
| --- | --- |
| "Put on then, as God's chosen ones, holy and beloved, heartfelt compassion, kindness, humility, gentleness, and patience, bearing with one another and forgiving one another, if one has a grievance against another; as the Lord has forgiven you, so must you also do. And over all these put on love, that is, the bond of perfection." (Col 3:12–14) | "But now you must put them all away: anger, fury, malice, slander, and obscene language out of your mouths." (Col 3:8) |

*Continued*

---

13. See Margaret Y. MacDonald, *Colossians and Ephesians* SP 17 (Collegeville, MN: Liturgical, 2000), 4–6, for a good overview of the literary relationship between Colossians and Ephesians. She notes, "Of all the letters in the Pauline corpus, no two works are so closely linked," 4.

---

### Virtues and Vices of Colossians and Ephesians *Continued*

| | |
|---|---|
| "With all humility and gentleness, with patience, bearing with one another through love, striving to preserve the spirit through the bond of peace." (Eph 4:2–3) | "All bitterness, fury, anger, shouting, and reviling must be removed from you, along with all malice." (Eph 4:31) |

The literary parallels between this list of virtues and vices found in Colossians and Ephesians has led some scholars to conclude that the author of Ephesians knew and used the list from the Letter to the Colossians.

---

## Outline of Ephesians

| | |
|---|---|
| 1:1–23 | **Greeting and Thanksgiving**<br>The letter was presented as sent by "Paul" to "the holy ones who are faithful in Christ Jesus" (1:1), indicating the universal intended audience. Paul offers an initial prayer of thanksgiving to God for the blessings and redemption received from Christ and for the gift of the Holy Spirit. A second prayer of thanksgiving is also presented, highlighting the faith of the recipients. Paul concludes by defining the church as the body of Christ. |
| 2:1–22 | **Life in Christ for Jew and Gentile**<br>The body of the letter begins with a discussion of the salvation offered by God through Christ to all who profess faith. Gentiles, who were once far off, are no longer "alienated from the community of Israel" (2:12). Christ, "our peace . . . made both one and broke down the dividing wall of |

*Continued*

| | |
|---|---|
| **Outline of Ephesians** *Continued* | |

| | |
|---|---|
| | enmity" (2:14). Jew and Gentile are now "fellow citizens . . . and members of the household of God" (2:19). |
| 3:1–21 | **Paul's Ministry and Prayer for the Church** |
| | Paul speaks next of his call and ministry, proclaiming the mystery that was revealed to him: "the Gentiles are coheirs, members of the same body and copartners in the promise in Christ Jesus through the gospel" (3:6). He concludes with a prayer for all believers that the Father may strengthen them with his Spirit, that Christ may dwell in their hearts, and that all may be filled with the fullness of God. |
| 4:1–24 | **Unity in the Body of Christ** |
| | Paul urges all members of the body of Christ to find peace in the seven unities of the church: one body, one Spirit, one hope, one Lord, one faith, one baptism, and one God and Father of all. He speaks of Christ as the head of the whole body, challenging members to build up the body of Christ and not to be influenced by human trickery and false teachings. These are remnants of the old self, no longer worthy of "the new self created in God's way" (4:24). |
| 4:25–6:20 | **Christian Moral Behavior** |
| | Paul begins the final section of the letter with instructions for proper Christian conduct, emphasizing compassion, love, and forgiveness for one another. He encourages disassociation from those who do evil, because God's wrath is coming upon them. Paul then presents household duties for wives and husbands, children and parents, and slaves and masters. He ends with an exhortation to "put on the armor of God" (6:13) in the struggle against evil, praying constantly in the Spirit. |

*Continued*

| | |
|---|---|
| **Outline of Ephesians** *Continued* | |
| 6:21–24 | **Concluding Remarks and Blessing** |
| | Paul concludes by stating that he is sending Tychicus so he can provide updated news of Paul and encourage their hearts. He closes with a final blessing. |

The general area of Asia Minor is often cited as a plausible place of composition for Ephesians, especially given Ephesians's extensive reliance on Colossians. One of the interesting features of Ephesians is the manuscript difficulties with the phrase "in Ephesus"[14] that appears in the greeting of the letter (1:1). Some of the earliest surviving manuscript copies of this letter do not contain this phrase. The absence of an intended specific congregation or person for this letter—if this is indeed the case—would be unique among the letters of Paul and reinforces the likelihood that its author intended this letter to be circulated around the numerous congregations in and around Asia Minor. The letter's greeting without the words *in Ephesus* would read: "Paul, an apostle of Christ Jesus by the will of God, to the holy ones who are faithful in Christ Jesus." The impersonal tone of the letter, along with its summaries of Paul's mission and theology (for example, Eph 3:1–13) and lack of greeting, travel plans, and personal reports, all contribute to the theory that Ephesians was intended to circulate to various churches, or in any case, to be a general reflection of Pauline theology, without reference to particular (or supposed) congregational problems.

Its literary dependency upon Colossians dates it to after 70 CE, as do clues in the text indicating a historical distance between the original apostles and the recipients of the letter (see Eph 2:19–20). Scholars often date Ephesians to sometime between 80–110 CE.

---

14. This phrase, "in Ephesus," is missing from early third- and fourth-century CE manuscripts.

# Historical Setting of 2 Thessalonians (Author, Audience, Date and Place of Composition)

As is the case with Colossians and Ephesians, the author of 2 Thessalonians is unknown. Furthermore, 2 Thessalonians offers no clues to its intended audience. Although 1 Thessalonians 1:9 indicates a Gentile audience, the concern of 2 Thessalonians—issues associated with the delayed Parousia—could apply to many Jewish and Gentile Christ-believers in the late decades of the first century CE. Nonetheless, scholars often identify Gentile Christ-believers as the recipients of 2 Thessalonians.

## Outline of 2 Thessalonians

| | |
|---|---|
| 1:1–10 | **Greeting and Thanksgiving**<br>In this letter, presented as co-sent by Paul, Silvanus, and Timothy to the church of the Thessalonians, "Paul" gives thanksgiving to God for their endurance and faith in the face of persecution and affliction and offers consolation to the Thessalonians by telling them that God will inflict punishment and eternal ruin on those causing them trouble. |
| 2:1–17 | **Warning against False Teachings on the Parousia**<br>Paul then raises the central concern of his letter: the false rumors that "the day of the Lord is at hand" (2:2). He informs the Thessalonians that these false teachings, in fact, precede the return of Christ and are necessary for the lawless one to be revealed. Paul reminds them to "stand firm and hold fast to the traditions" (2:15) that he and his co-workers taught them. |
| 3:1–16 | **Proper Conduct in the Congregation**<br>Paul requests their prayers for his success in ministry and assures the Thessalonians that God will strengthen and guard them from the evil one. Paul |

*Continued*

> **Outline of 2 Thessalonians** *Continued*
>
> | | |
> |---|---|
> | | urges them to shun those who act in disorderly ways (refusing to work, minding others' business) and to disassociate from them. |
> | 3:17–18 | **Farewell and Blessing**<br>The letter ends with a farewell "in my own hand"(3:17) and a final blessing. |

Identifying the date and place of composition for 2 Thessalonians proves challenging, because the letter itself offers few clues. Its main focus, responding to another pseudo-Pauline letter about the Parousia already having taken place (see 2 Thess 2:1–2), often leaves scholars to hypothesize a date of composition late in the first century, typically 90–100 CE. The depicted recipients—Christians in the city of Thessalonica in the province of Macedonia—leads scholars to guess Macedonia or even Asia Minor as the possible places of composition for 2 Thessalonians.

## Arguments for Pauline Authorship of Colossians and 2 Thessalonians

Scholars arguing that Paul is the author of Colossians raise some strong points. They note that Colossians follows the structure of the seven undisputed letters and exhibits numerous characteristics of each: it addresses a specific problem within the congregation of Colossae (false teachings, 2:8–23); it has a personal tone; and the greetings to specific individuals in the closing remarks (4:7–18) closely parallel those mentioned in Philemon 23–24. Scholars who believe Paul wrote Colossians often present a secretary hypothesis, which maintains that Timothy (a co-sender of four of the seven undisputed letters) wrote the letter late in Paul's ministry during

*Continued*

one of his imprisonments (often Rome), when Paul may have been unable to write himself. However, scholars arguing for Colossians as deutero-Pauline wonder if the significantly different writing style of Colossians (for example, much longer sentences) and the different theology of Colossians (for instance, presenting Jesus as the cosmic Christ) would come from the same author.

Scholars who defend Paul's authorship of 2 Thessalonians often note that 1 and 2 Thessalonians both focus on the Parousia (the return of Christ) and that they share a strikingly and somewhat unusual parallel structure. Explanations for Paul's different approaches to the question of Jesus' return in each (1 Thess: the Lord's return is imminent; 2 Thess: the Lord's return is delayed) range from the development of Paul's own thinking on the subject to the wide range of ideas associated with apocalyptic language. Scholars who argue for the deutero-Pauline status of 2 Thessalonians cite the different eschatologies of 1 Thessalonians and 2 Thessalonians. In 2 Thessalonians, the eschaton (end-time) includes apocalyptic signs before the end. In 1 Thessalonians, there is the prediction of a sudden end, like a thief in the night.

## Summary: Historical Settings of Colossians, Ephesians, and 2 Thessalonians

| Authors | Unknown (possibly a close co-worker during Paul's lifetime, with Timothy, Titus, and Epaphras being plausible candidates) |
| --- | --- |
| Audience | Gentile Christ-believers |
| Dates of Composition | Colossians: around 70–100 CE<br>Ephesians: around 80–110 CE<br>2 Thessalonians: around 90–100 CE |
| Possible Places of Composition | Colossians: southwest Asia Minor<br>Ephesians: Asia Minor<br>2 Thessalonians: Macedonia or Asia Minor |

## Summary: Historical Context of the Deutero-Pauline Letters

### CORE CONCEPTS

- Ancient Greek, Jewish, and Christian writers commonly practiced pseudepigraphy, writing in the name and with the authority of another.
- The theology, language, and style of Colossians, Ephesians, and 2 Thessalonians have led many scholars to conclude these are pseudepigrapha (deutero-Pauline) writings written after the death of Paul.
- The evidence is stronger that Ephesians is deutero-Pauline than Colossians and 2 Thessalonians.

### SUPPLEMENTAL INFORMATION

- Scholars can only speculate on the dates and places of composition of these letters because the letters themselves offer few clues.
- Some scholars offer the idea of Pauline schools to explain the writing of the deutero-Pauline letters.
- Colossians, Ephesians, and 2 Thessalonians contain many words not found elsewhere in the New Testament (*hapax legomena*).
- Colossians may be the earliest attempt at a pseudepigrapha writing of Paul.
- Ephesians depends heavily on Colossians as a literary source.
- Second Thessalonians is modeled after and reuses much material from 1 Thessalonians.

# THEOLOGY AND ETHICS OF COLOSSIANS, EPHESIANS AND 2 THESSALONIANS

The next section explores the theological themes of Colossians, Ephesians, and 2 Thessalonians in turn: Christ, the Church, and the Parousia in Colossians; Christ and the Church in Ephesians; and the Parousia in 2 Thessalonians, respectively. The ethical teachings, such as "household codes" and virtues and vices, however, are treated together, as Colossians and Ephesians contain many parallels in this regard.

## Theology

### Christ, the Church, and the Parousia in Colossians

Colossians's discussion of Christ's saving work in creation and in the universe reflects several developments beyond the undisputed letters of Paul. Although Paul mentions Christ's role in creation and supremacy in the universe (see, for example, 1 Cor 8:6; Phil 2:9–11), Colossians offers a sustained and expanded discussion of the subject. The letter's explanation of the sovereign role of Christ in the universe provided vital details to counter false teachings presented as influencing the congregation in Colossae (Col 2:8–23).

At the beginning of the letter (1:15–20), the author defines Christ as both "firstborn of all creation" (1:15) and "firstborn from the dead" (1:18), thus, defining his central role as mediator of creation as well as mediator of redemption for the believer. As firstborn of all creation, Christ is "the head of every principality and power" (2:10) whose death and Resurrection demonstrated Christ's sovereignty and public "triumph" over all other cosmic principalities and powers (2:14–15). As firstborn from the dead, Christ now shares his resurrected life with believers, who will be "raised with him" (2:12) and whose life is now "hidden with Christ in God" waiting to "appear with him in glory" (3:3–4). The author of Colossians provides a succinct summary of the letter's Christology: "Christ is all and in all" (3:11).

The author of Colossians also speaks of the church in a different way than in the undisputed letters. Whereas Paul spoke of the Christ

## An Eschatology of an Already Realized Resurrection

In Colossians 2:12–13; 3:1, the author defines the believer's resurrection as a *past*, existential or spiritual, event rather than a *future*, eschatological, event: "If then *you were raised* with Christ, seek what is above, where Christ is seated at the right hand of God" (Col 3:1) (emphasis added).

In his undisputed letters, the apostle Paul places the *resurrection* and *salvation* in the *future* (see, for example, 1 Cor 15:20–28). Ephesians, on the other hand, reflects a non-Pauline eschatology of *an already realized resurrection* (following Colossians): "[God] raised us up with him [Christ], and seated us with him in the heavens" (Eph 2:6). Colossians and Ephesians present a theology of an already realized resurrection. This innovative development is not Pauline.

as the "body" of the church (for instance, 1 Cor 12:12–13; Rom 12:4–5), in Colossians, Christ is the "head of the body" of the church (1:18). The church itself, as the body of Christ, now participates in the salvation offered by its head, Christ (1:18; 2:18–19; 3:15). This is a concept of church beyond what is seen in the undisputed letters: simply an assembly of the congregation of believers. Furthermore, the author of Colossians speaks of Paul, who suffers for the benefit of the church now (Col 1:24). This is one of the most striking non-Pauline theological points in the letter.

In terms of the Parousia or the return of Christ, its sense of imminence—characteristic of Paul's letters (for instance, 1 Cor 7:33b)—has shifted, as believers have already been raised (Col 3:1). The undisputed letters speak of the new being in Christ that will be revealed to believers at the eschaton (see, for example, 1 Thess 4:13–18; Phil 1:6); in Colossians, however, baptized believers have already died and risen with Christ (2:12–13; 3:1) and are encouraged "to think of what is above, not of what is on earth" (3:2). Although Colossians still hopes for the return of Christ (3:4), the letter's description of the role and function of the cosmic Christ

## The Opponents in Colossians

The letter to the Colossians was mainly written to deal with a threat of false teachings (2:8–23), which the author refers to as an "empty, seductive philosophy according to human tradition" (2:8). Scholars have debated over the content of this "philosophy" as well as the identity of the opponents spreading it. Clues from the letter suggest the opponents advocated a philosophy that combined Jewish dietary practices and observance of sacred calendar days (2:16) with some pagan religious customs (2:18,23). The author of Colossians challenges those in the congregation who accept this philosophy (2:20). He refutes the false teachings—its philosophy and its practices—by appealing to the rite of baptism (2:11–13) that initiates the believer into the death and Resurrection of Christ once and for all. In baptism, one joins the body of Christ, and Christ is both head of the body and "head of every principality and power" (2:10). The Colossian opponents are different from the Galatian opponents: the issue is no longer whether one must follow the Mosaic Law. Thus, a pseudonymous author takes up a problem that was not current when Paul lived.

shifts the focus to heaven, in which believers should direct their "hope" (1:5,23,27).

### Christ and the Church in Ephesians

Given its literary dependency on Colossians, it is not surprising that much of the theology of Ephesians also centers on Christ and the church. Just as Colossians focuses on Christ's sovereignty (Col 3:11), the author of Ephesians exalts Christ with the repeated phrase that "all things" in heaven and on Earth are found in his being (1:10,11,22,23; 3:9; 4:10). Christ's rule over the universe solidifies the "hope," the "riches," and the "surpassing greatness" for believers (1:18).

In Ephesians, Christ becomes "our peace" here on Earth (2:14), harmonizing the historic separation between Jews and Gentiles (2:11–13), breaking down the "dividing wall," "abolishing the law," creating "in himself one new person, in place of the two" so that he "might reconcile both with God" (2:14–16). Herein lies a likely impetus

Jesus and believers seated with God in the heavens is one of the powerful images the Letter to the Ephesians presents.

for writing Ephesians: to encourage the largely Gentile recipients of the letter to seek peace and reconciliation with fellow Jewish Christ-believers and with the Jewish roots that ground their congregations.

One of the novel ideas in Ephesians is God "seating" Jesus in the heavens (Eph 1:20). In this letter, believers are not only raised with Christ (Col 3:1) but also are seated with Christ in the heavens. Thus, the development of Pauline thought can be traced in two stages beyond the Paul of the undisputed letters.

Regarding Jewish and Gentile relations, the church plays a critical role. Because Jesus' death on the cross has reconciled Jew and Gentile (2:13,14,16), believers are called to "preserve the unity" (4:3). United in peace as one body, the church can make known "the manifold wisdom of God" throughout the universe (3:9–10) as it continues in "building up the body of Christ" in its "work of minis-try" (4:12). This defines the church's mission to the world (3:1–4:24), which will lead to its growth and renewal (4:17–24).

## Evidence of a Developing Tradition

Twice in Ephesians (2:19b–20; 3:4–5) the author's language implies a historical distance from Jesus and the original apostles, which supports a date of composition between 80–110 CE. In chapter 2, for example, Paul refers to the apostles and prophets as the foundation of the household of God and to Jesus as its capstone. Referring to the apostles as the "foundation" suggests that they lived a generation or two earlier than the audience of Ephesians.

### The Parousia in 2 Thessalonians

The occasion for writing 2 Thessalonians is singular and straightforward: to correct a misinterpretation of the description of the second coming and the end-time found in 1 Thessalonians. In 1 Thessalonians 4:13–18, Paul spoke to the Thessalonian congregation about the expectation of the imminent return of Christ and its associated events. He articulates a clear order of the end-time events in which Christ will first raise from the dead those who have already "fallen asleep" (4:15). Then, those still living will assemble and "be caught up . . . in the clouds to meet the Lord in the air" (4:17). Attempts to calculate the timing of the Parousia are fruitless (5:1). The most that believers can do is to live as "children of the light" and "stay alert and sober" (5:5–6).

The author of 2 Thessalonians departs significantly from the perspectives on the Parousia given in 1 Thessalonians and in the pseudonymous Pauline letter to which he responds (2 Thess 2:2b). Events associated with the end-time now include a number of new expectations. Before the return of Christ, first comes "apostasy" (renunciation of the faith), and then "the lawless one is revealed" (2:3), opposing God and misleading unbelievers (2:4–6). The lawless one is at work in the present and will remain active until the Parousia, when Christ will destroy him (2:7–8). Whereas the imminent Parousia of 1 Thessalonians focused on the glorified Christ and the resurrection of the dead, the future Parousia in 2 Thessalonians emphasizes the destruction of the lawless one and all nonbelievers who believe "the lie" of Satan (1 Thess 2:9–11; 2 Thess 1:5–10).

## The Lawless One

Engraving depicting the two beasts described in Revelation 13. Like Revelation, 2 Thessalonians associates an evil figure with the return of Christ.

© Album / Art Resource, NY

The idea of an evil figure appearing before the Second Coming of Christ as part of the eschaton appears in various writings of the New Testament. The Synoptic Gospels include predictions of false messiahs and false prophets in anticipation of the end of the age (Mark 13:21–22; Matthew 24:23–24; Luke 21:7–8). In the letters of John, this figure is actually called the antichrist (1 John 2:18,22; 4:3; 2 John 7). The Book of Revelation mentions two different types of "beasts": the evil ruler or the beast from the sea (Revelation 13:1–10; 16:13; 19:20) and the false prophet or the beast from the land (Revelation 13:11–18; 16:13; 19:20). Curiously, the Second Letter to the Thessalonians (2:1–12) is the only Pauline letter that mentions this evil figure, or "the lawless one," anticipating the return of Christ. According to 2 Thessalonians, the lawless one has not yet been revealed because someone or something is "restraining" him (2 Thess 2:6). Scholars speculate as to who or what is understood to be restraining the lawless one "for the present" time. Proposals range from Satan or some other supernatural force to the Roman Empire or the Roman emperor at the time of the writing of 2 Thessalonians.

Many scholars see the significantly different approach to the Parousia in these two letters as confirmation of the deutero-Pauline status of 2 Thessalonians. Second Thessalonians has shifted away from the more present-time, imminent expectations in 1 Thessalonians to a more indeterminate future arrival. The author encourages the recipients to "hold fast to the traditions that you were taught" (2:15) as a strategy to defend against false teachings on the Parousia. This approach to defending the faith suggests a late date (90–100 CE) for the composition of 2 Thessalonians because "tradition" language would have been a later development.

Second Thessalonians is only three chapters long. Generally speaking, chapters 1 and 3 are mostly drawn from 1 Thessalonians. As a result, scholars examine more closely 2 Thessalonians 2:1–12 to understand something about this author's theology and reason for writing. Somewhat ironically, this pseudonymous Pauline author writes to refute another pseudonymous Pauline letter (2 Thess 2:2b). Astonishingly, this other letter claimed that "the day of the Lord," including the Parousia, has somehow already taken place. Clearly, such a notion is non-Pauline. In effect, 2 Thessalonians is the refutation of a non-Pauline eschatology with another non-Pauline eschatology.

Both Colossians and Ephesians discuss virtues to practice and vices to avoid as well as household codes of conduct for parents, children, and slaves. Although 2 Thessalonians does not list virtues and vices or household codes, the letter does uphold Paul as a moral model and advocates following his example as the best means to avoid acting in a "disorderly way."

## Virtues and Vices

Colossians 3:5–17 presents a list of virtues to practice and vices to avoid. The undisputed Pauline letters contain similar lists (see, for example, Gal 5:19–23). Colossians couches these ethical norms of conduct in a comparable way. For example, the vices of human conduct cause "the wrath of God" to come (3:6); the virtuous way of being reflects "the new self" in Christ, no longer suitable for "the old self" and the former pagan way of life (3:9–10). Baptismal language of taking off the old self and putting on the new self (3:9–10) appears in the undisputed letters as well (compare 1 Cor 12:3 and

Gal 3:27–28). Ephesians 4:17–5:20 also catalogues virtues and vices and, like Colossians, emphasizes that the virtues reflect "the new self" (4:24) as a believer in Christ and a rejection of "the old self" (4:22) as a repudiation of their former lives.

These moral codes of conduct found in both the undisputed and the deutero-Pauline letters served an important function for the Christian communities. No longer under the Mosaic Law but under a newfound freedom in Christ and led by the power of Spirit, they needed a clear set of ethical principles to guide community life.

### Household Codes

Unlike the list of virtues and vices found in both the undisputed letters (for instance, Rom 1:29–31; 2 Cor 12:20–21) and the deutero-Pauline letters, the household codes of conduct are unique to the deutero-Pauline letters of Colossians and Ephesians (Col 3:18–4:1; Eph 5:21–6:9). Each letter pairs off members of the Christian household—wife/husband, child/parent, and slave/master—and offers a similar parallel set of instructions, first addressing the subordinate and then the main member. The letters detail expectations for each member of the pairs in relation to the other, with a rationale provided for these behavioral norms. In the section treating the relationship between husbands and wives, Ephesians adds an extended discussion on Christ and the church (5:22–33) that offers a model for Christian households to follow.

One of the striking features of the household codes in Colossians and Ephesians is their departure from Paul's more radical and countercultural views of women and slaves. Whereas Colossians and Ephesians speak of the submission of slaves and women/wives (Col 3:18,22; Eph 5:21–22; 6:5), Paul acknowledged women's leadership roles within the congregation (for example, Phil 4:2–3) and advocated treating believers who are slaves as brothers (Phlm 16).

### Paul as the Moral Norm

The author of 2 Thessalonians relies on the teachings received from Paul in his discussion of believers' ethical conduct (2:15; 3:6,14). In fact, 2 Thessalonians holds up Paul as the model of moral behavior (3:7–9). The author applies this standard of conduct as a means of confronting those believers who act in a "disorderly way" (3:7,11), such as not working for their own food or minding another's business (gossiping).

Second Thessalonians concludes with a stern admonition (3:14) to believers who may be unwilling to live up to the moral standards established in the letter. For example, it was expected that believers treat those who violate the ethical norms of the congregation as brothers rather than as enemies (3:15).

## Summary: Theology and Ethics of Colossians, Ephesians, and 2 Thessalonians

### CORE CONCEPTS

- Like Colossians, the Letter to the Ephesians emphasizes the saving work of Christ in creation and in the universe.
- Second Thessalonians approaches the Parousia differently from both 1 Thessalonians and the pseudonymous Pauline letter (now lost) that it aims to correct.
- Ethical norms in Colossians and Ephesians focus on virtues and vices and household codes of conduct.

### SUPPLEMENTAL INFORMATION

- The letter to the Colossians was written, in part, to combat the false teachings of an "empty, seductive philosophy" (2:8).
- Colossians describes Christ as the head of the body of the church.
- Ephesians stresses that the church should be a unified body of Christ for both Jews and Gentiles.
- In Ephesians, the church's mission is to make known "the manifold wisdom of God" throughout the universe.
- In 2 Thessalonians, both apostasy and the lawless one will appear before the return of Christ, indicating that the end is near.
- Second Thessalonians stresses avoiding "disorderly" conduct.

## Questions for Review

1. What does *pseudepigraphy* mean?
2. What does *hapax legomenon* mean? How does it apply to deutero-Pauline letters such as Colossians, Ephesians, and 2 Thessalonians?
3. How does the theory of Pauline schools help to account for the deutero-Pauline writings?
4. Give three examples that lead scholars to infer that Ephesians depends on Colossians as a literary source.
5. What can be known about the authors and the depicted audiences of these three deutero-Pauline letters?
6. What role does Christ have in creation and in the universe according to Colossians?
7. How does Colossians discuss the Parousia and the Resurrection of Christ?
8. How does Ephesians describe the mission of the church and believers' resurrection and session with Christ?
9. For what occasion was 2 Thessalonians written?
10. According to Colossians and Ephesians, what are some of the behavioral norms for family households?

## Questions for Reflection

1. How do you imagine these pseudepigraphic letters were received by their congregations? Do people today write pseudepigrapha?
2. What do you think would be some challenges in writing a letter in Paul's name?
3. If the authors of the deutero-Pauline letters were some of Paul's co-workers and delegates to various congregations (for example, Timothy, Epaphras, and Titus), how could Paul's theology change in these later letters?
4. What is your reaction to the household codes of conduct in Colossians and Ephesians?

# Recommendations for Further Reading

Ehrman, Bart D. *Forged: Writing in the Name of God—Why the Bible's Authors Are Not Who We Think They Are.* New York: HarperCollins Publishers, 2011.

This book provides historical and cultural background for the widespread phenomenon of forgery in the ancient world. Ehrman offers the provocative argument that some of the New Testament writings were deliberately forged in the name of the disciples of Jesus. In doing so, Ehrman is able to present the debates and arguments among the early believers of the first few centuries of Christianity.

Lincoln, Andrew T., and Alexander J. M. Wedderburn. *The Theology of the Later Pauline Letters.* Cambridge, UK: Cambridge University Press, 1993.

This book provides introductory material on the Colossians and Ephesians. Wedderburn begins with the background and theology of Colossians, with special attention given to Colossians in relation to the rest of the Pauline corpus. Lincoln focuses on Ephesians, emphasizing background material on its theology as well as its connection to the theology of the other Pauline letters. Both scholars reflect on the contemporary relevance of these letters.

MacDonald, Margaret Y. *Colossians and Ephesians.* Sacra Pagina 17. Collegeville, MN: The Liturgical Press, 2000.

MacDonald takes a social-scientific approach in her commentary on Colossians and Ephesians. Although she does judge both letters as deutero-Pauline, MacDonald presents the views of scholars who deem these letters to be authored by Paul. Her introductory material covers the basic historical questions of authorship, audience, and date and place of composition. She examines the opponents in Colossians and the nature and purpose of Ephesians as well as the religious significance of both letters for today.

Richard, Earl J. *First and Second Thessalonians.* Sacra Pagina 11. Collegeville, MN: The Liturgical Press, 1995.

Similar to other commentaries in the Sacra Pagina series, this book offers an extended introduction to Paul's letters to the Thessalonians, covering topics such as "New Views on the Pauline Mission and 1 Thessalonians" and "Circumstances of Mission and Correspondence according to Acts." Earl's attention to the language and rhetoric of these two letters helps readers better understand the nuances of Paul and his followers.

Witherington, Ben, III. *The Letters to Philemon, the Colossians, and the Ephesians: A Socio-Rhetorical Commentary on the Captivity Epistles.* Grand Rapids, MI: Eerdmans, 2007.

Witherington presents the rhetorical structure and argument of each of these letters written from prison. He includes a discussion of the different rhetorical styles and situations, as well as the social setting of Paul and his audiences. The book includes a very helpful annotated bibliography that outlines both the classic studies on these letters as well as some of the more recent scholarly works accessible for those interested in further study.

# CHAPTER 10

# First Timothy, Second Timothy, and Titus

## INTRODUCTION

The designation of the Pauline letters of 1 Timothy, 2 Timothy, and Titus as the Pastoral Epistles dates back to the early 1700s.[1] Most scholars today regard these three letters as pseudepigrapha and, therefore, classify them as deutero-Pauline. They contend that like Colossians, Ephesians, and 2 Thessalonians, these letters use Paul's name and draw upon his authority, but they were written by an unknown author or authors, addressing issues that developed a generation or two after Paul's death. The first section of this chapter explores the historical context of these letters—author and audience, date and place of composition, the occasions for writing the Pastoral Letters, and a profile of the opponents mentioned in them. The second section considers the theology of the Pastorals, including the author's Christology, Paul as a model of an ideal church leader and his qualifications for Church leadership as well as examines the ethics of the letters, covering such areas as the qualifications of bishops and deacons and rules for the members of the congregations.

### First Timothy and Titus

All three of the Pastoral Letters offer instructions to a particular church leader and reflect several common themes (for example,

---

1. Both Udo Schnelle, *The History and Theology of the New Testament Writings*, trans. M. Eugene Boring (London: SCM Press, 1998), 326–327, and Benjamin Fiore, *The Pastoral Epistles: First Timothy, Second Timothy, and Titus*, SP 12 (Collegeville, MN: Liturgical, 2007), 8, credit Paul Anton (1726) with coining the phrase "the Pastoral Epistles."

instruction on how to deal with false teachings). Among these letters, 1 Timothy and Titus are often grouped together because of their shared focus on church order. First Timothy outlines the qualifications and responsibilities of bishops, deacons, and presbyters, or elders, especially regarding refuting false teachers and promoting Paul's theology and ethics. The Letter to Titus discusses the duties and tasks of bishops who are to be vigilant in defending the faith as articulated by Paul.

This does not imply that the circumstances that occasioned the writing of 1 Timothy and Titus were identical. First Timothy, for example, claims to address the conditions and structures of the household congregations in Ephesus. Titus, on the other hand, is said to be a leader among the Christian communities on the island of Crete. However, enough parallels in content exist that justifies grouping these two letters together.

## Second Timothy

Second Timothy, although also addressed to Timothy, has an altogether different focus from 1 Timothy and Titus. Rather than referring to church order, 2 Timothy reads more like Paul's last will and testament: after the apostle's death, someone wrote an ideal version of Paul's final words to the church (and especially its leaders) on how to defend the gospel amid hardships and persecutions. In 2 Timothy, Paul is presented as both reflecting upon his ministry at the end of life as well as offering advice for the ongoing struggles sure to face Timothy and the Christian congregations in the future.

The sober tone and sense of finality of 2 Timothy have led some scholars to conclude that 2 Timothy was the last of the Pastoral Letters to be written. The letters offer no direct clues as to their order of composition, however.

## HISTORICAL CONTEXT OF THE PASTORAL LETTERS

Clues within the Pastoral Letters provide only limited help in answering questions of author and audience and date and place of composition. The reliability of the few clues (for example, the city of

Ephesus as the place of composition for 1 Timothy and 2 Timothy) is questionable because these are pseudonymous letters: an author who forged Paul's identity may also have fabricated the supposed situation these letters are to have addressed. In any case, what can be analyzed is a pseudonymous author's message and, perhaps, the circumstances of the later church that gave rise to the need for the later embellishment on Pauline theology.

## Author and Audience

Like Colossians, Ephesians, and 2 Thessalonians, the Pastorals are examples of early Christian pseudepigrapha. Considered deutero-Pauline, these letters are attributed to Paul and received by Timothy and Titus, two of Paul's co-workers. Although some scholars continue to advocate for Paul as the author and Timothy and Titus as the intended audience for these letters,[2] the vast majority of scholars acknowledge the actual author and audience remain indeterminate from the internal evidence.[3] This conclusion leads to such questions as, Is there one or more authors behind the Pastorals? Who were the intended recipients of these letters, if not Timothy and Titus?

In the case of Colossians, Ephesians, and 2 Thessalonians, most scholars infer that three different authors were behind these letters. The Pastorals, however, leave scholars somewhat divided on the question of authorship. The similar content in 1 Timothy and Titus, combined with the different focus of 2 Timothy, lead some scholars

---

2. Modern scholars who argue for Paul's authorship of the Pastorals include Luke Timothy Johnson, *Letters to Paul's Delegates: 1 Timothy, 2 Timothy, and Titus* (Harrisburg, PA: Trinity Press International, 1996), George W. Knight III, *The Pastoral Epistles* (Grand Rapids, MI: Eerdmans, 1992), and James D. Miller, *The Pastorals as Composite Documents* (Cambridge, UK: Cambridge University Press, 1997). Arguments for Paul's authorship often center on secretary theories (a secretary or scribe writing at Paul's direction; for example, Luke) or fragmentary hypotheses (the Pastorals containing fragments of undisputed Pauline letters).

3. Some external evidence for later dating does exist (for example, first mention of the Pastorals by Irenaeus late in the second century; the Chester Beatty papyri, which do not contain the Pastorals; and especially Marcion's prologues, which omit the Pastorals. These sources do suggest a later dating (or at least circulation) of the Pastorals than the other Pauline letters.).

## Timothy and Titus as Paul's Co-workers

Timothy is the co-worker Paul most often mentions in his undisputed letters. Five of Paul's seven surviving letters identify Timothy as a co-sender (1 Thess 1:1; 1 Cor 1:1; 2 Cor 1:1; Phil 1:1; and Phlm 1). Paul considered him a trusted and reliable ally in preaching the gospel message (1 Cor 4:17; 16:1) and, in Paul's absence, the person most qualified to serve as a problem-solver on community matters (1 Thess 3:2–3; Phil 2:19–24).

Paul's undisputed letters also name Titus as a valued co-worker in Paul's mission to the Gentiles. Titus, a Gentile Christ-believer, accompanied Paul and Barnabas to meet with the apostles in Jerusalem (Gal 2:1–3). Paul felt close to Titus (2 Cor 2:13; 7:6,13–14) and relied upon him to help organize the collection of money for the poor people in Corinth (2 Cor 8:6,16–23) and to resolve a conflict between Paul and the Corinthian church (2 Cor 12:17–18).

Addressing his letters to Timothy and Titus reflects a strategic choice made by "the Pastor." As part of Paul's inner circle of loyal delegates, they served as the ideal, if fictive, mediators of the Pastor's message. Addressing letters to these two co-workers increased the likelihood that these letters would be received and honored as stemming from the apostle himself.[4]

to attribute the Pastorals to two or more authors.[5] However, many others conclude that a single author, commonly referred to as "the Pastor," is behind all three letters.[6] This book takes the view that "the Pastor" wrote all three letters.

---

4. It is interesting to note the anomaly that although Paul views Timothy and Titus as his loyal and closest co-workers, in Acts, Luke highlights Barnabas and Silas in this role.

5. Even scholars arguing for Paul's authorship of the Pastorals acknowledge, on the basis of the secretary and fragmentary theories, the possibility of multiple authors.

6. Schnelle, 328–332; Fiore, 15–18.

## Outline of 1 Timothy

| | |
|---|---|
| 1:1–2 | **Greeting** |
| | The Pastor (the letter's unknown author) speaking in Paul's name describes Timothy, the letter's addressee, as Paul's "true child in faith" (1:2) Unlike in most of the undisputed Pauline letters, there is no thanksgiving. |
| 1:3–20 | **Instructions to Timothy on False Teachers** |
| | The Pastor, ostensibly writing to Timothy in Ephesus, immediately identifies one of his main reasons for writing: to confront those teaching "false doctrines" and "myths and endless genealogies" (1:3–4). The letter identifies Hymenaeus and Alexander by name as among those Christ-believers who promote false teachings and who, thereby, make "a shipwreck of their faith" (1:19). The Pastor uses Paul's life story (from persecutor to believer) to exemplify the life of a sinner saved by Christ. |
| 2:1–15 | **Men at Prayer** |
| | With his request that believers "lead a quiet and tranquil life in all devotion and dignity" (2:2), the Pastor indicates how men should gather and lift up holy hands to God in prayer. The Pastor assigns women to a subordinate role to men, stating that a woman is not permitted to teach or have authority over a man. |
| 3:1–16 | **Qualifications for Bishops and Deacons** |
| | Next, the Pastor lists qualities required for those seeking to serve as bishop or deacon, emphasizing high moral standards, a well-run household, and a good reputation within the larger society. The Pastor concludes with a hymn dedicated to Christ. |

*Continued*

| | |
|---|---|
| 4:1–16 | **Further Instruction to Timothy on False Teachings**<br><br>The Pastor again exhorts Timothy to combat false teachings and practices, such as the forbidding of marriage, the requirement of abstinence from sex, and the promotion of "profane and silly myths" (4:7). He urges Timothy to set a good example, use his gifts, and be diligent. |
| 5:1–6:2 | **Rules for Widows, Presbyters, and Slaves**<br><br>The Pastor then focuses on rules for the care of widows, outlining criteria for the congregation to follow. He sets forth guidelines for the office of the presbyter and concludes with instruction for slaves on proper behavior. |
| 6:3–19 | **True Wealth**<br><br>The Pastor draws his letter to a close by reminding Timothy to confront those who promote false teachings and by emphasizing that the wealthy should be responsible stewards of their money, supporting good works. |
| 6:20–21 | **Final Instructions and Blessing**<br><br>The Pastor concludes by encouraging Timothy to fulfill his instructions and be diligent in the defense of the faith. The letter closes with a brief blessing. |

## Outline of Titus

| | |
|---|---|
| 1:1–4 | **Greeting**<br>The Pastor, writing in the name of Paul, describes Titus, the letter's addressee, as Paul's "true child in our common faith" (1:4). As in 1 Timothy, this letter uncharacteristically contains no thanksgiving. |
| 1:5–16 | **Titus's Charge on Crete**<br>The Pastor begins by reminding Titus of his task to appoint qualified presbyters in the towns on the island of Crete. He also emphasizes the role of the bishops to promote the sound doctrine of the faith and to refute, reprimand, and silence the opponents, whose teachings are upsetting families. |
| 2:1–3:11 | **Instructions to Titus to Teach Sound Doctrine**<br>The Pastor charges Titus to teach specific elements of the sound doctrine of the faith to older men and women, to younger men and women, and to slaves. Special emphasis is placed upon obedience to the (Roman) civil authorities. The Pastor insists that the congregation perform good works and avoid heretics who continually spread false teachings. |
| 3:12–15 | **Final Directives, Greetings, and Blessing**<br>The Pastor concludes the letter with a mention of Paul's winter travel plans and with support for the travel plans of Zenas and Apollos, two coworkers. The letter concludes with a final greeting along with a blessing. |

## Outline of 2 Timothy

| | |
|---|---|
| 1:1–5 | **Greeting and Thanksgiving**<br><br>Similar to the greeting in 1 Timothy, the Pastor refers to Timothy as Paul's dear child. This second letter also contains a thanksgiving to God for Timothy's faith. The Pastor cites the faith of Timothy's grandmother, Lois, and his mother, Eunice, as a model to exemplify. |
| 1:6–2:13 | **Instructions to Timothy to Stand Firm in the Faith**<br><br>The Pastor encourages Timothy to remain true to his calling and be courageous in preaching the gospel. The Pastor holds up Paul as a model of endurance amid hardships and suffering and summarizes Paul's gospel about Christ. |
| 2:14–3:17 | **Further Instructions against False Teachings**<br><br>The Pastor urges Timothy to confront those Christ-believers who spread false teaching (for instance, Hymenaeus and Philetus) and to "avoid foolish and ignorant debates" (2:23). He advises Timothy to expect persecution for the faith and encourages him to see Paul as a model. |
| 4:1–8 | **Paul's Testament**<br><br>The letter closes with the pronouncement of Paul's impending death. These final words, or testament, attributed to Paul are to instruct Timothy to persist in proclaiming the word and fulfilling his ministry despite the inevitable opposition. |
| 4:9–22 | **Requests, Final Greeting, and Blessing**<br><br>The letter concludes by listing those who had abandoned Paul and a request for Timothy, along with other co-workers, to join Paul soon and to bring his cloak and writing materials. The Pastor presents Paul as sending greetings to various believers and ends with a blessing. |

Although the Pastorals identify Timothy and Titus as the intended recipients (1 Tim 1:2; 2 Tim 1:2; Titus 1:4), the real audience was likely later Christian congregations of western Asia Minor, including those in Ephesus (1 Tim 1:3) and on the island of Crete (Titus 1:5). The Pastor chose to address his correspondence to Timothy and Titus because they were already well known as Paul's delegates from the undisputed letters (Timothy in 1 Thess 3:2; 1 Cor 4:17; Phil 2:19; Titus: 2 Cor 2:13; 7:13–14; 8:23). As a result, both Paul and these co-workers serve as exemplars for current church leaders who would carry forth the Pastor's instructions to oppose false teachings in present-day communities.

Internal evidence from the Pastorals suggests congregations largely consisted of Gentile Christians (1 Tim 2:7; 3:16) with some Jewish members as well (2 Tim 3:8–9; Titus 3:9). These believers were people of means, described as householders (1 Tim 3:1–5; 2 Tim 4:19; Titus 1:11), with expensive furnishings (2 Tim 2:20) and clothing (1 Tim 2:9). The letters' warnings against love of money (1 Tim 6:6–10; 2 Tim 3:2; Titus 1:7), along with references to the congregations' ability to pay presbyters (1 Tim 5:17–18) and care for widows (1 Tim 5:16) all point to a community of believers who were financially well off. Directives to less lucrative professions, such as artisans (2 Tim 4:14) and lawyers (Titus 3:3) indicate, however, a mixed economic stratum among the believers of the congregation.

## Date and Place of Composition

The letters provide no direct evidence for the date of composition. Numerous clues, however, indicate a date for the Pastorals significantly later than the death of Paul. The differentiated functions of bishops, presbyters, and deacons (1 Tim 3:1–13; 5:17–23; Titus 1:5–9) and the accepted practice of transmitting authority to new leaders through the imposition of the hands (1 Tim 4:14; 2 Tim 1:6) point to developments beyond what is seen in the undisputed letters. References to sound teaching / doctrine (1 Tim 4:6; 2 Tim 4:3), a believer who causes divisions (Titus 3:10), and the debate over eschatology (2 Tim 2:17b–18) imply an apostolic tradition well underway in establishing a sense of orthodoxy among post-Pauline Christian communities. With these clues in mind, scholars often date the writing of the Pastorals to around 100 CE.

The place of composition of the Pastorals remains unknown. Each letter, however, offers some geographic references. First Timothy, for example, indicates concern for the situation in Ephesus (1 Tim 1:3); 2 Timothy implies the letter is composed from prison in Rome (2 Tim 1:17); and the Letter to Titus addresses the Christian congregations on the island of Crete (Titus 1:5). However, because the author and recipients of pseudonymous letters are fictitious, the same may also be said of the indicated geographic origin of these letters. For this reason, scholars cannot determine with any certainty the place of composition, although one common hypothesis suggests the general region of western Asia Minor as a possibility.

## The Pastorals as Pseudepigrapha

Multiple factors point to the pseudonymity of the Pastoral letters. The Pastorals differ from the undisputed Pauline letters in several ways:

### Theology

- Major Pauline themes such as the Spirit, the cross, and the church as the body of Christ are absent. The expectation of Christ's imminent return has faded, and the hope for his coming has shifted to an indefinite future time.
- Faith in Christ as a means of salvation has been recast into a set of virtues to be practiced, such as love, holiness, modesty, and purity.
- Faith (*pistis*) now becomes belief in correct doctrine.

### Vocabulary and Style

- Words and phrases, such as *didaskalia* (teaching), *epignōsis* (knowledge), and *muthos* (myth), not found in the undisputed Pauline letters, recur in the Pastorals.
- Personal information about Paul and his itinerary that is nowhere mentioned in the undisputed letters or Acts (for example, the mission on the island of Crete in Titus 1:5) is provided.

*Continued*

The Pastorals as Pseudepigrapha *Continued*

**Church Organization**

- The male and female leadership of the church of Paul's day was inspired by the various gifts of the Holy Spirit. Church leadership, defined as bishops, presbyters, and deacons, are now all male.
- The church leadership primarily functions to uphold the apostolic tradition of the faith.

**False Teachings**

- The nature of the false teachings (for instance, "myths and endless genealogies" ([1 Tim 1:4], a realized eschatology [2 Tim 2:17–18], and mandated asceticism in terms of marriage and food [1 Tim 4:1–4]) is unique to those letters and not mentioned in the undisputed letters.
- The reasoned arguments against false teachings found in Paul's undisputed letters are replaced by a general appeal to defend the "sound doctrine" and "true teaching" held in the deposit of faith.

# Occasions for the Writing of the Pastorals

The occasions for the writing of 1 Timothy and Titus differ from that which prompted the writing of 2 Timothy. First Timothy and Titus focus more on church structures, the duties and responsibilities of church leaders, and confronting false teachings. In contrast, 2 Timothy is more concerned with Timothy's fidelity to his call and his mission to carry on the traditions and teachings of Paul, particularly in light of false teachings and anticipated persecution. Paul's withstanding of persecutions offers a model to Timothy and other church leaders who must endure hardships to defend correct doctrine. Given that the context of the letter is Paul's impending death, 2 Timothy has a more somber tone.

Despite the different circumstances that occasioned their writing, the Pastorals find common ground in their intention to confront and refute false teachings, which continue to create internal crises for the Christian congregations. The Pastor sees Paul's life and theology as the best avenue for establishing a sense of continuity and connection between the apostolic traditions that serve to defend against heresy and the contemporary communities. Indeed, throughout these letters, the Pastor draws upon Pauline material, especially from Romans and 1 Corinthians, to support his positions. This can be seen in discussions of, for example, the goodness of the law (1 Tim 1:8–9 and Rom 7:12,16), the handing over of deviants in the faith to Satan (1 Tim 20 and 1 Cor 5:5), on not being ashamed of the gospel (2 Tim 1:8 and Rom 1:16), on drawing analogies between the work of the gospel and manual labor (2 Tim 2:4–6 and 1 Cor 9:7), and on how to handle heretical or immoral behavior (Titus 3:10–11 and Rom 16:17–18; 1 Cor 5:11). By drawing on several of Paul's writings, the Pastor hoped that Paul's contribution would continue to guide the life of the community and, in turn, help to secure Paul's legacy.

## Women in the Pastoral Letters

Scholars over the years have noted that the Pastorals do not hold a favorable view of women in terms of leadership positions in the church. For example,

> A woman must receive instruction silently and under complete control. I do not permit a woman to teach or to have authority over a man. She must be quiet. For Adam was formed first, then Eve. Further, Adam was not deceived, but the woman was deceived and transgressed. But she will be saved through motherhood, provided women persevere in faith and love and holiness, with self-control. (1 Tim 2:11–15)

This is a departure from the undisputed Pauline letters that, for example, spoke of female prophets (1 Corinthians 11:3–16) and of men and women as co-workers with Paul (Romans 16:3). In fact, some scholars argue that Pauline texts that speak of restricting women, such as 1 Cor 14:34–35, may be later interpolations reflecting the kinds of values seen by the Pastor in 1 Tim 2:8–15.

## Opponents in the Pastorals

All three Pastoral Letters frequently address the issue of false teachers and false teachings (1 Tim 1:3–7,18b–20; 4:1–5; 6:3–10,20–21; 2 Tim 2:14–18,23–26; 3:1–9; 4:3–4; Titus 1:10–16; 3:9–11). The continual focus upon the opponents likely indicates the serious threat these teachers and their teachings were seen to pose. Advocates for these teachings apparently attended congregational gatherings (2 Tim 2:16–17,25; Titus 1:7–9; 3:9–10), making an impact on entire households (Titus 1:11). The Pastor seems especially concerned about the impact these false teachers were making on the congregation: "For some of these slip into homes and make captives of women weighed down by sins, led by various desires, always trying to learn but never able to reach a knowledge of the truth" (2 Tim 3:6–7).

Although the Pastor consistently highlights the need to confront and disassociate from the opponents, he offers few details about their teachings. One feature of the opponents' message was the certain "knowledge" (*gnōsis*) they could provide to the congregations (1 Tim 6:20–21; 2 Tim 3:7; Titus 1:16). In response, the Pastor construes this "knowledge" as including mere "myths and endless genealogies" (1 Tim 1:4; 4:7; 2 Tim 4:4; Titus 1:14; 3:9). The teaching also seemed to include a demand for abstinence from marriage and a banning of select food (1 Tim 4:3) as well as the claim that the resurrection had already occurred—obviously not a Pauline concept, yet one attested to in Colossians and Ephesians (2 Tim 2:18; Col 2:12–13; 3:1; Eph 2:5–6).

The teachings of the opponents also contained Jewish elements. Indeed, the opponents claim to be teachers of the law (1 Tim 1:7), described by the Pastor as Jewish Christians (literally, "from the circumcision faction," Titus 1:10) promoting "Jewish myths and regulations of people who have repudiated the truth" (Titus 1:14). The exact identity of the opponents, however, remains unknown. It could be the case that there was more than one type of opponent or that the opponents reflected a variety of influences. Regardless of their profile(s), they clearly were of great concern to the Pastor at a time when the struggle for influence in the post-Pauline Christian congregations was in full swing.

## Names of the Opponents

On several occasions, the Pastorals identify by name the opponents spreading false teachings:

> Some, by rejecting conscience, have made a shipwreck of the faith, among them *Hymenaeus and Alexander*, whom I have handed over to Satan to be taught not to blaspheme. (1 Tim 1:19b–20) (emphasis added)

> Avoid profane, idle talk, for such people will become more and more godless, and their teaching will spread like gangrene. Among them are *Hymenaeus and Philetus*, who have deviated from the truth by saying that [the] resurrection has already taken place and are upsetting the faith of some. (2 Tim 2:16–18) (emphasis added)

> *Alexander the coppersmith* did me a great deal of harm; the Lord will repay him according to his deeds. You too be on guard against him, for he has strongly resisted our preaching. (2 Tim 4:14–15) (emphasis added)

The Pastor's willingness to identify some of the opponents by name suggests that at least some of the false teachers and teachings were active, and possibly recognized leaders, within the congregations over which the Pastor desired to have influence.

## Summary: Historical Setting of the Pastorals

| Author | Unknown (one or more authors possible) |
|---|---|
| Audience | Mostly Gentile Christians |
| Date of Composition | Around 100 CE |
| Place of Composition | Unknown (possibly western Asia Minor) |

## Summary: Historical Context of the Pastoral Letters

**CORE CONCEPTS**

- Nearly all scholars consider the Pastoral Letters to be deutero-Pauline letters.
- As early Christian pseudepigraphic writings, the letters offer few reliable clues to their historical setting.
- The Pastor construes the opponents and their teachings as a substantial threat to the Christian congregations receiving the Pastoral Letters.

**SUPPLEMENTAL INFORMATION**

- For the Pastor, Paul, Timothy, and Titus are models of endurance amid hardships.
- First Timothy and Titus share a common focus on church order.
- Second Timothy focuses on Timothy's fidelity to his call to carry on the traditions and teachings of Paul.
- The Pastorals were addressed to Christian congregations with mostly wealthy believers.
- All three Pastoral Letters are concerned about false teachers and false teachings.
- The exact identity of the opponents remains unknown.

# THEOLOGY AND ETHICS OF THE PASTORAL LETTERS

The theology of the Pastoral Letters focuses on promoting and defending the "deposit" (*parathēkē*) of the faith, the "good news" of Jesus Christ. The Pastor considers Paul the foremost apostle of Christ and believes that the Pauline gospel preserves the deposit of faith for all believers (2 Tim 2:8). Paul also serves as the model for subsequent church leaders in terms of ethical behavior and norms. The Pastor presents these norms mostly in the form of qualifications of church leaders (bishops, presbyters, and deacons) as well as duties for the presbyters, and community rules for the congregation, including for widows and slaves.

# Theology

## Christ

The various titles attributed to Jesus in the Pastorals shed light on how the Pastor understood Jesus' identity. Appearing a total of eighteen times, the title most often used is *Lord* (*kurios*), (1 Tim 1:2,12,14,15;

## This Saying Is Trustworthy

On five occasions, the Pastor assures his readers of certain sayings that are "trustworthy":

| | |
|---|---|
| 1 Timothy 1:15 | Christ Jesus came into the world to save sinners. Of these I am the foremost. |
| 1 Timothy 3:1 | Whoever aspires to the office of bishop desires a noble task. |
| 1 Timothy 4:8 | Devotion is valuable in every respect, since it holds a promise of life both for the present and for the future. |
| 2 Timothy 2:11–13 | If we have died with him we shall also live with him; if we persevere we shall also reign with him. But if we deny him he will deny us. If we are unfaithful he remains faithful, for he cannot deny himself. |
| Titus 3:4–7 | But when the kindness and generous love of God our savior appeared, not because of any righteous deeds we had done but because of his mercy, he saved us through the bath of rebirth and renewal by the holy Spirit, whom he richly poured out on us through Jesus Christ our savior, so that we might be justified by his grace and become heirs in hope of eternal life. |

These trustworthy sayings are a particular appeal to authority for a possibly controversial point on which, as the Pastor would have it, there ought to be agreement.

6:3,14; 2 Tim 1:2,8,16,18; 2:7,22,24; 4:8,14,17,18,22). As Lord, Jesus strengthens believers (1 Tim 1:12; 2 Tim 4:17), facilitates their understanding of the faith (2 Tim 2:7), rewards the faithful on the Day of Judgment (2 Tim 4:8) and punishes the unfaithful (2 Tim 4:14). The Pastor also refers to Jesus as *savior* (*sōtēr*) (1 Tim 1:1; 2:3; 4:10; 2 Tim 1:10; Titus 1:3,4; 2:10,13; 3:4,6). Although the Pastoral Letters refer to both God and Jesus interchangeably as "our savior," this is likely not a claim to Jesus' divinity. A third title applied to Jesus is *judge* (*kritēs*), for example in 2 Timothy 4:1,8, which portrays Jesus as the end-time judge (see also 1 Tim 6:14; 2 Tim 4:18; Titus 2:13).

The Christology of the Pastorals is embedded throughout numerous passages. The Pastor affirms Jesus' preexistence (2 Tim 1:9), as well as his humanity, death, Resurrection, glorification (1 Tim 3:16; 2 Tim 2:8), and his return one day as the end-time judge (2 Tim 4:8). The letters support the fundamental conviction that the Christ-event brought victory over death for all believers (2 Tim 1:10), accomplished by God and not from works on the part of believers (Titus 3:4–7). Jesus now serves as the mediator between God and humanity; his death on the cross has brought salvation to the world (1 Tim 2:5–6). For the Pastor, this is the good news of Jesus Christ.

## Paul

For the Pastor, the life and the theology of Paul best expresses the gospel message of Jesus Christ. He holds Paul in the highest esteem and acknowledges him as the apostle and teacher of the Gentiles, appointed by God (1 Tim 2:7; 2 Tim 1:11; Titus 1:3) and entrusted with the proclamation of the gospel (1 Tim 1:11; 2 Tim 1:12). Paul's theology and ethical instructions (the Pauline gospel) form the original teachings, the "sound doctrine" (1 Tim 6:1,3; 2 Tim 4:3; Titus 1:9; 2:1) that the Christian congregations are to preserve and proclaim when defending the faith from false teachers (1 Tim 1:10; 4:1,6; 2 Tim 3:10).

The Pastor expects Timothy and Titus to follow Paul's lead, so that they, too, will serve as models to the faithful (1 Tim 4:6,12; 2 Tim 3:10–11; Titus 2:7). By holding firm to the received tradition, handed down from Paul that unites the believers, Timothy and Titus stand in contrast to the false teachers who are accused of creating division within the congregations (1 Tim 6:3–5; 2 Tim 3:10–17; Titus 1:10–16). As the apostle's beloved children in the faith (1 Tim 1:2,18; 2 Tim 1:2; 2:1;

Titus 1:4), and in the exercise of their ministerial duties, Timothy and Titus are to manifest Paul's presence to the congregations they serve.

## Jannes and Jambres Opposed Moses

In his exhortations to Timothy to oppose false teachers (2 Tim 3:1–9), the Pastor refers to Jannes and Jambres (v. 8), the legendary magicians of the Egyptian Pharaoh. According to the Old Testament book of Exodus, Pharaoh used magicians to oppose Moses and Aaron in their attempts to release the Israelites from Egyptian slavery (for example, Exodus 7:11–13). The Old Testament mentions these magicians and their "magic arts" several times (for instance, Exodus 7:22; 8:3,14; 9:11), but does not refer to them by name. This has led some scholars to conclude that the Pastor may have had access to later Jewish writings that did include their names. The figures of Jannes and Jambres serve as archetypes in support of the Pastor's contention that opponents have always attempted to corrupt God's truth, but their ignorance and "depraved mind" will be eventually exposed for all to see (v. 9). In other words, the false teachers in certain Christian congregations known to the Pastor are no better than the Pharaoh's deceitful magicians.

### Church Leadership

The Pastor intended his exhortation to Timothy and Titus about following Paul's example and leadership to be heard and emulated by the leadership of the congregations to whom he was writing, which included presbyters, (1 Tim 5:17–23; Titus 1:5–6) bishops, and deacons (1 Tim 3:2–13; Titus 1:7–9). The undisputed letters of Paul make no mention of the *office* of presbyter. The offices of bishop and deacon, however, are mentioned in Philippians 1:1.[7] (See also Rom 16:1, in which Paul refers to Phoebe [a woman] as "a deacon of the church at Cenchreae.")

---

7. Modern understandings of the offices of bishop and deacon should not be projected back onto these ancient texts. Such a reading would be anachronistic. The reason the Pastor needs church leaders is for the management of change over time, which presumes a rather noneschatological vision of the church, especially as it conforms to Roman social values.

The Pastoral Letters provide evidence that an increased need for recognized church leaders was sensed after the days of Paul. A bishop's main task consisted of teaching and defending the deposit of faith (1 Tim 4:11,13,16; 2 Tim 1:13; 2:24; 3:14–17; Titus 2:1), refuting opponents with "sound doctrine" (Titus 1:9). Referred to as "God's steward" (Titus 1:7) and supported by deacons and the presbyters (1 Tim 4:14), a bishop was to function as the defender and teacher of the faith that Paul (purportedly) proclaimed and that was now under siege by false teachers.

# Ethics

Much of the ethical instructions in the Pastorals are addressed to the leadership of the congregations or specific groups within the congregations, such as widows and slaves. Although the Pastor often directs his moral exhortations to Timothy and Titus, the congregations' leaders are the real target audience.

## Qualifications of Bishops and Deacons

In 1 Timothy and Titus, the Pastor discusses the roles and responsibilities of bishops and deacons. Those seeking to be a bishop, or overseer, (*episkopos*) are held to a high moral standard (for example,

### "The Household of God"

One curious feature of the Pastorals is the relative absence of the word *ekklēsia* (*church*), a term that figures prominently in Paul's undisputed surviving letters. It occurs only three times in 1 Timothy (3:5,15; 5:16) and not at all in 2 Timothy or Titus. An important clue to understanding its absence from the Pastorals may lie in 1 Timothy 3:15: "But if I should be delayed, you should know how to behave in the household of God, which is the church of the living God, the pillar and foundation of truth." It is interesting to note how the Pastor takes over the patriarchy typical of a Roman household when calling for men to take charge of the responsibility of enforcing correct doctrine. For a potential bishop or a deacon, managing one's household shows that one is prepared to be a manager of God's household.

living above reproach, being married only once, and acting in a respectable and peaceable manner). This aligns with what the wider Roman society of that period would expect of fathers managing their households (1 Tim 3:2–7; Titus 1:7–9). The Pastor views the social institution of the household as the model of the church. Notably, the requirement of being married only once would exclude both unmarried (and, presumably, also younger) men as well as divorced men.

As "God's steward" (Titus 1:7), the bishop's major challenge is to hold "fast to the true message as taught" (Titus 1:9). One of his main duties is to serve as teacher of sound doctrine to the congregation and to refute opponents who spread false teachings (Titus 1:9). In the Letter to Titus, the Pastor excludes any "recent convert" (1 Tim 3:6) from becoming bishop, a restriction likely due to the desire that a possible future leader be observed over time to gauge his fitness to serve before being appointed.

A similar high standard of conduct is expected of those seeking to become a deacon (*diakonos*). A candidate must, for example, have married only once, be dignified, and manage his household well (1 Tim 3:8–13). Like the bishop, the deacon must be faithful to the traditions received; that is, hold "fast to the mystery of the faith with a clear conscience" (3:9). In addition to these behavioral norms, deacons should be "tested first" before being accepted as deacons (3:10).

## Congregational Rules

In 1 Timothy, the Pastor outlines his expectations of Timothy by explaining how to treat various groups within the congregation—men, women, widows, presbyters, and slaves. As in the discussion of bishops and deacons, these ethical standards set forth for Christian congregations combine the social norms of the day with some distinctively Christian elements.

The Pastor begins by exhorting Timothy to think of a congregation as a family, treating older men and women as one's father and mother, and younger men and women as one's brothers and sisters (1 Tim 5:1–2). In this way, the church models the household with parents and siblings.

He then focuses on three specific groups within the congregation: widows, presbyters, and slaves (1 Tim 5:3–6:2). First, the Pastor sets forth guidelines to determine who are "truly widows," that is, dependent upon the congregation's help, and which widows should seek assistance from their relatives (1 Tim 5:3–10). Younger widows are strongly encouraged to remarry and resume their traditional roles as wives (1 Tim 5:11–14).

Next, the pastor discusses the role of presbyter, or elder (*presbuteros*), who is charged with preaching and teaching at worship; he should also be paid for his services (1 Tim 5:17–18). Presbyters have a duty to carefully discern candidates before they "lay hands" and confer upon them Christian duties and responsibilities. The Pastor strongly encourages presbyters to perform good works in public (1 Tim 5:25).

Finally, the Pastor turns to slaves, whom he says, must be respectful of their masters, whether Christian or not, "so that the name of God and our teaching may not suffer abuse" (1 Tim 6:1). If the master is a believer, the slave is obliged to give even "better service" (1 Tim 6:2a).[8] The Pastor concludes by reiterating to Timothy: "Teach and urge these things" (1 Tim 6:2b).

## Shifting Strategies with Widows

Paul discusses the subject of widows within the early Christian congregations only in 1 Corinthians (dated mid-50s CE), in which he offers some straightforward and simple advice (1 Cor 7:8–9,39–40). He recommends that the widows and the unmarried remain as they are.

By the time 1 Timothy was written (around 100 CE), that approach had changed, at least within the Christian congregations to whom the Pastor wrote. First Timothy 5:3–16 provides a glimpse into how the congregations' leadership treated widows. "Real" widows were narrowly defined as those who were "all alone" (v. 5). The extended family (children or grandchildren) of a widow were expected to care for her: "If any woman believer has widowed relatives, she must assist them; the church is not to be burdened, so that it will be able to help those who are truly widows" (1 Tim 5:16).

Further, this letter places certain restrictions upon who qualified as a widow: more than age sixty, have married only once, and

*Continued*

8. This stands in contrast to the message in Philemon, which presumes a Christian master cannot have a Christian slave.

have a reputation for good works (vv. 9–10). The Pastor discourages younger widows from remaining single; rather, he instructs them to remarry, have children, and manage a home (v. 14). In the Pastor's view, the younger widows who remained unmarried too often created problems by being idlers, gossips, and busybodies (v. 13). Translation: They need to be under a husband's control so they will not be nuisances to the church.

Note the contrast between Paul and the Pastor in terms of widows. Paul wants them to remain unmarried, but the Pastor wants the very opposite—that they remarry. The Pastor leaves unanswered the question of what happens to women who become widows again.

## Summary: Theology and Ethics of the Pastoral Letters

### CORE CONCEPTS

- The theology of the Pastoral Letters focuses on promoting and defending the deposit (*parathēkē*) of the faith from false teachers.
- Church leadership is expected to teach and defend the faith.
- Ethical norms in the Pastorals are directed to the church leadership and to certain groups, such as widows, presbyters, and slaves.

### SUPPLEMENTAL INFORMATION

- The Pastor considers Paul the foremost apostle of Christ.
- The Pastorals commonly refer to Christ as *Lord* and *savior*.
- The Pauline gospel claims to be the basis of the "sound doctrine" that the Christian congregations are to preserve and proclaim.
- The Pastor views the bishop as "God's steward."
- The high moral standards expected of those who serve as bishop and deacon follow the social and behavioral norms of the larger Roman society.
- As "the household of God," Christian communities are expected to model themselves after households within the larger Roman society.

## Questions for Review

1. Why are scholars uncertain about how many authors wrote the Pastorals?
2. What is the profile of the Christian congregations receiving the Pastoral Letters?
3. Why do scholars think that the Pastorals were written around 100 CE?
4. What are the possible occasions for the writing of the Pastorals?
5. What is known about the opponents discussed in the Pastoral Letters?
6. How do the Pastoral Letters describe Christ?
7. In what ways is Paul considered central to the deposit of the faith?
8. What were some leadership positions during the writing of the Pastorals?
9. What were the duties and responsibilities of a bishop?
10. According to the Pastor, what made someone a true widow?

## Questions for Reflection

1. What difference would it make if the Pastorals were written by one author or by multiple authors?
2. What challenges do you think may have arisen for bishops who followed the Pastor's advice to defend the deposit of the faith?
3. Why do you think the author(s) of the Pastorals is such a huge proponent of the apostle Paul?
4. What is your reaction to the duties and responsibilities of the household members as presented in the Pastorals?

## Recommendations for Further Reading

Harding, Mark. *What Are They Saying about the Pastoral Epistles?* New York: Paulist Press, 2001.

> Harding surveys recent scholarship on the Pastoral Letters, giving special attention to how the Pastorals can be applied today. Harding divides his study of scholarship on the Pastorals into six categories: authorship,

relation to the Pauline tradition, social and literary setting, relation to ancient rhetoric, and the meaning of the Pastorals Letters for today.

Johnson, Luke Timothy. *Letters to Paul's Delegates: 1 Timothy, 2 Timothy, and Titus.* Harrisburg, PA: Trinity Press International, 1996.

Johnson presents his case for the authenticity of these three Pauline letters, arguing that Paul could have written each, especially 2 Timothy. While conceding that the theology of the Pastorals is clearly different in many ways from the undisputed letters of Paul in terms of style, Johnson maintains that the Pastorals contain many undisputed Pauline elements.

Kidd, Reggie M. *Wealth and Beneficence in the Pastoral Epistles.* Atlanta, GA: Scholar's Press, 1990.

Kidd challenges the notion that the wealthy audience of the Pastorals represents a new phenomenon for Pauline Christians (a "bourgeois Christianity"), noting the undisputed letters were addressed to believers on varying levels of the economic spectrum. Rather than accommodating these wealthy Christians, the author of the Pastorals challenges them to be generous in sharing their wealth with other believers.

Köstenberger, Andreas J., and Terry L. Wilder (eds.). *Entrusted with the Gospel: Paul's Theology in the Pastoral Epistles.* Nashville, TN: B & H Publishing, 2010.

This book offers twelve essays on the Pastorals from the perspective of Protestant evangelical scholars. The essays cover topics associated with the Pastorals, ranging from church leadership, the role of women, and the Pauline authorship of the Pastorals to the structure, ethics, and mission of the Pastorals.

MacDonald, Margaret Y. *Early Christian Women and Pagan Opinion: The Power of the Hysterical Woman.* Cambridge, UK: Cambridge University Press, 1996.

MacDonald examines how the larger Roman society tended to view Christian women in the first and second century CE. She begins her study with a cultural analysis of the ancient Mediterranean society. The book is then divided into three parts: pagan reaction to early Christian women in the second century CE; celibacy, women, and early church responses to public opinion; marriage, women, and early church responses to public opinion.

# CHAPTER 11

# Later Letters, Narratives, and the *Apocalypse of Paul*

## INTRODUCTION

In chapters 9 and 10, the legacy of Paul has been considered as reflected in the six New Testament deutero-Pauline letters. In this final chapter, that legacy is traced in even later Christian writings about Paul. The first section of the chapter traces the Pauline tradition in the Apostolic Fathers (Clement, Ignatius, Polycarp, and Papias) and the later apocryphal writings associated with Paul: the *Acts of Paul* (including the *Acts of Paul and Thecla*, *3 Corinthians*, and the *Martyrdom of Paul*), the *Epistle to the Laodiceans*, the *Apocalypse of Paul*, and the *Correspondence of Paul and Seneca*. Special focus is given to the historical setting of the later apocryphal writings. Each of these sources, ranging from the late-first through early-fourth centuries, helps scholars understand the legacy of Paul in the early church. The second section of the chapter provides an overview of the later apocryphal writings, including a summary and a focus on the main theological emphasis.

### Occasions for These Later Writings

The circulation of Paul's writings apparently began in the mid-second century (and possibly earlier). The letter of 2 Peter (dated early- to mid-second century) confirms knowledge of Paul and his letters with the author warning against those who would "distort" Paul (2 Pet 3:15–16). This circulation to wider audiences of Christians likely accounts for the Apostolic Fathers' mention of Paul and his letters in some of their writings. It may have also given rise to the production of these later letters, narratives, and apocalypses associated with Paul. Scholars today debate whether the later writings complement, compete with, or are largely independent of the New Testament literature.

Another reason for the composition of such writings stemmed from the letters of Paul themselves. The *Epistle to Laodiceans*, for example, seems to have been written to fill the gap in the correspondence between Paul and the Colossians. At the end of the Letter to the Colossians, Paul asks the Colossians to send greetings to the Laodiceans and refers to a letter from them (Col 4:15–16). The *Apocalypse of Paul*, which narrates Paul's vision of the afterlife, apparently responds to 2 Corinthians 12:1–5, in which Paul writes of being "caught up into Paradise." It may have also been the case that the circulation of the canonical Acts of the Apostles encouraged the later composition of the *Acts of Paul*.

## New Testament Apocrypha

Scholars today routinely classify Christian writings of the first few centuries that were not included in the canon as New Testament "apocrypha," a category that encompasses gospels, acts, epistles, and apocalypses. This chapter focuses on apocryphal acts (the *Acts of Paul*, which includes the *Acts of Paul and Thecla* and the *Martyrdom of Paul*), apocryphal epistles (*3 Corinthians*, the *Epistle to the Laodiceans*, and the *Correspondence of Paul and Seneca*), and an apocryphal apocalypse (the *Apocalypse of Paul*).

The modern designation *apocrypha* (hidden things) can be somewhat misleading, however. Whereas *apocrypha* means, "hidden, concealed, secret," many church fathers knew about these Pauline writings and, in some instances, even considered them part of the New Testament canon. (For example, the Christian church in Armenia considered *3 Corinthians* an undisputed letter of Paul.)

## THE CONTINUING LEGACY OF PAUL

After the undisputed letters of Paul, written between 50 and 60 CE, the legacy of Paul began with the six deutero-Pauline letters of the New Testament, 70 to 110 CE. Paul's legacy continued with echoes of "Paulinism" seen in some of the writings of the Apostolic Fathers of the early second century. Later Christian writings soon emerged in the wake of the Apostolic Fathers that developed further the "Pauls" of the early church into the early fourth century.

## The Pauline Tradition in the Apostolic Fathers

The generation of church leaders and authors following that of the apostles are commonly referred to as the Apostolic Fathers. They are considered the earliest post-New Testament witnesses to Paul; that is, these writings provide a "witness" to scholars that second-century Christians knew about Paul and his letters. Among those considered Apostolic Fathers are four bishops: Clement, Ignatius, Polycarp, and Papias. Their writings show deference to Paul and his authority as well as hold up Paul as a model of endurance and suffering for the faith.

*First Clement*, a letter to the church in Corinth dated to 95–96 CE, attributed to Clement, the bishop of Rome (but more likely written by the church of Rome), addresses the problem of schism in the church of Corinth, a major issue Paul had addressed already in 1 Corinthians. A disturbing change of leadership had occurred in the Corinthian community, and part of the author's strategy in coping with this problem is to celebrate Paul's endurance as a long-suffering missionary. Because of jealousy and envy the greatest and most righteous pillars were persecuted, and fought to the death. . . .

> Because of jealousy and strife Paul by his example pointed out the way to the prize for patient endurance. After he had been seven times in chains, had been driven into exile, had been stoned, and had preached in the East and in the West, he won the genuine glory for his faith, having taught righteousness to the whole world and having reached the farthest limits of the West. Finally, when he had given his testimony before the rulers, he thus departed from the world and went to the holy place, having become an outstanding example of patient endurance.[1] (*1 Clem* 5:5–7)

---

1. English translation taken from Michael W. Holmes, *The Apostolic Fathers in English*, 3rd ed. (Grand Rapids, MI: Baker Academic, 2006), 44–45.

Further, apparently referring to Paul's Letter to the Galatians (Gal 2:1–15), the author laments the divided state of the church even during Paul's time:

> Take up the epistle of the blessed Paul the apostle. What did he first write to you in the "beginning of the gospel"? Truly he wrote to you in the Spirit about himself and Cephas and Apollos, because even then you had split into factions. Yet that splitting into factions brought less sin upon you, for you were partisans of highly reputed Apostles and of a man approved by them. In contrast now think about those who have perverted you and diminished the respect due your renowned love for the brotherhood. It is disgraceful, dear friends, yes, utterly disgraceful and unworthy of your conduct in Christ, that it should be reported that the well-established and ancient church of the Corinthians, because of one or two persons, is rebelling against its presbyters.[2] (*1 Clem* 47:1–6)

Another Apostolic Father, Ignatius, bishop of Antioch, mentions Paul in two of his letters, dated between 110 and 117 CE. In the first passage, Paul is presented as an example for those who suffer (compare, for example, 2 Tim 3:10–12, 4:5–6). In the second, note Ignatius's deference to apostles Peter and Paul:

> You are the highway of those who are being killed for God's sake; you are fellow-initiates of Paul, who was sanctified, who was approved, who is deservedly blessed—may I be found in his footsteps when I reach God![3] (Ign. *Eph.* 12:2)

> I do not give you orders like Peter and Paul: they were apostles, I am a convict; they were free, but I am even now still a slave. But if I suffer, I will be a freedman of Jesus Christ, and will rise up free in him.[4] (Ign. *Rom.* 4:3)

---

2. Ibid., 64.

3. Ibid., 100.

4. Ibid., 114.

Polycarp was bishop of Smyrna and a friend of Ignatius and, like Ignatius, a martyr. After receiving Ignatius's letter, Polycarp wrote at the Philippian Christians' request, responding to their questions. (Ign. *Phil.* 3:1). They had asked for copies of Ignatius's letters, and Polycarp sent his own letter with those letters of Ignatius known to him, possibly all seven of them (Pol. *Phil.* 13:2). Polycarp reflects little knowledge of the Old Testament but does claim to know the letters of Paul, including the Pastorals and Hebrews. For example, Polycarp defers to Paul's letters and authority:

> For neither I nor anyone like me can keep pace with the wisdom of the blessed and glorious Paul, who, when he was among you in the presence of the men of that time, accurately and reliably taught the word concerning the truth. And when he was absent he wrote you letters; if you study them carefully, you will be able to build yourselves up in the faith that has been given to you, 'which is the mother of us all,' while hope follows and love for God and Christ and for our neighbor leads the way.[5] (Pol. *Phil.* 3:2–3a, citing Paul's Gal 4:26. See also Pol. *Phil.* 11:2b, citing Paul's 1 Cor 6:2)

Elsewhere, Polycarp celebrates Paul's endurance:

> I urge all of you, therefore, to obey the teaching about righteousness and to exercise unlimited endurance, like that which you saw . . . in Paul himself and the rest of the apostles. (Pol. *Phil.* 9:1)[6]

Additionally, Papias, bishop of Hierapolis, around 120 CE (as preserved by Irenaeus, *Against Heresies 5.5.1*, around 180 CE), refers to the "translation" of Paul to another place where the apostle received visions and revelations (compare 2 Cor 12:1–7).

Echoes of Paul are present in the select writings of these Apostolic Fathers. They provide some evidence of the legacy of Paul developing in the early church.

---

5. Ibid., 136.
6. Ibid.

## Overview: The Later Pauline Writings[7]

| Writing | Date and Place of Composition | Surviving Witness and Manuscript Evidence |
| --- | --- | --- |
| *Acts of Paul* | Approximately 180–200 CE, perhaps in Asia Minor | Third–fourth century Greek fragmented manuscripts; fifth–sixth century Coptic manuscripts; early Church fathers' witness: second and third century—Tertullian, Hippolytus, Origen; fourth and fifth century—Eusebius, Jerome, Augustine |
| *3 Corinthians* | Approximately 150–200 CE, place unknown | Greek and Latin fragmented manuscripts as early as third century CE, prior independent circulation, later incorporated into the *Acts of Paul* |
| *Acts of Paul and Thecla* | Approximately 180–200 CE, place unknown | Many Greek fragmented manuscripts, maybe original to the *Acts of Paul*, later circulating independently from the *Acts of Paul* |

*Continued*

7. The data for this overview is taken from numerous secondary sources: Bart D. Ehrman, *Lost Scriptures: Books That Did Not Make It into the New Testament* (New York: Oxford University Press, 2003); J. K. Elliott, *The Apocryphal New Testament: A Collection of Apocryphal Christian Literature in an English Translation* (Oxford, UK: Clarendon, 1993); Wilhelm Schneemelcher, *New Testament Apocrypha*, vol. 2 (Louisville, KY: Westminster John Knox Press, 1991).

| Overview: The Later Pauline Writings *Continued* | | |
|---|---|---|
| *Martyrdom of Paul* | Approximately 180–200 CE, place unknown | Greek fragmented manuscripts, likely original ending of *Acts of Paul* |
| *Epistle to the Laodiceans* | Approximately 200–300 CE, place unknown | Fragmented Latin manuscripts; early Church fathers' witness: possibly second century—Tertullian; fourth century—Jerome |
| *Apocalypse of Paul* | Approximately 250 CE, perhaps in Egypt | Fragmented Latin manuscripts from fifth–sixth century; early Church fathers' witness: third century—Origen; fourth and fifth century—Prudentius, Augustine, Sozomen |
| *Correspondence of Paul and Seneca* | Approximately 300s CE, place unknown | Many fragmented manuscripts dated as early as fifth century CE; multiple languages; early Church fathers' witness: fourth century—Jerome and Augustine |

Even centuries after Paul's death, some Christians continued to write letters in Paul's name. Second- and third-century Christians, following the Apostolic Fathers, produced a variety of writings associated with Paul, focusing on various aspects of his life, ministry, miracles, and martyrdom. These later Christian authors further enhanced the legacy of Paul. Although these writings probably tell nothing about the historical Paul, they are of great interest to understanding receptions and developments of Pauline traditions. The popularity of these apocryphal writings in the early church is seen in both the witness of the early church fathers to these writings and the extensive manuscript evidence that remains of these texts.

## A Description of Paul

The New Testament contains no physical description of Paul. The earliest depiction of Paul's physical appearance occurs in the *Acts of Paul and Thecla*, written at least a hundred years after Paul's death. According to the storyline, Titus offered a description of Paul to Onesiphorus, a fellow Christian waiting to greet Paul, because Onesiphorus had never met Paul:

> And he [Onesiphorus] went along the royal road which leads to Lystra, and stood there waiting for him, and looked at all who came, according to Titus' description. And he saw Paul coming, a man small of stature, with a bald head and crooked legs, in a good state of body, with eyebrows meeting and nose somewhat hooked, full of friendliness; for now he appeared like a man, and he had the face of an angel.[8] (*Acts of Paul and Thecla* 3.3)

Scholars do not necessarily regard this description of Paul as accurate. Ancient people often attributed physical characteristics to personality traits. For example, baldness was thought to be a sign of piety and eyebrows meeting (one eyebrow) indicated thoughtfulness.[9] Although by contemporary western standards Paul is not described with attractive features, the physical description in the *Acts of Paul and Thecla* may well have intended to be complimentary of Paul.

8. Wilhelm Schneemelcher, ed. *New Testament Apocrypha*, 2 vols. Rev. ed. trans. R. McL. Wilson (Louisville, KY: Westminster John Knox Press, 1991), 239.

9. For a good source on ancient personalities connected to physical features, see Bruce J. Malina and Jerome H. Neyrey. *Portraits of Paul: An Archaeology of Ancient Personality* (Louisville, KY: Westminster John Knox Press, 1996).

The writings of the church fathers from the patristic period (second through fifth century CE) verify the existence of these texts within the early church.[10] In most cases, however, the church fathers mention only select episodes or ideas from these writings and typically either condemn or support them as part of a larger discussion.[11] For example, the *Acts of Paul* was familiar to numerous early and influential church fathers, such as Tertullian, who lived in the late-second and early-third century. In his work *On Baptism* (17), which argues that women should not be allowed to baptize or preach, Tertullian criticizes Thecla, one of Paul's female co-workers from the *Acts of Paul*. (Apparently, there were Christian women known to Tertullian in North Africa who baptized and who used Thecla's example of baptizing herself before her martyrdom.) Hippolytus of Rome, in his *Commentary on Daniel* (3.29) from the early third century, likewise mentions a scene from the *Acts of Paul* involving a lion licking Paul rather than eating him. It remains unknown, however, whether Tertullian and Hippolytus had a complete text of the *Acts of Paul*, as neither mentions it by name. The writings of the early church fathers provide evidence that all of the apocryphal writings highlighted in this chapter existed.[12]

---

10. The first explicit mention of the *Acts of Paul* occurs in a mid-third–century writing by Origen of Alexandria (185–254 CE), a prolific third-century Christian scholar and theologian. In his work, *On First Principles* (215 CE), Origen mentions the *Acts of Paul*. Origen uses the *Acts of Paul* to support a larger theological argument about Wisdom and the Word of God (Christ). The text suggests that Origen had a favorable view of the *Acts of Paul*, but church fathers of the fourth and fifth centuries eventually deemed the work outside the realm of orthodox writings. Subsequent Church fathers from the fourth and fifth century (Eusebius, Jerome, and Augustine) reference the *Acts of Paul*, but ultimately reject it for not representing the orthodox faith.

11. See J. K. Elliott, *The Apocryphal New Testament: A Collection of Apocryphal Christian Literature in an English Translation* (Oxford, UK: Clarendon, 1993) and Wilhelm Schneemelcher, *New Testament Apocrypha*, vol. 2 (Louisville, KY: Westminster John Knox Press, 1991) for good background information on the attestation of the early church fathers for the later writings about Paul.

12. The *Apocalypse of Paul* is mentioned by numerous church fathers of the patristic period: Origen, Prudentius, Augustine, and Sozomen. In describing the destiny of souls after death in his homily on Psalm 36, Origen appears to draw from the *Apocalypse of Paul* (13). However, because he does not cite it by name, there are doubts about whether Origen knew the *Apocalypse of Paul* in its present form. This also appears to be the case with the fourth-century poet Prudentius, whose work, *Cathemerinon* (5), likewise may have drawn from the *Apocalypse of Paul*. The earliest direct references to the *Apocalypse of Paul* appear in Sozomen's *Church History*, dated to the

Although overall there is good manuscript evidence for these additional writings on Paul, the actual manuscripts exist today only in fragments. The sheer volume of fragmented manuscripts that do exist, however, along with the multiple languages in which they were written, testifies to their popularity in the early church. For example, fragments of the *Acts of Paul* are found in third- and fourth-century Greek manuscripts.[13] Three sections from the *Acts of Paul* (the *Acts of Paul and Thecla*, *3 Corinthians*, and the *Martyrdom of Paul*) exist in separate fragmented manuscripts, which suggests that these texts may have circulated independently.[14] The *Apocalypse of Paul* is found in fragmented Latin manuscripts dated to the fifth–sixth century.[15] The *Correspondence of Paul and Seneca* also survives in numerous fragmented manuscripts in multiple languages, but these manuscripts are quite corrupted, with the oldest dating back to the fifth century. The manuscripts of the *Epistle to the Laodiceans* exist today in only a few Latin fragments.

---

end of the fourth century, and in Augustine's *Tractate on John*, written in the early fifth century. Sozomen dismisses legends associated with the divine origins of the *Apocalypse of Paul* as "invented by heretics" (19.7), and Augustine refers to the *Apocalypse of Paul* as "forged" and "rejected by the orthodox Church" (98.8). Tertullian rejects the *Epistle to the Laodiceans* as an authentic letter of Paul in his treatise, *Against Marcion* 5.11, 17, but scholars are uncertain if the text Tertullian refers to in his treatise is the same as the present apocryphal epistle. In his work *On Illustrious Men* (5) dated to near the end of the fourth century, Jerome comments on the status of the *Epistles to the Laodiceans* as one of Paul's letters, saying the idea was "rejected by everyone." In contrast, regarding the *Correspondence of Paul and Seneca*, he maintains that the letters "are read by very many" (*On Illustrious Men*, 12). Jerome gives no indication that he viewed these letters as forgeries, so he may have considered them as authentic letters of Paul.

13. Nearly 2,000 fragments in Coptic, dated to the fifth and sixth centuries, have been assembled, providing a nearly complete version of the *Acts of Paul*.

14. More than forty fragmented Greek manuscripts of the *Acts of Paul and Thecla* exist today. The story's popularity, which gave rise to the cult of Saint Thecla, likely facilitated a later and separate circulation. Fragmented manuscripts of *3 Corinthians* exist in Greek and Latin, some dated as early as the third century. Early on, in fact, it appears that the Syriac and Armenian churches considered *3 Corinthians* an authentic Pauline letter. It seems probable that *3 Corinthians* was written earlier than—and later incorporated into—the *Acts of Paul*. Greek fragments of the *Martyrdom of Paul* also exist. Although originally written as the conclusion to the *Acts of Paul*, this story too may later have circulated independently of it.

15. One of the curious features of the manuscripts associated with the *Apocalypse of Paul* is the existence of numerous shorter versions or recensions that tend to focus on Paul's visions of hell. Scholars suspect these recensions may have provided fodder for some rather fiery sermons (see Elliott, 616).

## Pauline Forgeries

Some scholars classify the additional writings on Paul as forgeries. Written a century or more after Paul's death, they served various purposes, with some intended to fill in the gaps from the New Testament Pauline letters (the *Epistle to the Laodiceans*, the *Apocalypse of Paul*), and others to show the superiority of Christianity over pagan religions (the *Correspondence between Paul and Seneca*) or provide fanciful legends about Paul (the *Acts of Paul*).

The early Christians did not always recognize these writings as forgeries. Some Latin manuscripts of the New Testament, for example, included the *Epistle to the Laodiceans*; and the mid-third-century Christian poet, Commodianus, used episodes from the *Acts of Paul* in his work *Carmen Apologetic* (128). Eventually, the early church rejected these writings as un-Pauline and for running counter to the later orthodox teaching.

### Authors, Audiences, Dates, and Places of Composition

Like the New Testament Pauline letters, the apocryphal writings associated with Paul offer limited information about their historical setting. Indeed, scholars must rely almost solely upon the writings of the early church fathers to establish even broad parameters for dating them, a circumstance that only magnifies the problem. The following, therefore, represent some general observations about these writings:

The authors of these texts are unknown, with the *Acts of Paul* being one possible exception. According to Tertullian, the presbyter forged this document "out of love" for Paul and was subsequently "removed from his office."[16]

Just as little is known of the authors, the same could be said of the audiences. The authors do not indicate their intended recipients. Given their subject matter, however, one can assume that the audience for these later writings about Paul was largely Christian.

---

16. Tertullian, *On Baptism* 17. See Schneemelcher, Wilhelm, ed. *New Testament Apocrypha*, vol. 2 Rev. ed. trans. R. McL. Wilson (Louisville, KY: Westminster John Knox Press, 1991), 214.

The patristic writings provide some help in reconstructing the dates of composition. Origen made the first explicit reference to the *Acts of Paul*, which indicates that the text was already written by the mid-third century. If Tertullian's remarks derived from the text of *Acts of Paul*, then that can be dated to the late second century. The earliest direct attestation of the *Apocalypse of Paul* dates to the end of the fourth century with Sozomen, but scholars think the original Greek version (now lost) may date back to as early as the mid-third century.[17] Both the comments by Tertullian and Origen regarding the *Epistle to the Laodiceans* place the composition of this letter sometime between the late second and fourth centuries. Establishing the date for the *Correspondence of Paul and Seneca*, however, is somewhat complicated by scholars' question of the literary unity of these fourteen letters, viewing letters 11, 13, and 14 as possibly composed at a different time. Nonetheless, a fourth-century date for composition is a given, because Jerome knows of the letters.

Of special note are *3 Corinthians* and the *Acts of Paul and Thecla*. Although found within the larger narrative of the *Acts of Paul*, scholars suspect that these two writings circulated independently from the *Acts of Paul* as early as the middle of the second century.

Scholars also know little about where these texts were written. According to Tertullian, *Acts of Paul* was composed in Asia Minor, and scholars suspect that the *Apocalypse of Paul* may have originated in Egypt.[18]

## Summary: Historical Setting of the Later Writings

| Authors | Unknown (possibly unnamed presbyter from Asia Minor for *Acts of Paul*) |
|---|---|
| Audiences | Mostly Christians |
| Dates of Composition | Late second to fourth century |
| Places of Composition | Unknown (possibly Asia Minor for *Acts of Paul* and Egypt for *Apocalypse of Paul*) |

17. Elliott, 616.
18. Ibid.

## Summary: The Continuing Legacy of Paul

### CORE CONCEPTS

- The writings of the Apostolic Fathers offer echoes of "Paulinism" in the generation following the apostles and New Testament writers.
- Even centuries after Paul's death, some Christians continued to write letters in Paul's name.
- Later Christian authors wrote about Paul's life, ministry, miracles, and martyrdom. Although these later writings probably tell nothing about the historical Paul, they are of great interest to understanding later receptions and developments of Pauline traditions.

### SUPPLEMENTAL INFORMATION

- The generation of church leaders and authors following the apostles are commonly referred to as the Apostolic Fathers.
- The writings of the Apostolic Fathers are an important link in the legacy of Paul between the New Testament Pauline writings and the apocryphal writings on Paul.
- Some early church fathers mention the *Acts of Paul* and *Apocalypse of Paul* by name.
- There is good manuscript evidence for these additional writings on Paul, but the actual manuscripts exist today only in fragments.
- Although included as part of the narrative of the *Acts of Paul*, both the *Acts of Paul and Thecla* and *3 Corinthians* also circulated independently.
- These apocryphal writings about Paul were likely composed between the late second and fourth century.

# OVERVIEW OF THE LATER LETTERS, NARRATIVES, AND THE *APOCALYPSE OF PAUL*

What follows are brief overviews to the *Acts of Paul* (including the *Acts of Paul and Thecla*, *3 Corinthians*, and the *Martyrdom of Paul*), the *Epistle to the Laodiceans*, an *Apocalypse of Paul*, and the *Correspondence of Paul and Seneca*. Each overview includes a summary of the writing content and a focus on its theological character.[19] These writings offer insights into who Paul *becomes* and how his figure is *used* in later theological disputes.

## The Acts of Paul

No complete text of the original *Acts of Paul* exists. However, enough of the text remains intact to show that this narrative provided legendary accounts of Paul's travels to the cities of Jerusalem, Damascus, Antioch, Myra, Sidon, Tyre, Ephesus, Philippi, Corinth, and Rome. These cities span numerous regions (Syro-Palestine, Asia Minor, Greece, and Italy) and thousands of miles. Like Paul in the canonical Acts, the Paul of *Acts of Paul* travels extensively.

The gospel message of Paul found in his undisputed letters (for example, salvation offered to all—Jew and Gentile alike—through faith in Christ) is not the focus of the apocryphal *Acts of Paul*. In fact, the "gospel message" of the Paul in the *Acts of Paul* is far more focused on denying the body, renouncing the world, living an ascetic life, and most of all, abstaining from sexual relations. This Pauline gospel is evident in a number of Paul's thirteen beatitudes:

> Blessed are they who keep the flesh pure, for they shall become a temple of God. . . . Blessed are they who have renounced this world, for they shall be well pleasing to God. Blessed are they who have wives as if they had them not,

---

19. Both Elliott and Schneemelcher provide complete English translations for each of the later writings on Paul. These translations are highly recommended as sources for these additional letters, narratives, and apocalypses of Paul. This chapter follows the Greek edition of the *Apocalypse of Paul*. The "Coptic Gnostic" *Apocalypse of Paul* is not taken up in this chapter. See Schneemelcher, *New Testament Apocrypha*, vol. 2:695–712 (Coptic) and 7–12–748 (Greek).

for they shall be heirs to God. . . . Blessed are they who through love of God have departed from the form of this world, for they shall judge angels and at the right hand of the Father they shall be blessed. . . . Blessed are the bodies of virgins, for they shall be well pleasing to God, and shall not lose the reward of their purity.[20] (*Acts of Paul* 3:5–6)

One of the most notable adventures in this narrative occurs when Paul meets Thecla, a woman from Iconium whom he converts to the faith. After hearing Paul's gospel message, which included the beatitudes listed above, Thecla decided to break off her arranged marriage, remain a virgin, and become a disciple of Paul. She refused to obey her pagan father by marrying the man he had chosen for her. Instead of being loyal to a father or husband, Theca's loyalty was to Paul, and for this she became a martyr (but not before she baptized herself, of course). This section of the *Acts of Paul* apparently gained such fame that it circulated independently, as the *Acts of Paul and Thecla*. It may have appealed to Christians, especially women, who wanted liberation from arranged marriages and social structures that offered few choices.[21]

Also inserted into the narrative of the *Acts of Paul* is a letter between Paul and the Corinthians, known by some early Christians as *3 Corinthians*. This letter by "Paul" seems to respond to another pseudonymous letter sent to Paul from five Corinthian elders. They inform Paul of the false teaching being spread in Corinth that Jesus only appeared to be human (a second-century heresy known as docetism) and that Jesus was a man, born not of a virgin, and at his baptism became God's Son (another second-century heresy known as adoptionism). In *3 Corinthians*, Paul refutes these ideas as "tools of the evil one."[22] Manuscript evidence shows that this letter, like the *Acts of Paul and Thecla*, circulated independently from the larger work and that some early Christians believed this to be an authentic letter of Paul.

The *Acts of Paul* concludes with the narration of Paul's martyrdom. The *Martyrdom of Paul* presents the beheading of Paul under

---

20. Schneemelcher, 239–240.

21. For an interesting discussion on legends associated with Paul, see Dennis Ronald McDonald, *The Legend and the Apostle: The Battle for Paul in Story and Canon* (Philadelphia, PA: The Westminster Press, 1983).

22. Schneemelcher, 255.

Emperor Nero. Filled with legendary details such as milk (rather than blood) spurting out at his decapitation and the resurrected Paul appearing before Caesar, this story too enjoyed widespread popularity among Christians. Given that Acts of the Apostles in the New Testament concludes with Paul preaching in Rome under house arrest (Acts 27–28), these details may have been intended to satisfy the curiosity of Christians who wanted to know more about Paul's martyrdom.

This text was likely written to entertain and edify its target audience with adventures from the life of Paul that were not otherwise known to the community of believers. This is not to say it is lacking in a theological emphasis. The author's interest in sexual purity, with its implied detachment from this world and reward in the afterlife through the resurrection, is a recurring theme in the narrative. Theological language such as *Christ* and *Lord* is present, although not systematically developed in a clear or consistent way. The narrative's denunciation of false teachings (docetism and adoptionism) clearly indicates the author's theological preferences.[23]

## The Cult of Saint Thecla

The popularity of Thecla grew over the centuries after the widespread circulation of the *Acts of Paul and Thecla*. The legends associated with her reached a peak with a cult following in the fifth century and continued to make an impact through the Middle Ages. The production of literature and art associated with Thecla, especially in the regions of Asia Minor and Egypt, point to the attraction of Saint Thecla among Christians, especially women.[24]

23. See Schneemelcher, 233–234, for a good discussion on failed attempts by scholars to find a coherent theology present in the *Acts of Paul*. Later church fathers, such as fourth-century Augustine, tells us that the Manicheans, who preserved the five main Apocryphal Acts (including *Acts of Paul*), practiced *enkratism*, which advocated that one is only the bride of Christ and is to have no earthly spouse (and, of course, no sex, even within marriage). The Manicheans certainly found a theological emphasis in this apocryphal Acts.

24. See Stephen J. Davies, *The Cult of Saint Thecla: A Tradition of Women's Piety in Late Antiquity* in Recommended Readings.

Image of Thecla from a fourteenth-century Italian reliquary

## *Epistle to the Laodiceans*

The *Epistle to the Laodiceans* is a twenty-verse forgery of the now-lost letter to the Laodiceans alluded to in Colossians 4:16. The author drew heavily upon Paul's Letter to the Philippians and somewhat on Paul's Letter to the Galatians. The letter appears to have been composed simply to answer the question of where the missing epistle to the Laodiceans might be.

Because the *Epistle to the Laodiceans* draws heavily upon Philippians, it includes certain theological ideas, such as the expectation of the eschaton (the return of Christ and the day of judgment) and life in Christ as well as the ethical imperative for proper conduct. However, neither the letter's theology nor its ethics can necessarily be attributed to the occasion of its writing or the motives of its author. These may simply be the result of being a forged Pauline letter.

## A Final Biblical Warning and Curse

In the closing remarks from the Book of Revelation, the author issues a warning and a curse against those who might otherwise tamper with its revered text. Those who add words to the text will suffer from plagues, while those who omit words will lose their "share in the tree of life and in the holy city described in this book" (Rev 22:19).

Dated by scholars toward the end of the first century CE, the Book of Revelation offers further evidence (already seen in 2 Thessalonians 2:2 and 2 Peter 3:15–16) that as early as the writings of the New Testament texts there was a concern over those who forge letters in the name of the apostle Paul or meddle with writings considered by some as sacred.

## *Correspondence of Paul and Seneca*

The *Correspondence of Paul and Seneca* consists of a series of fourteen private letters—eight from Seneca to Paul and six from Paul to Seneca. A contemporary of Paul, Seneca was a first-century Roman moralist and political advisor to Emperor Nero, the Roman emperor considered responsible for Paul's martyrdom. Scholars deem these letters as pseudepigrapha writings; there is no evidence that the historical Paul and the historical Seneca ever met, much less any documentation or evidence of the conversion of Seneca to Christian beliefs implicit in the letters. The motive for creating the correspondence may have simply been to show the superiority of Christianity over the pagan religions and other philosophies of the day. For example, Seneca praises Paul for his depth of knowledge and understanding, even commenting that the emperor (Nero) is impressed:

> I confess that I was much taken with the reading of your letters which you sent to the Galatians, the Corinthians and the Achaeans, and let us both live in the spirit which with sacred awe you show in them. For the Holy Spirit is in you and above all exalted ones gives expression by your sublime speech to the most venerable thoughts. I could

wish therefore that when you express such lofty thoughts a cultivated form of discourse should not be lacking to their majesty. And that I may conceal nothing from you, brother, or burden my conscience, I confess that the emperor was moved by your sentiments. When I had read to him about the origin of the power in you, he said that he could only wonder that a man who had not enjoyed the usual education should be capable of such thoughts.[25] (*Correspondence of Paul and Seneca*, letter VII)

This friendly and respectful exchange has little or no theological substance, though scholars have recognized some historical value to the eleventh letter, in which Seneca discusses the burning of Rome and the subsequent persecution of Jews and Christians in the city. The specificity of detail (for instance, Seneca reports the destruction of "one hundred and thirty-two private houses and four thousand apartment-houses burned in six days"[26]) suggests that the author may have had access to an otherwise unknown historical source about the Neronian persecution.

## Apocalypse of Paul

The *Apocalypse of Paul* narrates the ascent of "Paul" into heaven and his visions of the afterlife. Most scholars suspect the unknown author of this apocalypse wrote it in response to Paul's comments in 2 Corinthians 12:4, in which he speaks of being "caught up into Paradise." The author apparently had a variety of sources for the compilation of this apocalypse, as he appears to draw upon the *Apocalypse of Peter*, *Elijah*, and *Zephaniah*.[27] This apocalyptic narrative also contains numerous parallels to the Old Testament prophetic tradition (Isaiah and Jeremiah, for example) as well as New Testament writings such as the Book of Revelation, the Gospel of Matthew, and the Pauline letters of 1 and 2 Corinthians.

---

25. Schneemelcher, 49.

26. Ibid., 51.

27. Elliott, 616.

The longest sections of the apocalypse are the visions of paradise (chapters 19–30) and the visions of hell (chapters 31–44). Here, a theology of divine judgment and mercy prevails. In paradise, Paul meets the predictable personages of Jewish and Christian history (for instance, Abraham, Isaac, and Jacob [chapter 47], Moses [chapter 48], and even the Virgin Mary [chapter 46]). In hell, Paul meets not only those deserving punishment (nonbelievers and idolaters), but also and perhaps surprisingly, damned presbyters (chapter 34), bishops (chapter 35), and deacons (chapter 36).

## The *Apocalypse of Paul* and Dante's *Inferno*

The visions of heaven and hell in the *Apocalypse of Paul* made an enormous impact on the imagination of Christians, especially in the Western Church of the Middles Ages.

In the fourteenth century, Dante Alighieri (1265–1321) wrote an epic poem titled *Divine Comedy*. Part of it, titled *Inferno*, tells of Dante's journey through hell, which it depicts as consisting of nine circles of suffering. Scholars suspect that Dante may have drawn on the images of hell in the *Apocalypse of Paul* for some of his inspiration. Rivers of fire and torment, as described in the *Apocalypse of Paul* (for example, chapter 32), figure prominently in Dante's *Inferno*.

Fourteenth-century illustration depicting the river of fire from Dante's *Divine Comedy*

© The Gallery Collection/Corbis

## Summary: Overview of the Later Letters, Narratives, and an Apocalypse of Paul

### CORE CONCEPTS

- These writings offer insights into who Paul *becomes* and how his figure is *used* in later theological disputes.
- The later writings appear to answer some of the questions and curiosities of second- and third-century Christians.

### SUPPLEMENTAL INFORMATION

- Thecla, the female disciple of Paul from the *Acts of Paul and Thecla*, had a cult following in both Asia Minor and Egypt.
- In *3 Corinthians*, Paul condemns the teachings of docetism and adoptionism.
- The *Epistle to the Laodiceans* draws heavily upon Paul's Letter to the Philippians.
- The *Correspondence of Paul and Seneca* was written, at least in part, to show the superiority of Christianity over the pagan religions and philosophies of the day.
- The *Apocalypse of Paul* narrates visions of heaven and hell.
- The *Apocalypse of Paul* has affected Christian imagination of the afterlife.

## Questions for Review

1. How do the Apostolic Fathers contribute to the legacy of Paul?
2. In what ways do the apocryphal writings continue the legacy of Paul?
3. How do the writings of the early church fathers provide a witness to these later writings on Paul?
4. In what general period were these writings produced?
5. Who authored these writings?
6. How is Thecla a main character in the *Acts of Paul*?
7. What do scholars think motivated the writing of the *Epistle to the Laodiceans*?

8. Who was Seneca, and what may have been the motive for the creation of the *Correspondence of Paul and Seneca*?

9. In what way do scholars think the *Apocalypse of Paul* is connected to 2 Corinthians 12?

10. What are some images of heaven (chapters 19–30) and images of hell (chapters 31–44) from the *Apocalypse of Paul*?

## Questions for Reflection

1. Why do you think the author of the *Acts of Paul and Thecla* highlights Thecla's courage and refusal to submit to a father or husband but, instead, to Paul?

2. What potential insights into these writings are lost by not knowing the date and place of composition?

3. Which additional writing on Paul do you most like, and why?

4. What is your reaction to the visions of heaven and hell as presented in the *Apocalypse of Paul*?

## Recommendations for Further Reading

Cartlidge, David R., and J. Keith Elliott. *Art and the Christian Apocrypha*. New York: Routledge, 2001.

This book contains more than 100 photographs of influential paintings, mosaics, and sculptures that have apocryphal texts and scenes as their inspiration. After an introduction that puts the enduring influence of text, art, and the Christian apocrypha in context, Cartlidge and Elliott have separate chapters on art and texts associated with Mary, images of the Christ, the life and mission of Jesus, Paul, Thecla, and Peter, and apostles and evangelists.

Davies, Stephen J. *The Cult of Saint Thecla: A Tradition of Women's Piety in Late Antiquity*. New York: Oxford, UK, 2001.

Davies assembles literary, artistic, and archeological evidence in his reconstruction of the cult of Saint Thecla in Asia Minor and Egypt. Special emphasis is placed upon the social practices and institutions of those devoted to the cult of Thecla in that region. Davies presents a compelling case for why Thecla became one of the most popular saints and martyrs among Christians in late antiquity.

Ehrman, Bart D. *Lost Scriptures: Books That Did Not Make It into the New Testament.* New York: Oxford University Press, 2003.

As his subtitle indicates, Ehrman provides a collection of early Christian writings not included in the canon of the New Testament. These writings, which reveal the diverse voices of early Christianity, are divided into fifteen gospels, five acts of the apostles, thirteen epistles and related writings as well as several apocalypses and revelatory treatises. Ehrman includes a brief introduction to each text.

Elliott, J. K. *The Apocryphal New Testament: A Collection of Apocryphal Christian Literature in an English Translation.* Oxford, UK: Clarendon, 1993.

Similar to Ehrman, but with more technical information, Elliot provides in one volume a collection of early Christian extracanonical gospels, acts, epistles, and apocalypses. This text offers a more extended introduction to these writings than Ehrman's as well as supplies patristic citations, extant editions, and a list of modern translations.

Schneemelcher, Wilhelm, ed. *New Testament Apocrypha,* 2 vols. Rev. ed. trans. R. McL. Wilson. Louisville, KY: Westminster John Knox Press, 1991.

This two-volume work contains apocryphal gospels (vol. 1) and apocryphal writings relating to the apostles (vol. 2). Schneemelcher's book contains detailed introductory notes to the writings, providing background on areas such as early church attestation, sources, and content summaries.

# INDEX

*Note:* An italicized page number indicates an illustration.

## A

Abraham
   *Apocalypse of Paul* and, 287*n*12, 298
   Galatians and, 20, 132, 138, 142, 144–47, 148
   Romans, Letter to, and, 70, 138, 159, 172–73, 174, 180
   scholarship on, 180
Achaeans, 297
Achaia, 42, 43, 58, 62, 113. *See also* Corinth
*Acts of Paul. See also* apocryphal (later) writings
   apocryphal, as, 29, 280
   author and audience, 289, 290
   beheading of Paul, 293–94
   date and place of composition, 12, 284, 290
   evidence for, 284, 287–88
   *Martyrdom of Paul* and, 285
   purity and, 294
   theology and ethics, 292–93, 294
*Acts of Paul and Thecla,* 12, 29, 279, 280, 284, 286, 288, 290, 293. *See also* apocryphal (later) writings; Thecla
Acts of the Apostles (Luke). *See also* letters, deutero-Pauline; narratives

   Artemis and, 33
   Chrestus and, 165
   Corinthians 1 and, 81, 85–86, 109*n*3
   Corinthians 2 and, 109
   co-workers and, 219, 258*n*4
   Galatians and, 137
   historical source, as, 10–11, 29, 58, 62
   imprisonment of Paul and, 182, 294
   life of Paul and, 9–10, 39, 43–44, 64, 86–87
   Lydia and, 186
   Macedonia and, 113
   Pauline Corpus and, 51–52
   Paul's training, on, 229*n*7
   Paul's travels and, 264
   Philippians and, 187, 189, 190
   Romans, Letter to, and, 162
   secondary nature of, 183*n*2
   Thessalonians 1 and, 64, 65, 67, 68, 109*n*3, 253
   Thessalonians 2 and, 253
   women and, 189
Adam and Eve, 98, 172, 180, 227, 266
Adams, Edward, 106–7
*adelphos* (brother), 140
adoptionism, 293, 294
affliction. *See* suffering
*After Paul Left Corinth: The Influence of Secular Ethics and Social Change* (Winter), 107